Improvising
Out Loud

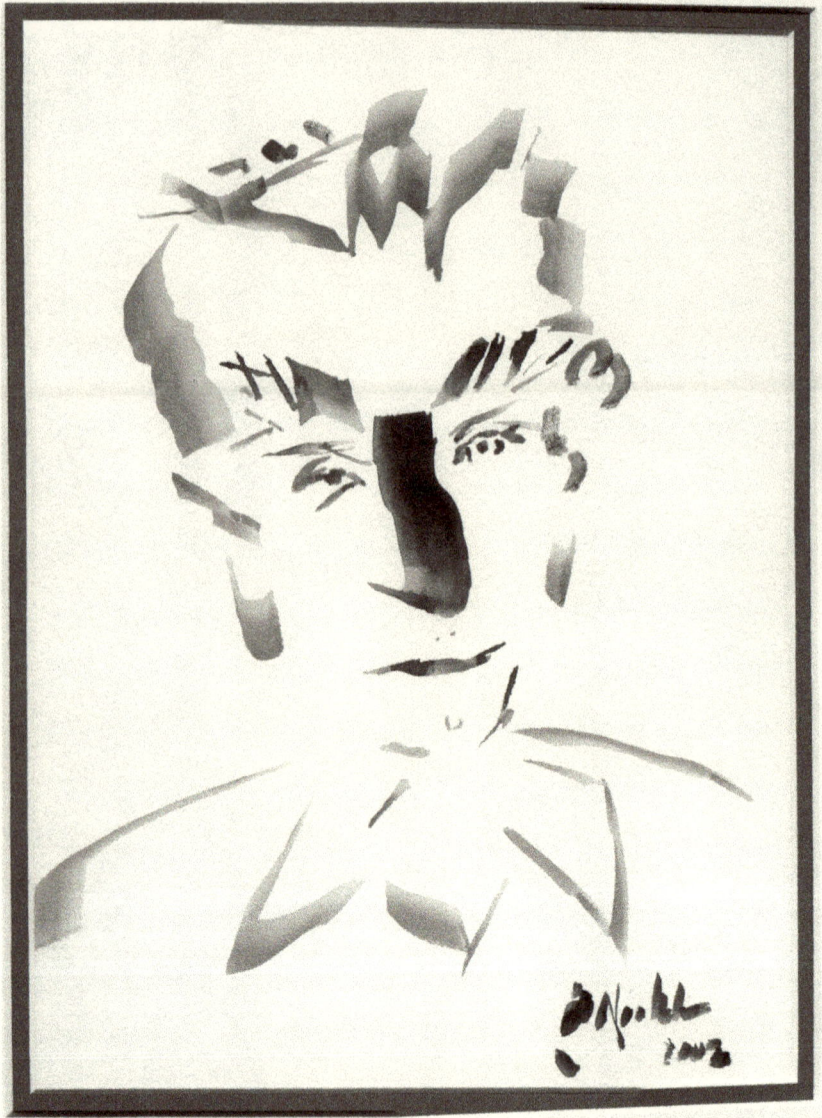

IMPROVISING OUT LOUD

My Life
Teaching Hollywood
How to Act

JEFF COREY WITH EMILY COREY

FOREWORD BY LEONARD NIMOY

AFTERWORD BY JANET NEIPRIS

UNIVERSITY PRESS OF KENTUCKY

Published by the University Press of Kentucky,
scholarly publisher for the Commonwealth,
serving Bellarmine University, Berea College, Centre College of Kentucky, Eastern Kentucky University, The Filson Historical Society, Georgetown College, Kentucky Historical Society, Kentucky State University, Morehead State University, Murray State University, Northern Kentucky University, Transylvania University, University of Kentucky, University of Louisville, and Western Kentucky University.

Editorial and Sales Offices: The University Press of Kentucky
663 South Limestone Street, Lexington, Kentucky 40508-4008
www.kentuckypress.com

Frontispiece: Portrait of Jeff Corey by Jack Nicholson.

Unless otherwise noted, photographs are from the private collection of Jeff Corey.

Cataloging-in-Publication data is available from the Library of Congress.

ISBN 978-0-8131-6983-5 (hardcover : alk. paper)
ISBN 978-0-8131-6985-9 (epub)
ISBN 978-0-8131-6984-2 (pdf)

This book is printed on acid-free paper meeting the requirements of the American National Standard for Permanence in Paper for Printed Library Materials.

∞

Manufactured in the United States of America.

Member of the Association of
American University Presses

For Hope, Eve, Jane, and Emily

Contents

Illustrations follow page 146

Note on Usage

Throughout this book, the word *actor* is used to refer to those working in this noble profession. The word is meant to be inclusive of the fine men *and* women in the field, and the use of the word, as well as the pronoun *he* throughout, in no way is meant as a slight to women. It is simply a nod to traditional English usage and the authors' collective dislike of the word *actress.* Men and women are actors. No insult or exclusion is intended. The observations made in this book refer to all actors.

Foreword

"You should take an acting class." I hated hearing that. Hated it. I heard it a number of times, from colleagues and occasionally directors. To me it was insulting. I was an experienced actor. A member of all the actors' guilds and unions, I'd been on stages since I was eight years old and even played the title role in a small boxing film in which I was well reviewed. I was in my late twenties when I began hearing this advice. Was I to walk into a class with others, even beginners, and pay money to be told things I already knew?

After two years away in the army, now married and father of my first child and expecting my second, I was picking up the thin threads of my career in Hollywood. The roles were often frustratingly small, but I was considered professional and dependable—a solid young character actor who could deliver the dialogue.

But something new was stirring. Marlon Brando had established a new level of work, and it was exciting. Other actors were following in kind, and I could see it happening. We were watching actors whose work I admired but didn't understand. What were they doing that I couldn't or didn't know how to do? How did this work differ from that which I recognized and could duplicate? These performances had an inner life. They simmered.

Jeff Corey was the name that came up repeatedly in actors' discussions about teachers. I decided to swallow my pride and made the call. Jeff gave me an appointment for an interview. On the day I arrived outside his studio, I was joined by several others. One by one we went in for a brief session. My turn came. Jeff invited me to sit. He had a yellow pad for notes. He quickly asked one question: "Have you done much acting?" This was something of a relief since I now had a chance to establish my credentials. I thought it went well. He told me he would be in touch: he was starting a new class and I would be considered. He was formidable, authoritative, and kind.

Within a couple of days I was called and told to be in class on the next Thursday morning at ten o'clock. The class was held in a small proscenium theater in Hollywood. There were approximately twenty students, balanced between males and females.

The exercise at this session was designed to explore the inner monologue of a character in a dramatic situation. Given a brief plot idea, students were asked to verbalize their thought process as the character. A young couple got up to work, and I was appalled. They stood in a faraway corner of the stage and mumbled. I could hardly see them and could not understand a word they said. When they were done, Jeff asked them to describe their experience. It wasn't a profound presentation.

At the break I told Jeff I was disturbed by what I had seen. I complained about the lack of form and style. Jeff said, "I cannot be held responsible for everything that happens in a class." I thought, "Fair enough. Let's back off and give this thing a chance."

When my turn came I was asked to do the inner monologue of a man who was a short order cook in a greasy spoon restaurant and hated his job. I thought I did okay, and Jeff was complimentary.

The following week I was very sick with a bad cold but decided I would go to class lest Jeff think I was a flake. When I got there, he approached me and said, "George Bernard Shaw described style as the way to do a thing in order that it be done best." I was impressed. He had taken the trouble to reflect on my concern.

I came to Jeff's class with a carpenter's tools. I had a solid basis of craft. Now, for the first time, I was exposed to the art of acting: to the concepts of theme, subtext, and character building. How does this character find his way in the world? What is he seeking in this scene that is not revealed in the dialogue? What is his social class? How does he help express or argue the theme of the play? What would he say if he decided to speak only his deepest truth? When he says, "I love you," is he being sincere or manipulative, ironic, sarcastic, or comic? Given the tools I came with, I was able to quickly apply what I was being given, and my work grew.

In a short time, Jeff moved me to an evening class in which there was thrilling work being done. His insights and suggestions were incisive and often electrifying. His comments were stimulating and never mean. His classes were a laboratory exploring an art form. Class was something I looked forward to and worked hard to make a contribution to.

Vic Morrow was a fellow student in the Tuesday night class. He was preparing to direct a play called *Deathwatch* by Jean Genet. On the basis of the work Vic saw me do in class, he offered me one of the three major roles. Genet was considered a literary genius in France. His work was much talked about but had never been produced in Los Angeles. The Hollywood community was interested and came to see the play. There were producers, directors, and casting agents in the audience every night. I began working regularly in better and more rewarding roles.

When the blacklist broke and Jeff began working in films, he hired me to teach classes in his absence. I did that for two years and then established my own studio, where I taught until the *Star Trek* series was sold and I no longer had the time.

I came alive as an actor under Jeff's guidance. So much is owed to him by so many like me. I'm so glad I put aside my ego and went to his class.

—Leonard Nimoy

Introduction

The Call to Act

"Jeff, do you think you could make an actor out of me?"

This question is often asked of me by accountants, schoolteachers, lawyers, and any number of men and women in conventional professions who harbor secret dreams of acting onstage or in film.

My answer is always an unequivocal "Yes."

Over the years, hundreds if not thousands of students have attended my classes and worked with me privately. Many of them have gone on to become the leading stars of the American stage and screen. But even more of them have been ordinary men and women who worked in other professions, hiding their secret desire to act from their colleagues, friends, and families.

When I assure people I can make them an actor, it usually brings on a sheepish grin, drenched in an equally embarrassed pleasure at the very idea. It is as if they had revealed some deep, dark confidence and never expected that anyone, particularly a reputable acting teacher, would take them seriously.

When I was working in England on the film *The Main Attraction*, I had an occasion to drop by the bursar's office. In England, the bursar is the person responsible for all the money that goes in and out of a film. Sitting behind an ornate, hand-carved wooden desk was a classically elegant man. His blue suit and starched collar gave him the aura of a banker, and there was no doubt in my mind that he was excellent at numbers and at keeping everything about the production in good financial order.

The bursar knew my reputation as an acting teacher. After we had conducted our business, he blushed slightly and in an almost hushed voice asked, "Jeff, do you think you can make an actor out of me?"

"Yes," I said. "I can show you how, right now."

His eyes widened with surprise, but he nodded his head in agreement.

"All right," I said. "Look at the clutter on your desk." There were sheaves of paper piled up all over his massive workspace, a scattering of memo pads, staplers, bills, receipts, wire baskets, and an array of gum labels and invisible tape.

"As a trained businessman," I continued, "how do you start your morning tasks? What makes you pick up this particular pile of papers rather than the one adjacent to it? Obviously, all these items have some relevance to your work. Why this one and not that one over there?"

"What has that got to do with acting?" he asked.

"I get a script," I continued. "I look at it. What makes me conclude that this line I'm looking at ought to be read in a particular way?"

"Because you're an actor and you know about those things," he said.

"How do I know those things?" I asked him.

"Weren't you trained?" he asked.

"Yes," I responded. "Just as you were trained to be an accountant. But your training doesn't tell you to pick up this particular receipt instead of this bank statement. Isn't that the result of your intuition, which tells you start here rather than over there? Wouldn't another man in your field give the work on this desk a different set of priorities?"

"Yes, a different person wouldn't approach it the way I do," he agreed.

"Do you think you're possibly a better businessman than this hypothetical other chap?" I asked.

"Yes," he said, starting to feel his oats.

"All right, that's the way it is in acting," I said. "You learn the nuts and bolts of your craft just as you took your business administration courses at university. But in the long run, it's the fellow who, with ease, follows his intuition and says, 'This is the best way to handle this accounting problem. Period.' That ability to connect to your second sight and make smart, convincing decisions for your character is really all good acting is about."

He looked at me with a smile as this information began to sink in. "Everything we do in life is really a form of playacting," I reassured him. "We just have to learn to trust it."

The mimetic impulse, that desire to embrace the make-believe, is born in childhood, and if we're lucky, we never quite relinquish our role-playing capacities. Whenever you tell a joke, you are essentially making someone believe it really happened. You take on the role of what "he" said and what "she" said and so forth. You are licensed to tell a whopping lie because the fabrication reveals a recognizable truth about us as humans. In our day-to-

2

day lives we make role adaptations to any and all situations we encounter. Our mimetic talent is engaged at the airport, handball court, church, mosque, or synagogue. Deciding what to wear to a business meeting or dinner with our friends entails "rehearsing" or imagining who will be there, what other people might wear, where we might go after the meeting or dinner, and countless other considerations. The actor simply codifies this process and shares it with his audience.

Part of this codification process has to do with our ability to communicate. The great icon of the Russian stage, the actor and theater director Constantin Stanislavsky, told his actors to "talk to the eye, not to the ear."

In working with students, I always encourage them to make their audience visualize what they are describing so their audience can see the future they propose. This holds true if you are speaking to a theater audience, boardroom, PTA meeting, coworkers, or any other situation you encounter throughout the day. We are able to visualize what we are talking about by accessing our insight and trusting our inner sensibilities.

I have worked with lawyers who were preparing oral arguments before the Supreme Court. I have worked with doctors who were struggling with ways to communicate with their patients. I have worked with politicians eager to convince the public to hand over their votes. And I have worked with countless actors who learned how to access their insight and intuition and transform those gifts into magnificent performances.

The longing to be in the spotlight should never be couched or hidden away by embarrassment or a feeling that the exhilaration of acting is reserved only for professionals. I encourage everyone I speak to who wants to act to take advantage of the many community playhouses, neighborhood theaters, and university venues that offer rich opportunities to express the desire to perform. One should always remember the Latin root of the word *amateur* is *amator,* which means "lover." Whether in our day-to-day lives, on a stage, or on the screen, we should all trust and embrace what we love.

I encourage everyone who has ever had a desire to act to throw off his or her self-conscious shackles and shout out a resounding, "Yes! I am an actor." Life cannot resist dramatization. All the world's a stage. No one should spend it hiding in the wings.

Part I

How to Live

Loss is unendurable until it becomes a fact.
—*Don Gordon*

I

Dreams of Acting

As a teenager, I saw the film *The Private Life of Henry VIII* starring the great Charles Laughton. The movie had a huge influence on me. As I exited the theater and walked through the streets, I tried to incorporate the stride, demeanor, and posture of the porcine sixteenth-century monarch I had just seen on the screen. I attempted not only to capture the outward mold of his character but also to absorb the moods, feelings, and attitudes of his personality. This was probably my first conscious brush with acting, and the energy and excitement of it stayed with me. After that, I spent many hours daydreaming about what it would be like to have people film me. I never shared these daydreams with anyone—it would have been too embarrassing—and I certainly never made my dreams of being an actor known to my family or friends.

My parents, Nathan and Mary Zwerling, were Orthodox Jews, and it was important to them that at least one of their sons received a proper Jewish education. My older brother, Lou, who was a bohemian from the day he was born, technically should have attended Yeshiva instead of me. But Lou would have none of it. He kept running away from home, searching for a better life beyond Borough Park and Brooklyn, so I was forced to attend Yeshiva in his place.

It was a remarkable yet utterly Dickensian experience. If you dropped a book on the floor, you had to say prayers. If you spoke back to a teacher, you had to say prayers. If you did anything unconventional, you had to say prayers. I felt very close to God but was bored by most of what was taught. I learned about *gett,* which is a divorce document in Jewish religious law. I didn't know what the word *divorce* meant in English—no one where we lived in Borough Park was divorced—so it was difficult to concentrate on something that had absolutely no meaning to me. I learned Aramaic and Hebrew and studied the Talmud, and though in retrospect it was a fairly stunning classical education, I was an all-American boy and all I wanted to do was go outside and play baseball. My parents wouldn't budge. My failures in the Yeshiva hit a tipping point: by tenth grade, my grades were a shambles and I had developed a nervous tic.

My mother was an immigrant from Latvia who was self-educated and full of strong opinions. No one in the family was fond of crossing her. When it became obvious that my tic was not going away and, in fact, was getting worse, she decided to take me to a specialist. I don't know how she found him, but together we took the subway to Manhattan and entered the dark, quiet office of a Freudian psychoanalyst.

Psychoanalysis was still in its early stages, and it was incredibly forward-thinking of my mother to take me there. His office was a world away from anything I had ever seen before and certainly far out of my mother's reality as well. Sadly, I do not remember his name, but I do remember his kindness. He spoke to my mother for a few minutes and then asked her to leave the room. The two of us sat and talked for a while. I was restless and unsure but finally felt safe enough to tell him I felt like a failure. When we finished talking, he called my mother back in and said, "This is a marvelous boy. There's absolutely nothing wrong with him."

My mother stared at him quietly for a moment. "Send him to public school and he'll be fine," he said, staring back at her. We left the office without saying a word. The next day, she enrolled me in New Utrecht High School in Brooklyn.

I was not a particularly good student at New Utrecht, either, and spent much of my time staring out the window between the buildings to the cargo vessels and ocean liners that sailed through New York Harbor. I was enamored of the plays that were performed at the school, but it never occurred to me that I could audition for one.

The only class that made sense to me was English, when, on occasion, I would be asked to recite a passage from Shakespeare. One I remember clearly was Marcellus's speech in the opening passage of *Julius Caesar*. I blasted out the opening lines with fervor: "Wherefore rejoice? What conquests brings he home?"

My ardor stunned my classmates, and after that I would often be greeted in the hallways with stentorian recitals of "Wherefore rejoice?" This small, random event made quite an impression and elevated my social stature, particularly with the coeds, who took a new interest in me. I had always been shy around girls, and my newfound fame was exhilarating. More important than my social status, my recitation had made an impression on Mr. Rosenswieg, my English teacher and the chair of the Drama Club. Mr. Rosenswieg had always wanted to direct a production of Goethe's *Faust* but had never found his leading man.

One day he announced I was the only student in the school who could play Mephisto. I was intoxicated at the thought and threw myself into the role, forgetting all else. The weeks of rehearsal were exhilarating, and the camaraderie of the cast and crew and the lessons in stagecraft gave me a quick glance into what life in the theater might be. *Faust* was a tremendous success, and I was hailed as a hero. Overnight, I went from relative obscurity to being known by everyone in school. This newfound popularity gave me an inner strength I had never felt before.

Regardless of my reinforced identity, when I graduated in the fall of 1932, I was eighteen years old and my options were slim. In spite of my theatrical victories, my schoolwork had continued to slip, and I didn't have the grade point average to attend City College, much less a university. With the success of *Faust* under my belt, I boldly auditioned for Eva Le Gallienne's Civic Repertory Theatre. Eva had been a star on Broadway but was devoted to the idea of theater as an art form rather than a business. She managed a 1,100-seat repertory theater slightly off the beaten path of Broadway. Her work paved the way for off-Broadway theaters to thrive in years to come. I was asked to prepare Malvolio's soliloquy from *Twelfth Night* and young Treplev's speech to Nina in Chekhov's *The Sea Gull*. I threw myself into the audition, rehearsing each line with the same fervor I had put into *Faust*. But to no avail. I was not hired.

Undaunted, I used the same material a few weeks later to apply for the Milward Adams Scholarship at the Feagin School of Dramatic Arts on West 57th Street. The Feagin School was one of the best acting schools of its day and turned out "real" actors. The award was named for Milward Adams, who had managed the Chicago Symphony and the Auditorium Theatre and was considered one of the movers and shakers of the theater world. The renowned lyrical poet Sara Teasdale was one of the judges of the competition, as was Hugh Miller. Miller was a well-known British character actor who had come to the United States in the role of Alfred Jingle in Dickens's *Pickwick Papers*. I was intoxicated to think of performing in front of such an illustrious gathering. It was a national scholarship, and I knew the competition would be fierce. I threw myself into my role, and to my delight—and utter relief—I won the two-year scholarship. Overnight, everything in my life changed.

On my first day of class at the Feagin School, President Franklin Delano Roosevelt closed the banks. It was the height of the Depression, and while I was deeply aware of the financial hysteria going on all around me, I was equally thrilled by my good fortune and opportunity. In no time at all, I decided to be the most profound theatrical artist on the continent. I took on a quasi-British accent and lowered my voice to its deepest decibels. My first role was the Constable in A. A. Milne's *Perfect Alibi,* a rather charming murder mystery. Milne was more famous for his children's books *Winnie-the-Pooh* and *Now We Are Six,* but he wrote over twenty-five plays in his lifetime.

Hugh Miller himself was to direct *Perfect Alibi.* Miller had been particularly complimentary about my audition pieces, and I wanted to impress him. At the first reading, I employed my newfound voice. Miller stopped me in my tracks. "Dear boy," he said amiably, "you must get out of that awful minor key. Everything you say sounds like 'Please pass the poison!'" My face flushed red, but I instantly understood what he was saying. Miller quickly moved on with the rehearsal in the most professional way possible.

Frankly, I was a bit relieved. On the spot, I excised my posturing and gimmicks and returned to my normal voice. As we rehearsed, Miller helped me take measure of my own indigenous capacities. It was the beginning of my finding myself as an actor and discovering that, indeed, I had a voice that was mine alone and that imitating anyone else's stance or performance was completely unnecessary.

The Feagin School had been founded in 1915 by Lucy Feagin. Lucy herself had studied with Milward Adams, the esteemed namesake of the scholarship I was in the midst of enjoying. Our curriculum incorporated the best of traditional dramatics, including the Delsarte Method, an approach to acting that promoted gesture as the "direct agent of the heart." The Delsarte Method was introduced in America by Steele MacKaye, a prominent actor who had studied in Paris with François Delsarte himself. We learned a full array of postures and what were supposedly the physical manifestations associated with each emotional state.

The gargantuan and splendid Jolson Theatre was just around the corner from the Feagin School. It was built by the Schubert brothers in 1921 as a gift to the singer Al Jolson, who at the time was America's most famous and highest-paid entertainer. After the crash, the Jolson, like many theaters in New York, was forced to close its doors. During my first year at the Feagin School, the great English actor and director Percy Vivian rented the vast venue, sitting empty and gathering dust, for a pittance. He renamed it the Venice Theater and founded a Shakespearean repertory company. Percy's company consisted of a group of very reputable British actors who had been stranded in New York in the early years of the Depression. Most had been members either of Sir Phillip Benson's traveling company or of the Sir Ben Greet Players, both great theater troupes of their time.

The actors who made up the eclectic troupe Vivian gathered for his theater at one time or another had shared the British stage with the most legendary actors of the nineteenth century, including Sir Johnston Forbes-Robertson, Ellen Terry, Mrs. Patrick Campbell, and Sir Henry Irving. The Feagin School encouraged its students to play minor roles in Vivian's productions, and we were delighted to chip in. During rehearsals, we young up-and-coming actors would test our betters by randomly tossing out opening lines from Shakespeare's plays. In unison, these old stage icons would resoundingly summon up the remaining dialogue with an articulate brilliance and artistic finesse that was awe inspiring. I used to get to the theater early, and I'd often see Percy sweeping the cyclorama himself. That made a deep impression and seeded in me a lifelong belief that it is important for an actor to get his hands into the manual work of a theater—set building, lighting, and, certainly, sweeping the stage when it was needed.

My first role was the First Citizen in *Julius Caesar*. Not completely cured of my desire to be the greatest actor on the continent, I played the First Citizen with such flagrant energy that Charles Dingle, one of the most prominent actors of the group, asked Percy, "Please tone down that young man who occupies upstage center as though he owned it."

Occasionally Percy would slip me two bits—that's all he could pay—but most of the time, I worked for free and was happy to do it. There was a glorious actor, Ian Maclaren, who had most of the leading roles. Watching him work was invigorating and set me on a lifelong love of Shakespeare.

Along with the Delsarte Method, my daytime training at the Feagin School included phonetics, foreign accents, soft-shoe dancing, art history, set construction, fencing, pantomime, stage lighting, and makeup. We put on plays before large audiences at least twice a month. That first year, after *Perfect Alibi*, I had roles in *Death Takes a Holiday*, which had been produced with great success on Broadway; the Greek classic *The Trojan Women*, by Euripides; *Coquette*, by George Abbott; and Hermann Sudermann's *Magda*. It was intoxicating for a young artist to have such a variety of roles to work with and to be so deeply immersed in his craft.

During my first summer break I worked in a factory at the Depression salary of eight dollars for a forty-eight-hour week. I put together laminated cardboard signs advertising the new beer companies that had emerged after President Roosevelt ended prohibition. My boss offered me a franchise for something called Schlitz's Beer for the entire borough of Brooklyn. I turned it down because they were going to pay only seven and a half cents per case, and I didn't think I could sell more than twenty cases a week. I would not have been a very good beer tycoon anyway. I was fine embossing signs and daydreaming of a more creative life.

One day we heard President Roosevelt was to drive in his open car down Fifth Avenue to celebrate the passage of the National Recovery Act. The parade was to end at Union Square. Our factory was on West 16th Street, a mere hundred yards from Fifth Avenue. Al Jolson himself was to walk in front of the president's car.

I was selected by my coworkers to approach the factory owners and ask for a twenty-minute break to watch Roosevelt's entourage pass by. The owners unequivocally said, "You stay at your workbenches!" I gloomily went back to my laminating chores. Then the rebel in me was activated, and I said to myself, "The hell with the bosses." I shouted out to my coworkers, "Let's go!" As my best Faustian voice resounded through the cavernous warehouse, one by one my fellow workers left their stations and gathered at the door. All nineteen of us proudly walked the short distance to Fifth Avenue.

The great Al Jolson did indeed walk just twenty feet in front of the president's touring car. He was carrying an American flag. Behind him was the elegant Roosevelt, waving right at us. For one quick moment, our eyes met. It was thrilling to be so close to him. He had the handsomest visage I had ever seen. After his car passed, our group silently walked back to the factory. Slowly, each one of us settled back to work. Whatever dread we felt at what was waiting for us upon our return was negated by the excitement of seeing Jolson and Roosevelt in person. We were quite proud of ourselves for defying our superiors. As we settled back down to our workbenches, we heard nary a complaint from our employers.

After Labor Day, I returned to the Feagin School. I was assigned the role of Malvolio in *Twelfth Night*. I got in touch with my buddies from the factory and invited them to a dress rehearsal. Most of them had never been inside a theater. They were very impressed with the building that housed the Feagin School. Our main playhouse occupied the second and third floors and had a commodious orchestra pit and balcony. The basement and ground level were owned by Stillman's Gym and were used by the world heavyweight champions Jack Dempsey and Jack Sharkey as their workout space.

I greeted my work buddies outside the building and led them inside. As we stepped onto the elevator to the fifth floor, where we were to perform *Twelfth Night*, we encountered the statuesque models engaged by the Russian avant-garde painter and sculptor Alexander Archipenko, whose studio was on the top floor of the building. None of us could take our eyes off these beauties. When we got out of the elevator, I pointed my friends to the theater door and made my way backstage. They loved the play, and the entire experience made quite an impression on them. They all asked if they could come back again. I invited them to every open rehearsal that year.

Part of my training at the Feagin School involved the preperformance tasks of hauling scenery flats, stage furniture, electrical equipment, and wardrobe and preparing makeup kits. We would arrive at the school in midmorning and carry stage paraphernalia to all the different auditoriums, large and small. I was the designated stage electrician and had to scrupulously check backstage fuses to avoid outages. When we performed, we had little dressing room space, so we often changed in the wings, if they existed at all.

I found a catalog from the Feagin School from 1953 in my files. As part of its mission, it states, "There must be a communication, a transfer of the actor's conceptions to his audience. For this, definite techniques must be learned, techniques that should be mastered and become an unconscious part of the artist's equipment. The actor, the entertainer, or the individual in daily life, if he would be an artist, must be a good craftsman. He must be the master of his tools."

I have always been deeply grateful for the tools I mastered at the Feagin School. Over time and as I grew as an actor, I dropped many of the more limiting dictates from my toolkit and replaced them with a more expansive view of the creative role, but I am forever grateful for the penetrating and formal education I received over the course of my study there. It was also nice to notice that in 1953, even though my career was deep in the doldrums of the blacklist, the Feagin School mentioned me in its catalog as one of its alumni, along with a list of my better film roles. I was grateful I was not a pariah in my alma mater's eyes.

I spent two exciting years at the Feagin School. At my graduation, our guest speaker was John Mason Brown, the distinguished drama critic of the *New York Evening Post*. In his speech he wished us good fortune but warned us of the difficulties of the highly competitive professional theater. I'm not sure what prompted him to deliver such a cynical speech to such an eager, hopeful group of graduates, but his final comment to us was: "Perhaps five years from now, only two or three of you will have made it, to some degree, in the profession." His prognostication was right. Five years later, only three of us were still working as actors. Luckily, I was one of them.

In the fall of 1935, I auditioned for Clare Tree Major's Children's Theatre. Clare was an English actor who had grown frustrated with the British stage and thought America might offer more creative opportunities. She was the first producer to provide professional touring plays exclusively for children, and her traveling troupe put on a variety of well-written plays that had been adapted for younger audiences. I was hired and given the role of Jeremy, the kitchen scullion in *Dick Whittington*. On the third day of rehearsal I told Clare I could not rehearse the following day because it was the Day of Atonement. She thought about it for a moment and reluctantly said, "Very well."

A few days later Lucy Feagin called me and said, "I had a phone call from Clare Tree Major, who complained that she did not know you were Jewish." Lucy had grown up in Aniston, Alabama, and was the epitome of a southern belle in every possible way. In her lovely, soft-spoken drawl, she said she told Clare, "He *is* Jewish and is one of the most gifted students I've ever had." Clare never made mention of it to me, and we got along famously. I earned $35 a week. I kept $15 and sent $20 back to my mother as a thank-you for all the years she'd been supporting me.

Most of my Feagin School teachers had talked glowingly about their youthful days as actors on the road. As my new troupe headed out of town, there were still legitimate theaters throughout the United States and boardinghouses that provided reduced rates for touring companies. Our stay in Providence, Rhode Island, was particularly memorable. The lobby of the theater we performed in displayed signed photographs and sketches of the reigning stars of yesteryear, including Sarah Bernhardt, Eleanora Duse, Tommaso Salvini, Katharine Cornell, Alfred Lunt, and his wife, Lynn

Fontanne. Every time I walked through the lobby, I felt myself swept up in their legacy. I loved the touring life. Along with four of my fellow cast members, I drove Clare's ancient but sturdy REO Speedwagon, filled to the brim with sets, props, and costumes. This was before freeways, and we would drive past farmhouses lit with kerosene lamps. It looked like such a cozy world and was far from the bustle of New York City.

We would arrive at a school in midmorning, and the entire cast and crew would pitch in. Because of my stagecraft training at the Feagin School, I was put in charge of electricity, and at each new performance space, I would carefully check out how much wattage we could safely pull from the fuse box.

We acted in elementary and high school auditoriums in towns like Wilkes Barre, Erie, Poughkeepsie, and Terre Haute. At Christmas we performed at the venerable Pabst Theater in Milwaukee for three performances of Shakespeare's *As You Like It*. I played four roles—Old Adam, William, Silvius, and the Elder Duke. I toured with Clare for two years. It was a marvelous way to see America and an even better way for a young man to learn more about acting.

After my stint with Clare, I was hired as a spear carrier in Leslie Howard's touring production of *Hamlet*. It was just a few years before Leslie's remarkable performance as Ashley Wilkes in *Gone with the Wind*. The play was directed by the majestic John Houseman and choreographed by the great lady of American dance, Agnes De Mille, and the neoromantic composer Virgil Thomson wrote marvelous incidental music. After a few months, the actor who played Rosencrantz had to leave the show. The producers wanted to bring in an actor from New York to fill the role. Leslie, showing the good judgment and kindness that permeated his personality, insisted they bring someone up through the ranks. On Leslie's suggestion, I was upgraded from spear carrier to Rosencrantz.

After several weeks in Chicago, we started our tour to Des Moines, Kansas City, Wichita, Salt Lake City, Ogden, Denver, and then westward to California, where we played in Fresno, San Jose, San Francisco, San Diego, and Los Angeles. We took the train from town to town, a traveling troupe of actors and technicians. As good as Leslie was in film, his stage presence was magnificent, and he was openhearted and supportive, especially to younger actors like myself. The tour was magnificent, and it launched my long-standing love of the American countryside and the small towns that housed good-hearted and eager theatergoing people.

Whenever there was a break in the tour, I was in New York, where I partook in performances at the Theatre Collective at the posh address of 2 Washington Square South. The Collective had a dining room where you could get a delicious meal for about twenty cents, which was a welcome relief since I had no income when the tour was on break. The atmosphere was intoxicating. The Theatre Collective introduced me to the work of Constantin Stanislavsky, the founder of the Moscow Art Theater and the father of so much that is good about acting today. His approach was a far cry from the Delsarte Method that had been central to my Feagin School training, and as I became enmeshed in his theories, I started to come alive as an artist.

The Theatre Collective rented the nearby Provincetown Playhouse on MacDougal Street in Greenwich Village for Lope de Vega's *The Pastry Baker* and *You Can't Change Human Nature* by Phil Stevenson and Maurice Clark. The Collective also did agitprop plays and booked programs featuring scenes from Irwin Shaw's *Bury the Dead,* Clifford Odets's *Waiting for Lefty* and *Till the Day I Die,* and the poet Alfred Kreymborg's *America, America!* The Collective had avant-garde training programs for its large acting membership, and we performed for free at union halls and the Hungarian Worker's Club, and we appeared at Madison Square Garden's *Political Pageants,* directed by my friend the imaginative and talented Jules "Julie" Dassin. I played one of the four narrators. It was thrilling to be performing in that prestigious venue. During this time I also met all the Theatre of Action performers, including Will Lee, who years later played Mr. Hooper on *Sesame Street,* and Nicholas Ray, who went on to direct *Rebel without a Cause.* Elia Kazan directed the Theatre of Action's first indoor theater production of *The Young Go First,* a play about young men working in the Works Progress Administration's Civilian Conservation Corps.

It was an ideal time to be immersed in theater. Creativity was high, and thinking outside expected approaches to art and imagination was encouraged. How I spent my days and nights was a far cry from anything I could have imagined as a boy struggling to find myself within the confines of the Yeshiva.

I counted my blessings every day and silently thanked Mr. Rosenswieg, my high school English teacher, for recognizing something in me that I was finally beginning to discover in myself.

2

Hope

I met my wife, Hope, in May 1937 when I walked my friend Naomi Schwartz home from a rehearsal. I can't remember what play we were working on, but I do remember it was great fun. As I entered Naomi's apartment, I saw the most beautiful woman I had ever seen curled up on the couch, reading a book. Naomi introduced me to her roommate, Hope Victorson. Hope and I talked very briefly. I asked her what she was reading and she replied, "*Old Calabria* by George Norman Douglas." She looked at me for a moment and then said, "I just finished it. Would you like to borrow it?"

"Yes," I said, unable to take my eyes off her.

Naomi, Hope, and I talked for a bit longer, and then it was time for me to leave. As I said my good-byes, Hope put *Old Calabria* into my hands. I slipped the small green book into my coat pocket and left the apartment, having no idea that my life had just been changed forever. I still cherish that copy of *Old Calabria* and keep it always on my bookshelf.

A few days after meeting Hope, I got a job doing summer stock at the Maverick Theatre in Woodstock, New York. I had to leave the production I was rehearsing with Naomi. I took *Old Calabria* with me. The Maverick was a wonderful theater. We'd do Ibsen's *Hedda Gabler* and Shaw's *Candida* with only one week's rehearsal. The performances were marvelous. Woodstock had been a successful artist's habitat since 1902, and our audiences comprised writers, painters, sculptors, and musicians who were always enthusiastic about our work. I spent five months in Woodstock and then worked odd theater jobs before returning to New York.

Six months after I met her, I returned *Old Calabria* to Hope. I had never known anyone like her. She was fascinated by art and art history. Even though I was a native New Yorker, I had spent little time in the city's many museums. Hope took me to the Metropolitan and introduced me to painters such as Brunelleschi, Leonardo, and Titian. I fell in love with the drama of El Greco and the passion of Botticelli. Hope introduced me to the Frick, which over time became our favorite museum to visit. She also introduced me to the Museum of Modern Art. MOMA hadn't landed at its permanent location in midtown Manhattan yet, but its early exhibitions offered a breathtaking glimpse into impressionist painters such as Cézanne, Gauguin, Seurat, and van Gogh as well as the abstract expressionist artists Kandinsky, Beckmann, and Klee. I discovered art through Hope's eyes. I learned to see the world through Hope's eyes.

We spent evenings walking in Greenwich Village, talking about culture, life, and politics. Hope had a passion for social justice, and we were both staunch trade unionists. We had come from very different backgrounds. Hope's mother had died when she was thirteen, and her grandparents, successful wine merchants in Manhattan, stepped in and raised her. They brought Hope up with a refined, cultured view of the world. She was Jewish but had been sent to a Catholic convent school after her mother died, so she had no experience with the Orthodoxy I was raised with. My days in the Yeshiva and my work in progressive theater had left me questioning many of the tenets my parents still lived by. I embraced my Judaism but was uncomfortable with the confines Orthodoxy insisted on. I vividly remember the first time I ate a ham sandwich. I was nineteen and studying at the Feagin School. As my teeth sunk into the thick, white bread layered with mayonnaise, lettuce, tomato, and ham, I truly wondered if I would be struck dead for my crime. I didn't die and it was delicious. From that moment on, it was impossible for me to keep kosher.

Regardless of the differences in our upbringing, Hope and I found common ground easily and we became inseparable. We were married on February 26, 1938. Hope was nineteen and I was twenty-three. We rented a cozy flat on 4th Street in Greenwich Village. On the ground floor, a lovely woman named Kate Brignoli owned an Italian grocery store. Kate introduced Hope and me to inspiring Italian cheeses, sultry olives, and dark coffees we had never heard of and taught us how to make her family's recipe for spaghetti sauce. That recipe became part of our family's culinary tradition, and my children and grandchildren still make it to this day.

Hope's grandmother Annie Eiseman would visit us from time to time. She was an extraordinary woman, self-made and self-taught. She and Hope's grandfather Morris at one time had owned six wine shops in Manhattan. They sold wines, brandies, and cordials they produced on their farms in New Jersey and California. Prohibition had taken away their fortune; they were reduced to distilling sacramental wine for religious purposes only. They were forced to close all six of their stores. Defined by an indomitable spirit, Annie would arrive at our door with an impressive stack of pink boxes from Ebinger's, filled to the brim with cakes and pastries. I adored Annie. She and I would spend the evening singing Gilbert and Sullivan together while we munched on the sweet delights she had marched up our stairs.

For the first few weeks of our marriage, I'd leave our apartment at ten in the evening, take the Eighth Avenue line, and walk to the basement of the Belasco Theatre on West 44th Street. My colleagues and I were rehearsing a staged reading of a play written by the actor Peter Frey. It was an autobiographical tale about his wartime experiences as a volunteer with the Abraham Lincoln Brigade during the Spanish Civil War. The Abraham Lincoln Brigade was an eclectic group of American volunteers who joined the International Brigade in Spain to fight against the fascist dictator Francisco Franco. The International Brigade was central to Ernest Hemingway's novel *For Whom the Bell Tolls*.

The Belasco was running a production of Irwin Shaw's *The Gentle People* with Sylvia Sidney, Franchot Tone, Sam Jaffe, and Roman "Bud" Bohnen. Sylvia had done a string of films in Hollywood and had returned to New York to appear on the stage. Franchot had been a founding member of the Group Theatre and was married to Joan Crawford at the time. Sam was a marvelous actor who went on to appear in *The Day the Earth Stood Still* and then costarred in the television series *Ben Casey* in the 1960s. The owners of the Belasco let us use the basement of the theater to rehearse after hours.

As soon as the curtain fell, we would begin our run-through. By then, it was close to midnight. My dear friend Bud Bohnen, who over time became my mentor as an acting teacher, would come down the stairs to our underground theater to direct us, and off we'd go until the wee hours of the morning. Our cast included Martin Ritt, who went on to direct films like *Hud* and *Norma Rae,* Karl Malden, and Will Lee. We were booked for Sunday afternoon performances at the Nora Bayes Theatre on West 44th Street. The reading went well, so we started in on our second midnight project, Ben Bengal's *Planet in the Sun*. After that, we did Phil Stevenson's *Transit,* based on a prizewinning short story by Albert Maltz. We scheduled a performance of Marc Blitzstein's musical paean to the American workingman, *May Day*, at Orson Welles's Mercury Theatre. Art Smith was our director and Carl Lerner was our stage manager. We did a run-through for Orson, and he graciously offered suggestions that we eagerly incorporated into our performance.

It was a heady time for theater in New York, and while we were all driven by a deep commitment to creativity and art, I cannot recall a single colleague of mine from that period who was not, to some degree, caught up with the vigor of left-wing theater. The New Theatre League had been established in 1935 and was a beehive of social activism. The group set up branches in Chicago, Philadelphia, Los Angeles, and San Francisco. A whole generation of American actors read *New Theatre Magazine* and looked forward to the publication of innovative plays such as Odets's *I Can't Sleep* and Albert Maltz's *Private Hicks*. There were scoffers who categorized the new drama as propaganda, but slowly, over time, mainstream theaters became interested in the high caliber of work coming out of our movement.

Before long, Broadway was producing plays with social content by Elmer Rice, Maxwell Anderson, Clifford Odets, Sidney Kingsley, S. N. Behrman, Sherwood Anderson, Sophie Treadwell, Irwin Shaw, and Robert Sherwood. It was a wonderful time to be immersed in theater, and it seemed that new, bright plays were being written and produced almost every day. There was ample opportunity to perform in splendid productions with an equally high caliber of talented directors and composers, supported by an audience eager to be there. Film had not yet cannibalized the dreams of young actors, and our focus on craft and our desire to appear in quality theater productions seemed unending.

Our interest in politics was an organic offshoot of what was going on around us. We all had experienced the poverty of the Great Depression, when it was almost impossible for anyone to have any aspirations beyond "What are we going to eat for breakfast?" I had just turned fifteen when the Depression hit. Overnight, my family was poor. I knew what it was like to be hungry. I remember begging my mother for money. She gave me eight cents. I went straight to the bakery and bought a loaf of rye bread and ate it on the spot. My parents had owned our house in Borough Park for over twenty years, and suddenly they were unable to pay the mortgage. The bank evicted us. They evicted everyone on our block. My father was a very honest man, but I think the Depression did him in. We lost our house because people who owed him money couldn't pay him. What can you do about that kind of chain of events but go on anyway? What can you do but hope for a better world with better solutions?

My experience was certainly not unique. Everyone in the theater scene in New York had a similar story, and unless you have a cold heart, those kinds of experiences soften you to the well-being of the Everyman. We wanted everyone to be raised up and counted as valuable. As a result, we were politically aware and, more important, strongly antifascist. Many of us, including Hope and me, raised money on street corners in Manhattan to support our friends who had joined the Abraham Lincoln Brigade. We believed in the abundance of the world around us and understood the plight of the worker. We also believed art could make a difference in people's lives. If that made us political, then indeed we were.

Harry Hopkins was the director of President Roosevelt's Works Progress Administration (WPA). The WPA and its sister project, the Civilian Conservation Corps (CCC), put thousands of Americans back to work during the Depression. The WPA constructed bridges, roads, and hundreds of marvelous buildings all across America that are still in use today. The CCC focused on America's natural resources and constructed national and state parks; it also planted nearly 3 billion trees to help reforest America. Fortunately, Harry Hopkins also believed society had an obligation to support the arts and made the astute observation to President Roosevelt that "unemployed actors are as hungry as anybody else."[1] To address this concern, Roosevelt created the Federal Theatre Project in 1935.

The Federal Theatre was not a revolutionary idea. As early as the 1800s, there had been strong support for theater in the United States. Our first theater structures were built in the port cities of Charleston, South Carolina; Philadelphia; New York; and Boston, and the great British stars of the nineteenth century, such as John Philip Kemble and his sister Sarah Siddons, William Macready, Edmund Kean, Sir Henry Irving, and Ellen Terry, would present premiere performances before taking their plays on the road to the newer towns sprouting up toward the west. American stars such as Joseph Jefferson, Edwin Booth, Clara Morris, James O'Neill, Julia Marlowe, Minnie Maddern Fiske, Charlotte Cushman, Adelaide Neilson, Lillie Langtry, Lola Montez, and John McCullough soon followed suit. In *Democracy in America,* written in 1835 by Alexis de Tocqueville, the French historian and social commentator observed that even in the wild frontiers nearly every house he visited had a Bible and a few odd volumes of Shakespeare. He further observed that the size of audiences attending Shakespearean plays in the United States far exceeded that of British audiences. This familiarity with Shakespeare served Americans for many generations and allowed the reading public to "get" and laugh at Mark Twain's Dauphin in *Huckleberry Finn* as well as the random extracts from *Hamlet, Romeo and Juliet,* and *King Lear* Twain wove into his mongrelized soliloquies. This curiosity and commitment was still true in 1935. It was a time in America when art in all its forms was viewed as a necessity, and going to see live theater was part of the fabric of everyday life.

My friends and I were ecstatic when we heard about the formation of the Federal Theatre and signed up to work. My first assignment was in 1937 with a traveling circus. I played the suitor Lomov, in clown makeup, for Chekhov's one-act farce *A Marriage Proposal.* We performed for free in public parks all over New York City to enthusiastic crowds. Our big-time date was in Washington Square Park in Greenwich Village, just a few blocks away from where Hope and I would eventually live. After we were married, the Federal Theatre assigned me the role of one of the four narrators in George Sklar's expressionistic *Life and Death of an American* at the Maxine Elliott Theater. J. Arthur Kennedy, who later went on to win a Tony Award for the role of Biff in *Death of a Salesman* on Broadway, played the lead. The production was very inventive for its time and included multimedia projections, jazz, vaudeville, singing, and dancing, all interlaced with the story of a World War I veteran who was shot and killed by the police while picketing at a steel mill. The play was based on the true story of a 1936 Memorial Day shooting of twelve trade unionists who demonstrated outside Republic Steel in Chicago. *Life and Death of an American* and other Federal Theatre productions that urged social action drew attention to corporate insensitivity and the rights of the American worker. These productions were also lightning rods for conservatives in Congress who supported corporate greed.

In 1938 the House Un-American Activities Committee (HUAC), chaired by Congressman Martin Dies of Texas, aggressively went after President Roosevelt's federal arts programs. The committee searched out a small number of witnesses who testified that communists were running the Federal Theatre. Writers, actors, musicians, directors, and scene designers spontaneously organized protest meetings. After the final curtain calls in Broadway houses, the stars of almost every play would step forward and urge audiences to protest HUAC by joining them at midnight protest meetings. One night I attended a particularly impassioned Actors' Equity meeting at the Music Box Theatre that was chaired by Raymond Massey and Tallulah Bankhead. Raymond had just starred on Broadway in *Abe Lincoln in Illinois*, and Tallulah was starring in Lillian Hellman's *Little Foxes* on Broadway. Their input gave great weight to the cause. As the meeting ended, the entire gathering rose to its feet, en masse, and joined up with another equally spontaneous meeting that had gathered at Times Square. Along the way, mounted police graciously cooperated and directed traffic to alternative routes so that we could make our way in peace.

Hallie Flanagan, the national director of the Federal Theatre Project, wrote repeatedly to Chairman Dies asking for an opportunity to reply to the allegations of communism, but it was months before she was finally allowed to appear. When she did, one committee member, Congressman Joe Starnes from Alabama, referred to an article Flanagan had written for *Theatre Arts Magazine* in which she described the emergence of trade union theaters and their enthusiasm as having a "Marlowesque madness." "You are quoting from this Marlowe?" observed Starnes. "Is he a communist? Tell us who Marlowe is, so we can get the proper reference."[2]

Starnes then asked Flanagan whether this "Mr. Euripides" was also a communist. Starnes, ignorant as the day is long, was referring to William Shakespeare's contemporary Christopher Marlowe and to the classical Greek playwright Euripides, who died in 406 BC. In her book *Arena: The History of the Federal Theatre,* Flanagan bemoaned the danger of Starnes's ignorance. "The room rocked with laughter but I did not laugh. Eight thousand people might lose their jobs because a Congressional Committee had so pre-judged us that even the classics were 'communistic.'"[3]

Later that year, the Federal Theatre was skewered by Dies and his committee when they convinced Congress to cancel the Federal Theatre's funding. Overnight, more than twelve thousand actors, musicians, chorus girls, stagehands, costumers, writers, and directors who had produced more than 2,700 stage productions for their fellow Americans lost their jobs. I was one of them.

The Federal Theatre's four-year existence had offered dignified employment to many whose work had evaporated because of the combined forces of the Depression and the success of the talkies. In the days before talkies, in movie theaters across America, live vaudeville acts performed before the silent films began. This offered a living wage to thousands of American artists. *The Motion Picture Almanac* states that in 1932, close to 14,000 silent movie houses that had once booked live vaudeville shows were wired for sound, and the live pre-shows the public once adored were sacked.

Indifferent to the job losses, Congressman Dies saw the utility of Red-baiting and used it to attack President Roosevelt's entire Works Project Administration. Using the demise of the Federal Theatre Project as his linchpin, he went after the WPA. In time, thousands of American workers in a myriad of professions, from bricklayers to machinists, carpenters to electricians, lost their jobs in the wake of his aggressive and mean-spirited witch hunt. Like those of his later counterpart, Senator Joseph McCarthy, many if not all of Dies's accusations about communists in government programs proved to be untrue. The damage had been done, however.

With the evaporation of the Federal Theatre, I counted myself lucky when I found work promoting the Berkeley Marionettes, a group that performed in public schools in New York and New Jersey. This brought in a very scant wage. Hope had steady work as a secretary in a Wall Street consulting firm, and her income sustained us for many months. But acting was beginning to seem futile. My father owned a sash, door, and trim factory in Brooklyn, so I enrolled in a blueprint-reading course at the Brooklyn Engineering Institute with a plan to find employment in the construction industry. Although it was a bitter pill, I was determined to find solvency in some other area and was ready to forgo the unstable life of an actor.

Hope presented another plan.

3

California

Before the demise of the Federal Theatre Project, Hope and I purchased a Model A Ford. It cost seventy-five dollars at a New York Garbage Collection Department auction. Hope proposed we sublet our apartment and drive west to California. The idea ignited my imagination. I tacked an ad on the Actors' Equity bulletin board, and the next day a very likable couple agreed to stay in our apartment. Off we went.

We spent a few days visiting Hope's father in Clarksburg, West Virginia. While we were there, I decided that our olive drab Ford needed a fresh paint job. I went to a general store and bought a ten-cent can of stove polish and a five-cent paintbrush. Our Model A Roadster beamed shiny black.

From Clarksburg we headed south. Hope's former roommate Naomi had married a delightful man named David Robison. David was teaching musicology at Fisk University in Nashville, Tennessee. Naomi was pregnant with their first child, Paula (now a world-class flutist). We spent several exciting days with them exploring the all-black university and hearing about David's teaching experiences before we continued our drive out west. Our maximum speed across the country was never more than forty miles an hour. Our headlights were unstable, so we had to stop by dusk. The trip took eighteen days. Our stay in modest motels usually cost us a whopping $.75 a night, and, on occasion, we'd pay the high rate of $1.50. When we added up motels, toll bridge crossings, gas, oil, cigarettes, and meals at roadside diners, the trip cost a total of $82.25—and that included a flywheel replacement at a small repair shop in the Ozarks.

On June 15, 1939, Hope and I followed Route 66 as it merged with Vermont Avenue into Hollywood. I made a left turn at Sunset Boulevard and impulsively made another turn as we reached the entrance to Barnsdall Park. There was a sign in front of a very modest house that read, "Room for rent." We stopped, made inquiries, and rented a room with bathroom privileges for $3.75 a week. We had been in Hollywood for less than an hour and already had a home.

On our second day in Hollywood, quite by chance, our friend Lee J. Cobb drove by in a convertible. I had not seen Lee since we had done Odets's *Till the Day I Die* together at the Theatre Collective. Lee eagerly pulled over and briefed us on whom we'd find in town. He gave us Julie Dassin's phone number and told us there was a weekly poker game at Julie's house on Mound Street in the Hollywood Hills. A whole range of New York wunderkind artists and social activists, including the playwright Clifford Odets, was regularly drawn to Julie's card table. Julie was on the RKO roster as a director-in-training and was about to start work on *They Knew What They Wanted*, directed by Garson Kanin and starring Carole Lombard and Charles Laughton. I called Julie and he not only invited us over, but he also asked if Hope and I would be willing to move into the commodious house he shared with his wife, Bea, and their three-year-old son, Joey. Bea was pregnant with their second child, and Julie was leaving the following day for location. He didn't want Bea to be alone.

The arrangement was serendipitous. We gave up our one-room flat and moved into the Dassins' house on a quiet cul-de-sac. It was furnished with great taste. Hope and I slept in the very large library, which connected to a bathroom. The day after Julie left, Bea went into labor. We drove her to Cedars of Lebanon Hospital, where she delivered their daughter, Rachel. Hope and I looked after Joey while Bea was in the hospital. Julie came home for a visit but had to return to filming in Northern California. He asked if we could stay until he returned. Our trip to California had been decided on a lark. We were feeling very footloose and fancy-free, and I was relieved not to be in the doldrums of blueprint studies in New York. Staying seemed like a fine idea.

Hollywood was beautiful back then. Hollywood Boulevard was lined with pepper trees that waved gently in the breeze. Hope and I enjoyed walking to the Thrifty Drugstore for the Blue Plate special. We ate meals of soup, entrée, salad, assorted pies, and coffee for thirty-five cents. We both loved to walk to the beautiful expanse of the wood-framed Hollywood Hotel on Highland Avenue and enjoyed the delights of nearby C. C. Brown's Ice Cream Parlor, which served inspired ice cream sundaes that came with their own little brown pitcher of hot fudge that you could never get enough of. From time to time, we had picnics at the base of the massive artesian well at the end of Vine Street and looked down on the picturesque Lake Hollywood Reservoir.

One morning I decided to walk to the Sunset Strip, about two miles west of the Dassin house. I'd heard that all the agents had offices in that area. In New York, actors "did the rounds." That meant dropping in at random agencies to see if anyone was casting plays. Unaware that that wasn't how agents worked in Hollywood, I decided to do likewise to see what might come of it.

My only respectable jacket was a Harris tweed, fit for wintry climes. On this particular day, California was at its sunniest, and while I was clearly overdressed, my enthusiasm was high. I walked into the first agency and told them of my theater background. They were moderately interested and said they'd let me know. The second agency was not interested at all. My third sojourn was the Paul Wilkins Agency. Paul signed me as a client on the spot. He had never even seen me act.

Paul arranged for the two of us to meet at MGM the very next day. He introduced me to a casting director named Leonard Murphy. After speaking with me for only a few minutes, Murphy told me to report to wardrobe the following day. I had been hired for the role of a Viennese music student in Noël Coward's musical *Bitter Sweet,* starring Jeanette MacDonald and Nelson Eddy and directed by W. S. Van Dyke, a prestigious director who had worked on the *Thin Man* series. I went home, ecstatic, to tell Hope the good news. I was told I had one line, which was fine with me. This was more work than I had had in months of looking for work in New York. And it was acting. And it was in film.

The next day I took the bus to MGM. The lot was a glorious place with cavernous soundstages that captured my imagination. I could not believe my good fortune. This was a time when the line between movies and theater was still fairly seamless. Good actors populated Hollywood and even B movies were well written and had stellar musical scores and excellent cinematography. It never occurred to me that by taking a role in a film, I might be leaving my stage career behind. Everyone I knew did both without either form's being diminished or disgraced.

At the conclusion of my brief one line, the assistant director handed me a chit and told me to report to the payroll department. The woman behind the desk handed me a check for $42.50. Five dollars went to my agent and $2.50 to social security. The remaining $35.00 was mine to keep.

The most I had ever earned as a Junior Equity member was $40.00 for an entire week's work. The sum in my pocket seemed enormous.

I had little time to ruminate over my good fortune. Two days later Paul asked me to meet him at Paramount Studios on Melrose Avenue. He introduced me to a casting director named Joe Egli. On the spot Egli sent me to wardrobe, and that same day I "starred" in a coming attraction vignette as a young man who has just seen the new movie called *I Want a Divorce,* starring Dick Powell and Joan Blondell. My role was to stare straight into the camera and tell audiences in every American movie house that they absolutely *must* see this film. It took only a few hours, and this time I went home with fifty dollars in my pocket. Hope and I were truly rich. Paul introduced me to Dick Stockton, RKO's chief casting director. Two days later I landed a three-day stint in Kay Kyser's *You'll Find Out,* directed by David Butler. Butler went on to direct the string of Bob Hope and Bing Crosby *Road* films.

In the wake of our good fortune, Hope and I decided to stay in fertile California. We rented the lower level of a little house just around the corner from the Dassins', at the intersection of Vine Street and Ivar Avenue. We had our own backyard, a screened-in breakfast nook, pretty birch trees outside our window, and a well-equipped kitchen. The rent for our hillside love nest, furniture, utilities, and all, was a mere thirty-five dollars a month. It was true California living and nothing like our little apartment back in New York.

One evening, over dinner with a group of friends, and with the advent of my newfound film career, we collectively decided it would be a good idea to change my name from Arthur Zwerling to Jeff Corey. I had been up for a role in Erskine Caldwell's *Tobacco Road,* and the producer asked me, "What kind of name is that?" I realized that he had a mind-set for the character and the name Zwerling didn't fit the part, even if I did. He was looking for something more bucolic. At the time there were no Jeffs in Hollywood, and this new name flew out of thin air. I was born on August 10, 1914, and my immigrant parents named me Albert. When the United States entered World War I in 1917, to show their loyalty to their adopted country, my parents legally changed my name from the Germanic Albert to the more American Arthur. I grew up knowing this story, and I think on some level my name was less important to me than who I was as a person. Hope moved easily into the new nomenclature, and overnight we became Hope and Jeff Corey. It is a name I have cherished since then and a surname my three daughters carry to this day.

Shortly after that, I heard from MGM again. They wanted me to play a Swedish newlywed in one of the last Metro zany comedies called *Third Finger, Left Hand.* It starred Myrna Loy and Melvyn Douglas and was directed by the silent film maestro Robert Z. Leonard. This was a much bigger part, but I still didn't get screen credit. I got the script and endeavored to acquaint myself with a Swedish accent. I stopped in at a nearby Swedish Lutheran church, but the minister and his flock all spoke perfect English. Fortunately, Greta Granstedt, who had been cast as my wife, was also represented by Paul Wilkins. Greta's parents were Swedish immigrants, and she read my dialogue to me with a perfect Swedish intonation. Greta also suggested I bleach my hair and recommended a reliable beauty parlor on Ivar Avenue. My heavy Harris tweed jacket was perfect for my newlywed role. I still cherish the photo of myself with Greta, Myrna, and Melvyn. My hair is blond and I look like an eager Swedish newlywed. It's a charming film although, sadly, rarely shown.

After my debut as a Swede, Universal wanted me to play the Swedish cook in *Mutiny in the Arctic* with Andy Devine and Richard Arlen. The background footage for *Mutiny in the Arctic* was lifted from Leni Riefenstahl's documentary *S.O.S. Iceberg.* Riefenstahl's film had originally been released in Europe by the German film company UFA. Throughout our filming, Andy, Richard, and I slid down a fabricated snow-covered incline into a large tank of water. In the final editing, they merged the two scenes together so what the audience saw was the three of us sliding down the icy footage from *S.O.S. Iceberg.*

After that, I was up for a part in *Two-Faced Woman,* starring the great Greta Garbo. I was to play a Swedish skiing instructor. I lied to the producers and told them I knew how to ski and then immediately got a lot of sound theory from a friend who had won a national skiing tournament in New Hampshire. I learned all that could be taught on a Persian rug in a house in Beverly Hills, and while I was pretty confident that I would be able to fake it, I think the odds were against me because skiing is harder to learn than it looks. When I didn't get the part, Paul reassured me there were more feature films in the offing.

Delightfully, there were.

4

Hollywood at Its Finest

In New York it had been my belief that as a stage actor I needed to have a good part in a hit play so that I could be put under a studio contract in Hollywood. In Hollywood acting in films fueled all my desires to continue to investigate the art of the stage. I had heard that Mary Virginia Farmer, who had been associated with the Group Theatre and the Theatre Collective and had overseen the Federal Theatre Project on the West Coast, was living in Los Angeles. Upon the demise of the Federal Theatre, Virginia rented space at the Falcon Dance Studio on Sunset Boulevard and established an acting class there. Hope and I went to visit her and had a delightful time. Through her we met Dick and Marjorie Fiske. The Fiskes had worked with the Seattle Repertory Playhouse, and Dick was under contact to Columbia Pictures. He and Marjorie invited us to a Christmas dinner in their pasteboard cabin on a cul-de-sac off Beachwood Drive. Through Virginia we also met the writers Alfred and Helen Levitt and actress Mary Davenport, who later married the screenwriter Waldo Salt.

We all became fast friends and our mutual interests brought us together in discussions about setting up acting classes for professional actors—much as the New Theatre League and the Theatre Collective had in New York. A large group of us met with Julie Dassin in the lobby of the League of American Writers on Vine Street. Julie agreed to teach a class, and a month later the board of directors of the Music Box theater (today known as the Fonda Theatre) gave us the use of their balcony foyer on Monday nights, when their very successful revue, *Meet the People,* was dark. There must have been about thirty of us in that first class. I rehearsed excerpts from George Kaufman's *Dinner at Eight* and Lynn Riggs's *Russet Mantle.* Veteran actors such as Alexander Granach, who had been a leading performer for Max Reinhardt in Germany, joined us as well. Since all our classes were in the evening, those of us fortunate enough to be working in film during the day had no problem maintaining regular attendance.

In 1940 the exiled German director William Dieterle was casting his RKO production of Stephen Vincent Benét's *The Devil and Daniel Webster*. Dieterle had seen my photo in the Screen Actors Guild's *Players Directory* and, without auditioning me, hired me for the part of Tom Sharp, the young leader of the Farmers' Grange. Dieterle and his wife believed in numerology, and the figuration of my new name, Jeff Corey, augured good fortune. Dieterle didn't know I had changed my name, but apparently that didn't matter. What mattered was that the letters of my name fit some configuration he had in mind for the role of Tom Sharp. The script was delivered to my home, and I was instructed to arrive at the set at 2:00 p.m. on the following Wednesday for the first day of filming. Dieterle had chosen the time and date in compliance with his numerological forecasts. The great Walter Huston played the Devil, and Edward Arnold played Daniel Webster.

Again, I couldn't believe my good fortune. It was a little more than a year since I had decided to forgo acting as a career. I gloated when I read my first press release in the *Los Angeles Times,* "Jeff Corey, 26-year-old character actor, will undertake the second juvenile lead in *The Devil and Daniel Webster* with William Dieterle directing. He weighs 175 pounds and is 6′2″ and this is his seventh assignment since coming to Hollywood."

I was truly an actor now and felt I had a career I could count on.

The following year, Dieterle hired me again, for RKO's *Syncopation,* a story about the birth of jazz in New Orleans. After that, he cast me in *Tennessee Johnson* at MGM. Just before the blacklist, Dieterle hired me again for Hal Wallis's Western *Red Mountain*. It was shot in Arizona and starred Lizabeth Scott and the now famous Alan Ladd. I had worked with Alan in *Petticoat Politics* at Republic Studios in 1940. At the time, he was relatively unknown. He was a down-to-earth guy who had worked as a grip to support his young family and slowly graduated to acting in B movies and then ultimately moved into Hollywood's A-list with his stunning performance in *Shane.*

Right after I filmed *The Devil and Daniel Webster,* our friends Mike and Elizabeth Gordon rented a large house with a tennis court on Woodrow Wilson Drive in the Hollywood Hills. They asked Hope and me if we would like to share it with them. It was an incredible house with a stellar Hollywood lineage. The house had been built for Lew Ayres and Ginger

Rogers. At one time, Orson Welles and Dolores del Rio had also lived there. We loved the idea. Mike had just started directing for Columbia. He had a good background, coming from Yale University, where his fellow students included Elia Kazan, Albert Maltz, George Sklar, and Molly Day Thatcher. Mike had directed at the Theater Union and, at its demise, was invited to do lighting for the Group Theatre. On weekends, all the old Group Theatre folks who had come west took over our kitchen and tennis court. Martin Ritt and his wife, Adele, Bud Bohnen, Alan Baxter, Tony Kraber, Phil and Ginny Brown, Anthony Mann, Eddie Dmytryk and his wife, Madeleine, all joined our Woodrow Wilson Drive coterie. We talked about film and theater and the great prospects of our acting workshop at the Music Box.

Around this time our classes moved from the balcony foyer to the large stage of the Music Box. When *Meet the People* closed, we decided we needed a home of our own. We all chipped in and rented a space above Sharkey's Saloon in a redbrick building at the corner of Bronson and Franklin avenues in Hollywood. All of us were handy from our stagecraft days, and together we built a platform stage, found appropriate velour curtains at an ancient theater warehouse, and put up some rudimentary lighting equipment. We agreed that a good name for our new theater would be the Actors' Laboratory Theatre, a name inspired by Richard Boleslavsky's American Laboratory Theatre in New York. Delighted with our newfound adventure, we became known as the Actors' Lab.

We had so much room that we were able to add a class taught by Mary Virginia Farmer. When Julie Dassin began to direct at RKO, Bud Bohnen took over teaching for him. Every morning, the actor Daniel Mann, Lloyd Bridges, and I would play a couple of sets of tennis in a nearby North Hollywood park, pick up some lunch, and drive to Bud's house in Studio City. Lloyd and his wife, Dottie, were Hope's and my closest friends. As our movie careers began to come into focus, Lloyd and I often appeared together in the same films, and it was always great fun to work with him. Lloyd and Dottie's son Jeff is named after me, and when my daughter Emily was born, Lloyd and Dottie were the first people to visit Hope in the hospital. Sadly, later on, when HUAC raised its ugly head, Lloyd and I chose different paths and our warm friendship, which I truly valued, abruptly ended.

But back in those halcyon days of Hollywood before the blacklist, Lloyd, Danny, and I would head over to Bud's house, eager to hear what he had to say. Bud would sit at his piano and play a random Chopin or Beethoven piece, and then we'd talk about our plans for a vital theater community in Los Angeles. We were fortunate to have Art Smith, J. Edward Bromberg, and Martin Ritt serve as backup teachers. Orson Welles came by from time to time to air his views on independent theater. His observations were always cogent and inspiring.

In those exciting and creative years before World War II, my film career kept growing apace. Twentieth Century Fox engaged me for *The Man Who Wouldn't Die*, starring Lloyd Nolan. After that, Fox hired me for *Small Town Deb*, *The Moon Is Down*, *Roxie Hart*, and *The Postman Didn't Ring*. The director Harold Schuster hired me to play the wrangler Tim Murphy in *My Friend Flicka*. I spent three months on location in the High Country near Buford, Wyoming. Upon my return, I resumed work at the Actors' Lab and immediately started rehearsing for our first public offering, the second act of Odets's *Paradise Lost*, directed by Howard Da Silva. We set a date for a single performance. It was to be on Monday, December 8, 1941.

On the morning of December 7, 1941, Hope and I decided to take a drive through the San Gabriel Valley and out toward the desert. It was a beautiful, sunlit December day with sylvan views of the mountains and soft winds blowing through orange groves. We were enjoying our conversation so much, we neglected to turn on our radio. We didn't learn of the terrible events at Pearl Harbor until we returned home later that evening.

Among the many discussions we had with friends about the day's tragic events was what to do about our performance. After much debate, we decided to put on our production. A blackout order had been issued for Los Angeles. Automobiles could be used at night with only their parking lights on, and those lights had to be covered by three dark blue sheets of gelatin. We found enough dark fabric to cover the windows in the theater and used one puny seven-watt nightlight onstage to illuminate our performance. I believe we had an audience of twenty-four.

A few days after Pearl Harbor, Helen Slote, the Actors' Lab's secretary, helped set up the Hollywood Canteen for servicemen. All our members, including myself, worked with the Red Cross and planned performances of *Brother Rat*, a popular play about shenanigans at a military academy. Red Cross volunteers drove the Actors' Lab's cast, crew, and wardrobe to veterans' hospitals all over the Los Angeles and Orange County areas, where we performed for patients and staff.

Not too many months later, many of us from the Actors' Lab went into the service ourselves. Gene Reynolds and I went into the navy. Daniel Mann served with the army in Burma, and Dick Fiske, who was the first chairman of the Actors' Lab, volunteered for the Rangers. Dick was killed in action after D-Day in Normandy. Another friend of the Actors' Lab, the screenwriter Robert Meltzer, was killed in Brittany during the Battle for Brest. Meltzer was married to our dear friend Jacobina Caro, the modern dancer.

Our daughter Eve was born on January 3, 1943. Three weeks after her birth, I was sent to boot camp in San Diego. From boot camp I went to Photo School in Pensacola, Florida. I still have my notebook filled with copious notes on how to take photos under fire. Four months later I was assigned to the USS *Yorktown* as photo mate 3rd class. I was originally assigned to what they called a Kaiser's coffin, which was a small ship used strictly for transporting airplanes and never would have seen combat. We were supposed to leave for Alexandria, Egypt, but two days before we were set to sail, the photo first mate on the *Yorktown* broke into the captain's alcohol cabinet and got stone drunk. In a huff, the skipper said, "Get that man's ass off my ship," which they did and assigned me to the *Yorktown* instead.

I spent two years in the Pacific on the *Yorktown* and was in fourteen major combat engagements. I photographed and filmed all of them. During the war, Hope used to go to the movies to watch the newsreels on the off chance she might see footage I had shot. On board the *Yorktown,* from time to time, I would emcee entertainment designed to boost morale on the ship. I wrote jokes and performed. It felt good, particularly under our circumstances, to get over 3,300 guys laughing, but the majority of my time was spent behind a camera, documenting death and destruction.

While I was overseas, my colleagues at the Actors' Lab, many of whom were too old to be inducted into the service, worked with military special services and performed productions such as *Three Men on a Horse* to entertain the troops on R&R. A particularly impressive war film, *A Walk in the Sun,* was directed by Lewis Milestone and employed every available actor from the Actors' Lab. Lewis had won an Academy Award for Best Director in 1930 for *All Quiet on the Western Front.*

During the war, the Actors' Lab moved to a larger location on Laurel Avenue and, through the Hollywood Canteen, offered free tickets for servicemen and servicewomen. *Life* magazine did a feature on the Actors'

Lab's wartime program and reported, "Some of the most skillful acting in the U.S. today is being done in Hollywood . . . by members of the Actors' Laboratory Theatre."[1]

I was proud to be a part of the Actors' Lab. With all the accolades and successes we experienced before and during the war, nothing could prepare us for the disaster that was soon to befall us.

5

The War Ends

At war's end, the *Yorktown* dropped anchor in Tokyo Harbor next to the USS *Missouri,* where the Japanese formally accepted surrender terms. We were the first American liberty party to land on Japanese soil. It was an amazing experience to walk through Japanese neighborhoods that only a few days before had been part of enemy territory. I took my camera with me and shot photos of the newly surrendered Japan. A local man stopped me and indicated he had been a war photographer—for the other side. He invited me to his home to show me some of his photographs. There was a surreal quality to looking at the war through such a different lens. As I prepared to leave, he handed me a set of watercolors his son had painted of the naval fleet of the Rising Sun. They were a remarkable view into a world I could only imagine.

The next day, my commanding officer told me to pack my gear and get "my ass" aboard the USS *Iowa.* I was suddenly headed for Hawaii. In October 1945 I sailed into San Pedro Harbor on the battleship *New Mexico.* It took three days to go through the discharge procedure. Hope and Evie met me at the pier, and in no time at all, we were at our lovely board-and-batten house on Hillcrest Road in the Hollywood Hills that Hope had rented during the last year of the war.

During those first blissful months after my discharge, I frequently commented to Hope how happy I was to be adapting so easily from my wartime experience to my renewed connection with the Actors' Lab and the resumption of my film career. I told her, "It is as if I had never gone away." After I shared that same sentiment with friends and associates over a period of months, one day Hope quietly told me there were changes. "When you fall asleep at night," she said, "you frequently get the shakes." She described how my whole body would tremble as I muttered incoherently, and that it had been going on for almost a year. What a revelation. They were kamikaze dreams! I was completely unaware of them.

Shortly after that, I had a dream I did remember. Hope and I were with three-year old Evie at the top of the Griffith Park Observatory. We had a clear view of downtown Los Angeles. Suddenly, a huge airplane crashed into City Hall and exploded. I had another dream in which I was sitting in Greenblatt's Delicatessen on Sunset Boulevard, directly across from the Actors' Lab. Again I watched as a plane crashed into the building across from me. The implication of those dreams became clear to me. This was well before doctors had identified post-traumatic stress syndrome (PTSD) as a condition resulting from combat. In the kamikaze dreams I mourned the death of friends and clearly worried about its happening again. Talking to Hope and realizing the nature of the trauma helped me, and over time my kamikaze nightmares went away.

Hope and I learned to juggle work and family life. Hope was supportive and patient. She never complained about the long hours I spent filming or the months I often spent shooting on location. We were living the life of a successful Hollywood couple. Life was good, and the future held great promise.

In the postwar years I had significant roles in more than thirty films, including *The Killers,* starring Burt Lancaster, and *Brute Force,* directed by my friend Julie Dassin. When I peruse the cast of *Brute Force,* I see at least a dozen members of the Actors' Lab in the cast, including Bud Bohnen, Art Smith, Jimmy O'Rear, Ruth Sanderson, Howard Duff, Kenneth Patterson, Will Lee, and others. It wasn't nepotism. Studio casting directors regarded the Actors' Lab's professional productions and GI student performances as a treasure trove.

Bryan Foy, who had been a producer at Warner Bros., hired me to play one of the leads in *Canon City,* a film based on an attempted prison break. I played Carl Schwartzmiller, one of the leaders of the break. Schwartzmiller and his fellow prisoners were all caught and sent to solitary confinement. Bryan contacted the warden and arranged for me to meet Schwartzmiller. It isn't often an actor gets a part in a screenplay and then is flown to meet the man he is about to play. It is rarer to find your man in a cramped, windowless cell in a prison building called Little Siberia. It is a further shock to discover that the man in that cell escaped from Joliet after four convictions and was arrested again in Colorado for armed robbery and assault to commit murder.

Schwartzmiller and I talked to each other through a slit in an iron door about five inches wide and perhaps three and a half inches high. His cubicle had no lights at all—he lived in darkness, save for some very faint reflected light from a small window in a corridor diagonal to his cell about twenty feet away.

"How come the guards hate your guts so much?" I asked Schwartzmiller. His face brightened.

"That's exactly the right dope, chum. I see right through them," he replied. In a confidential tone he asked, "Are they going to put me down as a pretty mean guy?"

I responded, "You're the heavy, all right." He thought about this for a moment. "I could have killed five screws [guards] by just giving our guys the nod."

He told me he knew this was the "end of the road" for him. He regretted not having been shot in the breakout. He asked them to kill him when he was captured in a farmhouse after a little old lady snuck up behind him and beat him unconscious with a claw hammer. Schwartzmiller and I talked in hushed tones because the captain of the guards was standing close by. I ended my conversation saying, "Sorry they couldn't get a prettier guy to play you, Schwartzmiller." He stopped for a beat and said, "You'll do me okay."

After *Canon City* came *Kidnapped, Wake of the Red Witch*, with John Wayne, *Hideout*, with Lloyd Bridges, *Bright Leaf*, directed by Michael Curtiz and starring Gary Cooper, Lauren Bacall, and Patricia Neal, and *Home of the Brave*. In the bustling postwar years, after filming all day, I rehearsed plays at the Actors' Lab at night. We had special Monday night performances of rarely produced plays, such as Aeschylus's *Prometheus Bound*, August Strindberg's *Miss Julie*, Gerhart Hauptmann's *The Weavers*, Goethe's *Götz von Berlichingen*, and Gotthold Lessing's *Nathan the Wise*. In January 1946 Julie Dassin was asked to direct *Piper Paid*, the first play written by the well-known short story writer Viola Brothers Shore. Viola was famous in her time as cohort of the humorist Dorothy Parker and an occasional member of the famed Algonquin Round Table. I joined the cast with Karen Morley, Howard Duff, Kenneth Patterson, Adrienne Marsden, and Jocelyn Brando, Marlon's sister. It was a drawing room comedy with social overtones. We played our scheduled week's run at the Actors' Lab, and by public demand, the performance was extended to a theater in Westwood for an additional week.

The Actors' Lab's classes qualified under the GI Bill, so a large number of war veterans enrolled in our programs. Fortuitously, the Actors' Lab had purchased the rights to *To the Living*, written by a combat veteran, Tony Palma, who had been in a German P.O.W. camp. Daniel Mann directed the production and cast it with many of the GIs who were taking classes at the Actors' Lab. We played to full houses at the renovated Las Palmas Theatre off Hollywood Boulevard. After each performance, veterans would come backstage and swap battle stories with us. It was a cathartic event for all.

In 1949 I costarred with Bill Lundigan in RKO's semi-documentary film noir *Follow Me Quietly*. The last day of shooting coincided with opening night of the Actors' Lab's production of Robert Sherwood's *Abe Lincoln in Illinois*, in which I played the leading role. We spent the day shooting at the remote East Los Angeles Water Works. It was a tough day. Shooting was behind schedule, and they needed a great deal covered, particularly shots of Bill and me racing up and down the cast-iron stairways of the waterworks as the villains, firing their guns, pursued us. Curtain time for *Abe Lincoln in Illinois* was 8:00 p.m. We stopped shooting at 7:10 p.m., and by 7:15 p.m. I was speeding along Hollywood Boulevard from East L.A. I arrived with ten minutes to shed my clothes, put on Lincoln's rustic apparel, and glue the familiar Lincoln wart to my right cheek. I made it onstage seconds before the curtain went up for my scene with Lincoln's teacher, Mentor Graham, played by David Wolfe. I still shake my head with disbelief as I remember that night and those hidden resources that kept a young actor going. The play ran for sixteen weeks.

During the war, the Actors' Lab had moved to a building around the corner from Schwab's Pharmacy. Sidney Skolsky, the movie and gossip writer for the *New York Daily Mirror* and, later, the *New York Post*, garnered much of his Hollywood gossip at Schwab's famous soda fountain, where fact and fiction conspired and tales of young stars being discovered abounded. Sidney loved our production of *Abe Lincoln in Illinois*. Any evening he had free, he would take the short walk from Schwab's to the Lab, where he would borrow a woman's shawl from the wardrobe mistress and walk onstage as one of the townsfolk who had gathered at the railroad station to hear Lincoln's farewell speech to his Springfield constituents. Sidney ranked with Hedda Hopper as the premier Hollywood gossip columnist, but unlike Hopper, who was just mean-spirited and vicious, Sidney actually understood the craft he was writing about and went on to produce a couple of films and star in his own television show.

The Actors' Lab had a stellar reputation and drew interest from a wide range of talent. Our numbers were enriched by the presence of the Group Theatre's cofounder, Morris Carnovsky, and his wife, Phoebe Brand. Art Smith, Ruth Nelson, Lee J. Cobb, Anthony Quinn, Phil and Ginny Brown, Hume Cronyn, Jessica Tandy, Vincent Price, Mary Tarcai, Robert Lewis, Mervyn Williams, Whitford Kane, Frances Williams, Sara Allgood of the Abbey Theater, Norman Lloyd, and Hugo Haas were all members. For a while, Michael Chekhov joined us and directed *The Inspector General*, which we put on at the Las Palmas Theatre in Hollywood. Even the conservative *Los Angeles Herald Examiner*, part of the Hearst syndicate, wrote, "We have been waiting a long time for a new life in the Los Angeles Theater. This is it. Casting and directing [at the Actors' Lab] sets a new standard for California productions."

Many studios sent their starlets to take classes at the Actors' Lab, taught by Phoebe Brand, Art Smith, and Mary Tarcai. A beautiful Marilyn Monroe showed up, along with the screenwriter Fay Kanin. UCLA professors Kenneth Macgowan, Ralph Freud, William Melnitz, and other faculty members from UCLA's Theater Arts Department regularly attended the Actors' Lab's classes and productions.

But our success could not protect us from disaster. In spite of our exceptional productions, in spite of the Actors' Lab's many performances for military personnel during World War II, and in spite of our stellar reputation for launching high-quality theater on the West Coast, conservatives still viewed the Actors' Lab as a hotbed of political criminals. While many of us at the Actors' Lab did have socialist leanings, none of our political thinking drove our productions or our classes. We were too interested in producing great art to try to propagandize anyone.

None of this mattered to Jack B. Tenney, the state senator who chaired the California Senate Fact-Finding Subcommittee on Un-American Activities. Tenney trolled for political capital using hate and fear as his hook. Labeling the Actors' Lab a "typical Communist front organization," on February 19, 1948, Tenney put the Actors' Lab on his calendar. The Lab's executive board members, Bud Bohnen, J. Edward Bromberg, and Rose Hobart, were subpoenaed. Ira Gershwin, who had allowed his name to be used as a sponsor of the Actors' Lab, was also on their list. In his opening statement, Tenney referred to the Actors' Lab as a "red front" and accused the Lab of producing plays by Anton Chekhov, Sean O'Casey, and George Bernard Shaw. Somehow, Tenney and his cronies deemed these great playwrights subversive. Eddie, Rose, and Bud were called to the stand, and all three of them, invoking their First Amendment rights, refused to respond to the committee's queries about their political affiliations.

The next night, the Actors' Lab opened Phil and Janet Stevenson's living newspaper docudrama, *Declaration,* a historical exposé of the heinous Alien and Sedition Acts that President John Adams signed into law. Bud played Adams; Lloyd Gough played the protagonist, Thomas Jefferson; and I was the Narrator. I stood on a balcony above the stage. Paul Robeson, the great African American actor and singer, was in the audience. I was able to observe this giant of a man absolutely absorbed in the story. It was a dramatic account of Jefferson's contretemps with Alexander Hamilton, Adams, and Aaron Burr. Daniel Mann directed the cast of thirty-five actors, many of them playing multiple roles. The *Los Angeles Examiner's* review proclaimed *Declaration* to be "a vivid and powerful drama . . . [that] offers thrill packed scenes, each a well-planned rung in the ladder that leads to strong entertainment."

Sadly, the review also mentioned Bud's appearance before the Senate Fact-Finding Committee on Un-American Activities. At the behest of the committee, the heads of all the studios categorically blacklisted all three of these good and principled performers, immediately ending their film careers. From then on, the Actors' Lab was the only place they could perform. And this was only the beginning.

A year later, the Actors' Lab produced the English translation of the Dutch play *A Distant Isle* by A. Defresne, directed by Morris Carnovsky. On February 24, 1949, in the middle of the second act, Bud Bohnen and Art Smith were sitting next to each other onstage when Bud collapsed in Art's arms. The stage manager called for the curtain to be lowered. Moments later, the audience members, who thought the action was part of the performance, were advised that Roman "Bud" Bohnen had died in the arms of his longtime friend and Group Theatre colleague Art Smith. I am quite sure Bud's death was brought on by the stresses caused by Tenney and his wicked investigations. His death left us all emotionally bereft and at artistic loose ends.

We held Bud's memorial at the large El Patio Theatre, run by the Women's Press Club, near Hollywood and Highland avenues. Bud was a fine actor and an even finer acting teacher. He was also my mentor and friend. Since his death, I have kept a large black-and-white photo of him on my studio wall. The photo is a publicity shot from *The Best Years of Our*

Lives. His kind eyes beam down on me and remind me to strive for the astonishing but never to make it too complicated. I miss him dearly. Many of my methods as a teacher stem directly from Bud's wisdom and ability to cut through the crap and get straight to the soul of good acting.

The Actors' Lab prevailed for a short time after Bud's death, but the Red scare gradually took its toll. Subscriptions to performances dwindled, and weak box office sales diminished our resources. As our reputation slid down the drain, fewer students were eager to enroll, and our GI Bill subsidy evaporated. In 1950 the Actors' Lab closed its doors. It was a tremendous loss for theater in Los Angeles.

It was a great personal and artistic loss for me.

6

Galileo

Everyone, regardless of his or her profession, has a list of "things that might have transpired but didn't." At the top of my list is an opportunity in late 1945. I had recently received my honorable discharge from the U.S. Navy and was eager to resume my acting career. The director Joseph Losey was preparing a stage production of Bertolt Brecht's *Galileo* at the newly built Coronet Theatre in Beverly Hills. The great Charles Laughton was to play Galileo, and Brecht, who was living in exile in Los Angeles, would be directly involved in the production. I had a remarkable meeting with Losey and Brecht, and they asked me to play two roles in *Galileo.* I was over the moon with excitement. Not only was it work, but it was also an opportunity to glean what I could, in direct proximity, from two iconoclast dramatists. I had read everything Brecht had written, and I could trace my desire to be an actor directly to seeing Charlie in *Henry VIII* when I was a teenager.

I had not yet committed to the parts when my agent, Paul Wilkins, called and told me that the producer Harry (Pop) Sherman wanted me for four weeks of work on *Ramrod,* starring Joel McCrea and Veronica Lake. We would shoot on location at Zion National Park in Utah. I had to weigh my options, but the scale tilted quickly in favor of the film when Hope and I found out she was pregnant with our second child, Jane. *Ramrod* would get me back to a generous motion picture salary after my two years of meager navy stipends. With a heavy heart, I turned *Galileo* down.

A few weeks later, Hope and I went to see the production. Laughton was brilliant. Charlie's love of acting was unbridled. In the heyday of the Actors' Lab, he would come to every production, big or small, and he graciously mentored many of the ex-military men who attended classes at the Lab on the GI Bill. He even went so far as to cast a number of the Lab's students in his marvelous production of Chekhov's *The Cherry Orchard.*

Charlie was certainly one of the busiest and most successful film actors in the Western world, but he presented *The Cherry Orchard* in a storefront theater on Santa Monica Boulevard in Hollywood that had no more than sixty seats. Charlie played Leonid Gaev, and the great Russian actress Eugenie Leontovich played Madam Andryeevna. Hope and I were fortunate to have seen that production. In *The Cherry Orchard,* Gaev addresses the family's bookcase: "My dear, venerable bookcase! I salute you!" He then confesses to the bookcase that he has had an insupportably failed life. Charlie's rendering of that speech was heartbreaking.

Although it was almost impossible to believe, his performance in *Galileo* was even more intoxicating. During the first intermission I ran into Sam Levine, Ruth Gordon, and Garson Kanin. I asked them, "Is it as great as I think it is?" They all nodded a very vigorous "Yes." Garson had directed Charlie in *They Knew What They Wanted* with Carole Lombard and was familiar with his talents. After the show, Ruth wrote an article for *Theatre Arts Magazine* about Charlie's *Galileo* performance. A few days later I left for Utah. Filming *Ramrod* was a great deal of fun and put necessary funds in our coffers, but I have always regretted not being able to be in *Galileo.*

The British playwright, novelist, and screenwriter Ted Willis describes a morning when Brecht arrived at Charlie's home to work on *Galileo.* Charlie was in his garden feeding his goldfish. As they talked, Brecht posed the question, "Charlie, why did you want to be an actor?" Without hesitation Charlie replied, "Because people don't know what they are like, and I think I can show them."

To my mind Charlie's response is the most succinct and compelling reason to be an actor.

7

Maelstrom

My years of teaching acting are an honorable footnote to the catastrophic Hollywood blacklist. It began in 1947, when the House Sub-Committee on Un-American Activities (HUAC), chaired by Congressman J. Parnell Thomas of New Jersey, subpoenaed nineteen of the most successful Hollywood writers and directors on the suspicion that they were trying to infiltrate Hollywood with communist principles. The first ten witnesses (Alvah Bessie, Herbert Biberman, Lester Cole, Edward Dmytryk, Ring Lardner Jr., John Howard Lawson, Albert Maltz, Samuel Ornitz, Adrian Scott, and Dalton Trumbo) vigorously challenged the committee's right to probe into their personal, social, and political beliefs and, invoking their First Amendment right to free speech, refused to answer the committee's questions.

It was an uproarious hearing, punctuated by the splenetic Thomas bellowing the now famous words "Are you now or have you ever been a member of the Communist Party?" Prone to the theatrical, Thomas marked off every word he roared with a powerful thud of his gavel. Designed to keep order at hearings, his poundings instead laid the foundation for the clamor and disorder that were to be the hallmark of the HUAC hearings over the next five years.

HUAC charged the ten with contempt of Congress for refusing to cooperate with the investigation. The Hollywood Ten, as they came to be known, took their case to the federal courts, but to no avail. Their lawyers were confident they could win their case in front of what was considered a liberal Supreme Court. Unfortunately, within three months, two of the more liberal justices, Frank Murphy and Wiley Rutledge, died. The conservative President Harry Truman filled their vacant seats with Justices Sherman Minton and Tom Clark. Clark had been instrumental in the wartime internment of Japanese Americans, and Minton was a staunch oppo-

45

nent of civil liberties. The newly conservative court refused to review the Ten's convictions. In 1950 all these upstanding and ethical men were sentenced to prison terms ranging from seven months to one year and fined $1,000 each.

Congressman Thomas, in the meantime, had very little time to revel in his search for Reds. Shortly after the Hollywood Ten's appearance, the syndicated columnist Drew Pearson published an article alleging Thomas had padded his congressional payroll with friends and family, and they, in turn, kicked back a portion of their fake salaries to him. Summoned before a grand jury, Thomas availed himself of the same First Amendment he had been unwilling to allow the Hollywood Ten to use. Found guilty of fraud and sentenced to nine months in prison, Thomas was sent to the federal penitentiary in Danbury, Connecticut—the same place Ring Lardner Jr. and Lester Cole, two of the Hollywood Ten, were serving their time.

A few years later, Lester Cole told me about his first encounter with the felonious ex-congressman. Lester was in the prison yard cutting grass with a sickle, and Thomas was scraping out the chicken coops. "Hey, Bolshie," Thomas yelled across the yard. "I see you still got your sickle." Lester gleefully shouted back, "And I see you're still knee-deep in chicken shit!"

I was well acquainted with the Hollywood Ten. We were friends and colleagues. Our wives all knew each other, and our children played together. We shared many of the same political and social beliefs. As Hope and I watched the Ten unravel before us, we knew the frenzy and fear surrounding the Cold War were not going to go away anytime soon. While we could have never predicted the destruction HUAC would eventually wreak on our lives, we knew that an ill wind was blowing our way.

After the Ten's conviction, HUAC resumed its hearings in Washington, D.C., and then abruptly decided to relocate to Hollywood. Federal marshals began issuing subpoenas to producers, directors, actors, composers, and musicians. An additional sweep of schoolteachers, clergymen, doctors, lawyers, ophthalmologists, and dentists immediately followed. It seemed no one was safe. I had been a professional actor onstage and in films for more than fifteen years, but I knew my days as a performer were numbered.

Somewhere out there, there was a subpoena with my name on it.

8

The Possibilities Narrow

Once the Hollywood Ten appeared before the committee, everyone in Hollywood knew the political tide had changed. I first heard the report of the Ten's appearance on the radio. I literally trembled uncontrollably as I heard the news. The power of the committee was undeniable, and it was clear that nothing would stop its fury, righteous indignation, or misplaced sense of patriotism. While I could not shake the feeling of doom, I also knew there was no other choice but to go on anyway.

In spite of the troubles of the Ten and the demise of the Actors' Lab, the postwar years were good to me, and from the spring of 1947 through early 1951 I was featured or costarred in thirty-one films. It was a busy time, personally, for Hope and me as well. Our daughter Emily was born in December 1950, and between the steady flow of film work and a household filled with the lively sounds of three growing girls, Hope and I both felt life was pretty wonderful in spite of the dark cloud hanging over our heads.

Early in 1950, my agent, Paul Wilkins, got a "hurry up" call from William Cagney's production office at Warner Bros. William had produced several of his brother James Cagney's films, including *Yankee Doodle Dandy,* and he was about to start production on *Only the Valiant,* starring Gregory Peck. The old vaudevillian James Barton was set to play Joe Harmony, the cavalry scout. Barton had become critically ill, and, though I was half his age, they wanted me for the role.

I was rushed to wardrobe, makeup, and hairdressing and then discovered that my first scene was the following morning. I picked up my script and zealously prepared for my first day of shooting. Others in the cast were Gig Young, Ward Bond, Lon Chaney Jr., Barbara Payton, and Terry Kilburn. Gordon Douglas was directing. Ward and I often found ourselves eating lunch together at the commissary at Warner Bros., where we'd talk a great deal about Westerns. We had acted together the year before in *The Singing Guns* at Republic Pictures, directed by R. G. Springsteen and starring Walter Brennan, Ella Raines, and the cowboy balladeer Vaughn Monroe. I seemed to have passed muster with Ward because I had done several Westerns with Joel McCrea, Randolph Scott, Tyrone Power, and Bill Boyd and, most important, had appeared with John Wayne in *Wake of the Red Witch.*

One day Ward and I had a conversation about *Death of a Salesman.* I had just seen Thomas Mitchell in the role of Willy Loman at the Biltmore Theatre and thoroughly enjoyed his performance. Ward, who had worked with Tommy in many John Ford films, offered a gratuitous opinion that took me aback. "Of course Tommy was better than Lee J. Cobb. Cobb played him too Jewish."

This was my first glimpse of Ward's rabid bigotry and conservatism. Our conversation was just one year before Ward and the infamous Roy Brewer, president of Hollywood's powerful International Alliance of Theatrical Stage Employees, Moving Picture Technicians, Artists and Allied Crafts (IATSE), joined forces and became the gauleiters of HUAC-occupied Hollywood. As head of IATSE, Brewer often sold out the membership to producers and became infamous for commissioning *Red Channels,* a pamphlet that Brewer said identified 151 writers, directors, and actors as subversive. *Gauleiter* was the name the Germans gave the men and women they appointed to run their affairs during the Nazi occupation of France. Gauleiters were considered collaborators and held in great disregard by the loyal French. Ward and Brewer certainly fit the description.

As the dark days of Hollywood grew dimmer and dimmer, these two men became the clearinghouse for people who chose to spill their guts to the committee. Together they made the final judgment on who was employable in Hollywood and who was not. Ward and Brewer had the power of the Roman tyrant Nero at the Colosseum in ancient Rome, who could indicate with a "thumbs up" or "thumbs down" the death or life of a gladiator.

On the other end of the social spectrum, during the filming of *Only the Valiant* I became quite close to a delightful young actor named Terry Kilburn. Terry had played several English schoolboys in the original screen version of *Goodbye, Mr. Chips,* starring Robert Donat. He was a charming, intelligent, and talented young man.

After we completed *Only the Valiant,* Terry was asked to direct Philip and Julius Epstein's dramatization of *The Brothers Karamazov* at the Players' Ring Theater in Hollywood. Terry was having trouble casting the female lead role of Grushenka. He asked me if I would help him by improvising with actors during their auditions. Most of the young women who worked with me were quite impressive. The last applicant for the role was Marilyn Monroe. She was a timorous young woman who spoke in a semi-whisper. She seemed both eager and apologetic. In a breathy voice she asked, "Can I take my shoes off?" Terry and I assented, and she walked to a corner of the stage and kicked off her heels. Terry explained the scene to be improvised, and she and I began to work.

She was inquisitive but very tentative and uncertain. We kept reworking the scene until a bit of courage started to surface as she slowly began to take charge of the role. When she left, Terry told me that he had known her for some time and that she had just completed her first good role as a contract player at Fox in John Huston's *Asphalt Jungle.* For reasons unknown to me, the dramatization of *The Brothers Karamazov* was abandoned. Over the years and in countless interviews, Marilyn often mentioned her wish to play Grushenka on the stage. I think she would have been marvelous.

During these years, I also had important roles in the Lux Radio Theatre shows *Philip Marlowe, Suspense, Night Shift,* and *Favorite Story,* along with a host of other shows. Before the advent of television, Hollywood screen luminaries often went on the air to reprise their successful film roles. From 1934 to 1955, 926 major films were presented in one-hour versions on Lux Radio Presents Hollywood. Every Monday evening at six o'clock Pacific and nine Eastern, over thirty million Americans listened to broadcasts that were performed in front of live audiences at the Lux Radio Playhouse on North Vine Street in Hollywood.

Rehearsals were held on Sunday afternoons. They brought in an audience for those as well. The studio was always filled to capacity—close to 1,000—because people from all walks of life were delighted to see the show's host, Cecil B. DeMille, and a parade of movie stars in person. I worked with Lionel and Ethel Barrymore, Ronald Colman, Charles Boyer, Cary Grant, Alan Ladd, Hedy Lamarr, Wallace Beery, and Merle Oberon. It was exhilarating work, and it was easy to apply my skills as a stage actor to radio. I used to love to watch Charles Boyer, in particular. Onscreen he was often subdued, but on radio he would get deeply involved emotionally and move around and gesture while he spoke. One Sunday afternoon we were rehearsing *All This, and Heaven Too,* starring Boyer and Bette Davis. I played the role of a relentless prosecuting attorney. Bette was hungry, so the producers had a wonderful Brown Derby hamburger with everything on it delivered to the studio. Bette proceeded to eat it as we rehearsed. In my role, I continued to badger her in cross-examination, and she began to cry. It wasn't the onions. Real tears poured down her cheeks as she munched that hamburger.

I appeared in twenty-six Lux Radio broadcasts before, during, and after the war. My last show before joining the war effort was the part of Joe in an adaptation of George Kelly's *The Show-Off.* The broadcast was on February 3, 1943, the day I was sworn into the navy. As I was leaving the theater, Cecil B. DeMille grasped both my hands and said, "Son, I envy you!" C. B. meant it, too. He would have loved to be put in charge of producing World War II.

After the war, I continued to work in radio and film. In spite of the difficulties, these were banner years and my career was growing. In February 1951, the *Los Angeles Herald Examiner* ran an article that proclaimed, "Jeff Corey is the most successful young actor in Hollywood."

While the pronouncement was delightful and should have heralded even more work, as it turned out 1951 was not going to be such a great year. In fact, the year turned on me completely. On a cold March morning in 1951, I was awakened by a call from an attorney in Washington, D.C. He told me he represented the actor Marc Lawrence. Marc had a minor career in Hollywood playing heavies and gangsters. He told me that Marc would be appearing before HUAC and asked what I would do if I received a subpoena. I told him I didn't care to answer and hung up the phone. I stood there wondering, "Why the preliminary call?" Was Lawrence's lawyer going down a list of as-yet-unmentioned actors to find one who wouldn't cooperate so Lawrence could look good to the committee? If you were a friendly witness, it was assumed you would name a few names the committee already had. To stay in their good graces, however, you had to deliver at least two new names for their list. That's how they kept their sham alive.

As I stared at the phone, I asked myself if his call had been some sort of ghoulish etiquette delivered out of shame and guilt on the part of his client, giving me a head's-up that I was closer than ever to the committee's bull's-eye. I have no way of knowing. Regardless of the motives for the call, I knew it meant Lawrence was seriously considering offering my name to

HUAC. I walked around the room trying to deal with the implications. I had known Lawrence tangentially. We had seen each other at numerous social engagements, but he was not a friend and certainly had no personal knowledge of my political inclinations, actions, or beliefs.

The phrase "My goose is cooked" floated before my eyes like a cartoon message. I had been dreading this dire moment for three and a half years, and now the dark clouds of HUAC were heading directly toward me. I realized, painfully, that I had been performing on borrowed time. Many of my friends had decided to duck the inevitable and had gone to Canada, Mexico, France, England, and beyond, hoping to find work as writers, directors, or producers. Hope and I had made the decision that when the time came, I would not leave the country. Instead, I would hide out at some remote area in Southern California and try to avoid the pink subpoena with my name on it.

Before I joined the navy, Hope and I had laid claim to a five-acre homestead in the barren desert wasteland southeast of Los Angeles. Under the provisions of the Homestead Act, we had five years to "prove up" our claim. Because I had served in the Pacific during the war, the government had given me additional time to improve my property. With the voice of Lawrence's lawyer still ringing in my ear, this seemed as good a time as any to visit my homestead and start my improvements.

My good friend the screenwriter Ray Spencer owned the five acres adjacent to our tract. Ray cheerfully offered to leave besieged Los Angeles and join me in constructing my humble abode. We put our building tools, pots and pans, canned food, and drinking water into the car and made our way to the desert. Phil Gersh was now my agent. Phil represented a lot of the bigger stars, including Humphrey Bogart. On my way out of town, I stopped briefly at a run-down phone booth off a two-lane road and called him. I knew the threat of a subpoena was almost as powerful as the subpoena itself, so I was not surprised when Phil advised me that two roles I had been up for—William Cagney's next feature at Warner Bros. and Stanley Kramer's *High Noon*—had both been nixed by the studios. Phil went on to tell me MGM would retract the deal they had already made for *Angels in the Outfield* unless I agreed to cooperate with the committee. On top of that bad news, the television show *Joe's Place,* in which I played the title role, had also been scuttled. *Joe's Place,* written by John Vlahos, was one of the first shows filmed for the new medium of television. We had shot one episode. It had turned out beautifully, and we were waiting to start work on the series. If it had not been for the blacklist, it is very likely *Joe's Place* would have been a big hit and my career would have taken a dramatically different turn. I do not say this with bitterness, but it is worth mentioning in order to understand the enormity of losses HUAC wreaked not only on my life, work, and income but also on the lives of so many other decent, hardworking men and women in Hollywood.

I said good-bye to Phil. This flood of bad news descended on me as I put the receiver back on the hook and started walking to the car over the sandy road. I suddenly slipped on the gravel and barely caught myself. How appropriate, I thought. No traction! All the happy aspirations I had coddled over the years, all my hard work to build my craft and career, had gone astray and my dreams had come undone. I was truly beleaguered, and, to add to my despair, I had no safe access to my wife and children.

Ray and I continued our journey to our isolated stretch of desert land in silence. Together we passed the days working on my homestead shack. We had to bring in adobe bricks and hardware on a four-by-eight galvanized metal sled that we dragged about half a mile from the very narrow road where we parked our car. Every hour, on the hour, we would turn on our battery-operated shortwave radio to hear the news about who had informed and who had refused. It brought to mind King Lear's description of the realm's captious gossip, "And hear poor rogues talk of court news. . . . Who loses and who wins, who's in, who's out."

On April 25, 1951, the radio picked up the HUAC noon hour report. Over the short waves came the news that Marc Lawrence had testified before the committee. Lawrence put on a vulgar charade before HUAC, playacting an illiterate who told the committee the only reason he went to Red meetings was to "meet broads." In the course of his rambling testimony, Lawrence formally offered them my name.

Even though I knew the moment was inevitable, the reality of its arrival was sudden and deep. I walked around my desert compound observing the rudimentary carpentry that had engaged our energies and had helped maintain equilibrium in this HUAC jumble. What had all this busy building activity to do with the abysmal predicament I was in? Suddenly, fatigue overcame me. I rested my head on a sack of raw cement and fell into a stupor. During the war, I encountered this same syndrome after the strain of battle. After every Japanese attack on our fleet, the flight deck personnel would stretch out on the deck, still wearing their kapok life jackets and helmets, and fall into the deep sleep of post-adrenaline oblivion. But here, on my five acres of homesteaded government land, I felt a hapless stupefaction. Everything I had come to count on was gone: my stable family life, my upstanding role in my community, my income, and my career. None of these important elements of my life was available to me now. Instead, I was thrust into an outlaw nightmare by the machinations of a liar and an equally disreputable congressional committee.

A few months before either of us knew about the forthcoming HUAC debacle, Marc Lawrence and I had bumped into each other on the Paramount Studio lot. I had been there for a wardrobe fitting. He mentioned he needed a ride to his mechanic, and I volunteered to drive him there. En route we engaged in shoptalk, and in response to his question about how things had been for me, I told him I was happy to have gotten a great deal of work and attributed much of it to my performance as the psychiatrist in *Home of the Brave*. In the wake of that assignment, I made seven films in 1950. I was not bragging. I was merely describing an upswing in my career. When we reached the repair shop I stopped my car and we both got out. Lawrence looked at me for a moment, made a fist, and playfully jabbed at my solar plexus and said, "You son of a bitch. You're working all the time." Well, he certainly put a stop to that.

I found out later Lawrence had sworn under oath that he had seen me at a Communist Party meeting at Karen Morley's home in Hollywood in 1944. This was completely untrue. In 1944 I was on the USS *Yorktown* shooting footage of kamikaze fighters who were making every attempt to kill everyone aboard ship, including me. Out of curiosity, one day I decided to check out the engagements for the *Yorktown* for that year. Our amphibious assaults, as the navy called them, began on January 16, 1944, when we sailed out of Pearl Harbor toward the battle for the Marshall Islands. This began what turned out to be a very long and grueling twelve months of the War in the Pacific, and if memory serves, we barely even sailed into port that year to replenish our supplies or make repairs. Most of 1944 consisted of fiery engagements, and I spent much of that year behind the lens of a camera, documenting attacks and risking my life for my country. I saw kamikazes hitting the *Missouri*. I saw the *Enterprise* hit. I saw the *Intrepid* hit twice. I shot 180 feet of film of a kamikaze attack on the *Yorktown* itself. After every battle the destroyers would pick up the bodies of the dead—many of them not more than eighteen years old. They looked like cherubs floating in the water in their life jackets. It was a nightmare. I was not, as Lawrence glibly stated, attending Communist

Party meetings in Hollywood. But the committee members did not fact-check. They were only too eager to promote their cause, and if that was built on lies, it made no difference to them. They gleefully added my name to their roster.

I decided to go back and look at Lawrence's testimony in the *Congressional Record.* It's hard to read because he so easily rattles off the names of the dearest and best people I knew back then, particularly those associated with the Actors' Lab. He appears to have no remorse or regret as he does it, and the committee is eating it up and, in fact, eggs him on. At Lawrence's hearing the congressmen took a backseat and allowed Frank S. Tavenner Jr., the chief counsel for the committee, to interview him. At one point, Tavenner, shamelessly probing the witness, says, "Let us see if we can identify more persons who were members of the cell within the Actors' Lab. You have named three. Can you recall any others?"[1]

It is as this point, as if he is ordering dinner at his favorite restaurant, Lawrence says, "Well, there was an actor called Jeff Corey who attended these meetings." It was an effortless response on his part, but that was the exact moment my career in Hollywood ended.

But in the desert that afternoon I did not know the details. I did not know that Lawrence had lied about my whereabouts. I did not know whom else he had named. All I knew was that my goose was finally cooked. At dusk, Ray and I decided to pick up some supplies in Indio, just east of our desert land. Ray parked our station wagon some distance from the store's entrance. I stayed in the car so as not to draw attention. By now, I was sure my photo was on the front page of the evening papers with the caption "Jeff Corey named as Red." As I sat waiting for Ray, a uniformed sheriff slowly approached the car. A man in a dark suit walked with him. The sheriff poked his head through the open window and said, "You're Jeff Corey, aren't you?"

"I am," I said, fearful of what was to come next.

He turned to the man in the dark suit and said, "There! I told you!"

"Jeff," he continued, "I want you to meet FBI Agent Sullivan. I *told* him you were Jeff Corey," he said, triumphantly. "But he didn't believe me."

Agent Sullivan shook my hand enthusiastically and told me how very happy he was to meet me. He was a "big fan." He had just seen me as Joe Harmony, the Indian scout in *Only the Valiant,* starring Gregory Peck, and was crazy about the film. While they continued to talk, I caught sight of Ray leaving the hardware store. When he saw the uniformed sheriff, he began to withdraw backward like a film on rewind. He reached the store's entry and stayed there until my admiring fans bid me good-bye.

Obviously, my great news had not yet hit the desert newsstands. Ray and I talked it over and decided it was time to go home. I had to talk to Hope and figure out what would be our next move. We arrived in Los Angeles just as the sun was setting. I didn't dare go near our house, fearful of surveillance. Ray called Hope and asked her to meet me at the very remote end of the bridle path in Griffith Park. After I dropped Ray off at his home in the Hollywood Hills, I wrapped myself in a blanket, covering as much of my face as possible, and made my way into the park to our meeting place. When Hope arrived, we were despondent. Nothing in our life plans could have prepared us for this terrible turn of events. Hope updated me about what had been happening with the children, and we discussed all matters of what to do next. We had enough money to get us through the next few months, but anything beyond that seemed hopeless. I looked at this sweet, lovely woman taking care of three children by herself and said, "We're going to make it work. We're going to be all right." We stood in the dimming light of the afternoon hugging each other. I whispered, "We'll figure it out." As the sun began to set, Hope drove off alone to our Cheremoya Avenue house. I picked up Ray from his home and we headed back out to the desert. It was a heartbreaking drive.

My hiding strategy soon wore thin. A few more weeks in the desert drove both Ray and me mad. We slept out under the stars, ate rudimentary meals, and continued to listen to more sad news on our shortwave radio. We missed our wives, our children, and our lives. Finally, we declared our respective shacks finished. Ray arranged for the government inspector to review our handiwork. We received affirmative reports and were handed slips of paper stating that the homesteads were now legally ours. As I stared at the official seal of the United States embossed on my deed of ownership, I wondered how this very same government could also be taking away my life and my livelihood. Ray and I packed up our belongings and drove back to Hollywood in silence.

The next day, I converted our mortgage payment of a $112 a month into an FHA loan of $80 a month. Ironically, I was able to demonstrate my solvency to the federal government with the record of my earnings in films and radio from 1950. As a distraction, I began writing a screenplay about a phantasmagoric baseball game, but, in the face of my circumstances, it seemed utterly irrelevant and I scrapped it. Someone suggested I consider selling an automatic refrigerator defrosting apparatus. I could not bear the thought.

I was up the proverbial creek without a paddle. One thing was certain. There wasn't a studio in town that would hire me. I hadn't even taken the Fifth, but being mentioned qualified me for the gray list and brutal unemployment. My agent told me categorically, "You either oblige the committee or forget it." I knew I wasn't going to cooperate, and Hope supported me 100 percent. But I dreaded the next static day and all the ensuing days that would follow. I was in flight from a reality I could not plumb. Hope and I devised an exit plan. We revised our thinking about leaving, and I decided to try my luck in Mexico. Our friends the writers Dalton Trumbo and Hugo Butler had already moved their families to Mexico City and were making contact with European and Mexican production companies. They encouraged Hope and me to do the same. I made a reservation for a midnight flight to Mexico City. The Butlers offered to put me up while I looked for some fringe occupation south of the border.

Halfway through packing, I stopped and asked myself, "What the hell are you doing?" Hope was still nursing baby Emily. Evie would soon enter the third grade, and Janie was about to start kindergarten. How realistic was it for me to leave my family and run off on a quixotic adventure? I emptied my suitcase, went downstairs, put my arms around Hope, and said, "We will do whatever we need to do, here. The kids will continue to go to Cheremoya Avenue School. We won't let HUAC hound us out of the place where we choose to live."

Hope immediately agreed and was equally relieved. Just because everything around us was topsy-turvy didn't mean we had to be equally chaotic. We agreed to dig in, together. We had built a good life for ourselves, surrounded by wonderful neighbors and friends. We resolved to hang on no matter what and continue to make a good life for our children and for ourselves in America.

The next day, I approached a contractor friend, who put me to work on a construction job making fourteen dollars a day. While I was grateful for the income, it was a significant drop from my movie salary, which by then was well over one thousand dollars a week. Things were tight and it was rough, but I had a wife and three kids to take care of, so I didn't complain. I had grown up around builders, so it felt a little bit like home. I constructed concrete forms, shingled rooftops, and was constantly reminded I was "not building pianos." I felt a fair degree of pride that I was working with my hands. More important, knowing that I was doing something about our predicament rather than falling into an abyss kept me going.

A childhood friend, Moshe Brilliant, was a *New York Times* correspondent in Tel Aviv. He sent me a letter suggesting I could get steady work as an actor with either the Habima National Theatre or the Chamber Theatre in Israel. I paced up and down the living room all morning, toying with the idea. Hope and I talked about it. She was supportive and willing to go if I was. As I looked around our house—this beautiful home Hope and I had purchased so enthusiastically only a few years earlier—I knew I didn't want to leave. I knew I didn't want to leave the United States. I thought to myself, "I love this country. I'm an exemplary citizen. I'm not the problem. I'm not leaving." It was the second time I reaffirmed to myself my true devotion to my homeland, my community, and my life. It felt good to make the decision to stay.

I decided to take a test run at the idea of returning to school, and in June 1951 I enrolled for the summer session at UCLA. Since I was a veteran, the GI Bill, passed by the same Congress that was stalking my career, paid for my tuition, books, and notebooks and provided me with a monthly stipend of $120. The irony did not escape me, but I was grateful for the help as well as for the distraction sitting in a classroom offered me.

College life was significantly different from my life as a successful Hollywood actor. The ideas interested me, but listening to lectures and taking notes felt out of context with the rest of my life. It was as if I had entered a time machine, only I was being sent back to a place I had never been before. Since I was technically a freshman, one of the classes I enrolled in was English I. My first assignment was to write a paper on the topic of my choice. I chose the history of censorship and blacklisting throughout the ages. Researching this subject helped me retain my sanity and allowed me to view my misfortunes through a historical lens.

It comforted me to learn that my situation was not simply a new plague fabricated just for my colleagues and me. Socrates was forced to drink poison in 399 BC as punishment for his thoughts and actions. Galileo's books were banned in 1616, as were hundreds of books over the ages, including Walt Whitman's *Leaves of Grass*, Mark Twain's *The Adventures of Huckleberry Finn*, and John Steinbeck's *Grapes of Wrath.* The Spanish Inquisition, the great cultural centerpiece of censorship, started in 1478 and lasted more than 350 years. The Salem witch trials jump-started censorship in the New World and were pulled off by a group of men who had fled England for the sake of religious freedom.

The witch hunts that were beginning to run Hollywood were just another brilliant flash in an already fiery censorship pan.

9

The Stage Society

Early in the summer of 1951, J. Arthur Kennedy, who had acted with me in the Federal Theatre's production of *Life and Death of an American,* called and asked if I would like to play the role of Captain Keeney in Eugene O'Neill's one-act play *Ile.* It was to be the first production of the newly formed Stage Society in Hollywood. In spite of my heavy schedule at UCLA and part-time construction work, I felt the need to act again. My colleagues were glad to see me, and people individually and in groups were most solicitous in regard to my murky HUAC situation. The eminent Russian actor-director and teacher Michael Chekhov, or Mischa, as we fondly called him, taught a master class at the Stage Society on Monday nights. Mischa was Anton Chekhov's nephew and had worked with Stanislavsky at the Moscow Art Theatre. His inventiveness intrigued Stanislavsky, and he appointed Mischa director of the Second Moscow Art Theatre.

I began rehearsing *Ile* and allowed myself the time to attend Mischa's Monday night classes. I had met Mischa briefly before the war, and it was a delight to meet up with him again. His presence was compelling. He had the most profound conviction that theater is not a trifling societal indulgence, but that the mimetic instinct exists in us, almost by necessity. He was not only a marvelous actor himself but he was also an amazing, intelligent teacher, and attending his classes helped focus what were rapidly becoming extremely difficult days.

The Board of Directors of the Stage Society wanted to establish a second class to work in tandem with Mischa's Monday night sessions and asked if I would teach a Tuesday night class. There's a cryptic line in Hamlet's greeting to the visiting players when he says, "Well e'en to 't like French falconers, fly at anything we see."

This is exactly what I did. In the 1940s I had substituted at the Actors'

Lab when Art Smith, Phoebe Brand, Daniel Mann, or Mary Tarcai wasn't available to teach a class, so the occupation of instructor wasn't completely foreign to me. The Stage Society could not afford to pay me, but considering the derailment of my career and my wish to remain active in my craft, I was grateful for the opportunity. I agreed to teach the class.

The Stage Society had obtained a theater built for Mae West by her manager in the 1930s. Mae was really Hollywood's first sex kitten. Known for her double entendres and bawdy delivery, she had a lot of clout with the public. The theater was a barnlike structure with a pitched roof and massive wooden beams. It had a good-sized proscenium stage and seated 150 people. It was here that I taught my first class. As I started to outline what I proposed to accomplish at our sessions, Gary Cooper and Patricia Neal entered the theater and sat down in the first row of the side aisle. It was an incredible and kind act of support. I had first met Pat and Coop when we worked together in *Bright Leaf* at Warner Bros. Coop had become a huge star after his performance in *Mr. Deeds Goes to Town* and went on to win the Academy Award for his remarkable performance in *High Noon*. Pat was a wonderful actor who years later won an Academy Award for her starring role in *Hud* with Paul Newman. I acknowledged their presence and, knowing Coop's reticence, did not ask either of them to join us onstage.

Back in 1949, before hiring me for the role of John Barton, the man who invented the cigarette-rolling machine, the director of *Bright Leaf*, Michael Curtiz, called me in for a screen test. I was amazed that Coop was doing the test scene with me. I had some long expository speeches, and Coop responded in his lovely, taciturn manner. Curtiz had us rehearse and then dismissed us while they laid tracks for the camera and lit the scene.

Coop and I stepped out of the soundstage and lit our cigarettes. To my amazement, he began to downplay the work he had just done. He told me that he'd been on a safari in Africa with Ernest Hemingway and away from a camera for about a year. He confessed to me he was a little uncomfortable about what he was doing. He then in a most self-effacing manner said, "You know, I've only got two or three tricks at best and that's not enough, is it?" It made me think of Trigorin in *The Sea Gull* telling Nina that when he dies, people will say he was clever and charming but he was no Turgenev or Tolstoy.

As I stood next to this splendid and revered movie star—who had so graciously agreed to work with me on my screen test—I felt compelled to reassure him. I told him that while a lot of New York stage actors may have patronizingly regarded him as only a movie personality, from my observation every one of them had employed the irresistible "Cooperisms" and homespun qualities he displayed in *Mr. Deeds Goes to Town* and other Capra films in their performances. I confessed that when I prepared for the title role in *Abe Lincoln in Illinois* at the Actors' Lab, I thought of the appealing simplicity that characterized his work. He smiled that affable smile, and we went back into the soundstage to film the screen test.

Some weeks into the filming of *Bright Leaf,* Coop and I were on a high knoll in the Hollywood Hills above the Warner's lot for some exterior shots. We started talking about the time and place of the film. *Bright Leaf* takes place in North Carolina, thirty years after the Civil War. Our talk brought about a discussion of Lincoln and what might have been but for his tragic death. Coop told me, with considerable hesitation, about his own Lincoln "what might have been." Before *Abe Lincoln in Illinois* opened on Broadway, Robert Sherwood asked Coop to play the great president. *Stage Magazine* even went so far as to print a full-page sketch of Coop as he would appear in the role. Coop told me he was reasonably sure he could have played the role on film but felt his lack of stage experience might have been a hazard, so he turned the part down. He told me not playing Lincoln onstage was one of the great frustrations of his life. I always loved Coop's work and thought he was a marvelous actor; I imagine he would have been as wonderful onstage as he was on film.

I thought about what Coop had said about Lincoln as I started working with my students that first night. It gave me a deeper sense that helping film actors in Hollywood feel comfortable onstage was a worthy endeavor. We began working on some scenes I had typed out. I felt pretty good about my evaluations of what they were doing. I decided the best thing to do was to curb a lot of talk and focus our energies on reworking the scenes by shifting assumptions and suggesting alternative thematic implications. It seemed to work, and I was very relieved. Throughout the evening, I must confess, I was more than just peripherally aware of Pat and Coop's presence even as I tried to stay focused on my new role as a teacher. I was extremely grateful and touched by Coop's willingness to show up for class and be seen in public with me in spite of the HUAC mess hovering on my horizon.

Pat and Coop returned for the next session and took their seats down in the orchestra again. Some students brought in a piece from *Julius Caesar.*

I commented on what they had done and then we proceeded, as in the first session, to play around with it and rework the scene to see what we could bring out of it. I elicited comments from the class. I then turned to Coop and asked if he had anything to add. It was immediately evident that he was not going to proffer any sort of critique to any actor under any circumstance, and he certainly was not going to give anyone pointers. He reverted to his most reluctant "Yep" and "Nope" mode that was so famous in the courtroom hearings in *Mr. Deeds Goes to Town*. I was both astonished and admiring of Coop's inordinate modesty. Perhaps that simple and kind good nature was at the root of his popularity. Years later, Coop sent his daughter, Maria, to work with me. She said, "Daddy told me that if I ever wanted to learn about acting, I should come to you." I was deeply touched and flattered.

When I started teaching, I dutifully committed myself to the basic études, or exercises, on attention and concentration. It was my understanding that this was the way good acting was taught. Furthermore, tradition dictated that sensory work and related exercises in concentration and relaxation be explored before scene work could even begin to take place. Try as I might, I soon tired of this method; my own disposition both as a teacher and an actor inclined me toward an unfettered willingness to forgo the preliminary disciplines and get up and have my students do the scene work. I longed to find a means to incorporate learning about acting into the act of acting. While this may seem an obvious approach today, back then it was novel.

I explained my new plan to my students. Bringing scene work into class would require spending time outside class rehearsing. Together we pulled scenes from favorite plays, and, eager to abandon the stiffer disciplines, they got to work. As I watched the work they brought in, it immediately became clear to me that the time put into rehearsals outside class was paramount to my students' artistic development, and that the quality of their performances served as a gauge for whatever sensory, concentration, or relaxation techniques they might require. This, ultimately, became the basis for my years of teaching.

I continued attending Mischa's Monday night classes at the Stage Society, which were absolutely marvelous. I loved Mischa, and while I didn't always concur with his theoretical conclusions—they seemed excessively mystical to me—that did not diminish my respect or affection for him. On some occasions, when impatient with an actor's inability to follow

through on a particular moment, Mischa would hasten to clarify the problem by illustration, either by incorporating the language of the scene in a
new context or by improvisation. He often asked me or my fellow student
Anthony Quinn to demonstrate the exercises he was talking about. His
illustrations were electrifying. Mischa was a slight man but became a giant
at those moments, and it was thrilling to work with him.

Mischa and I talked endlessly about the Moscow Art Theatre and its
astonishing successes in France, England, Germany, and the United States.
He told me that while the artistry of the company was extraordinary, the
impositions and outright censorship by the Soviet bureaucracy were
unbearable. He recommended I read Juri Jelagin's *Taming of the Arts*, a
book about repression of the arts in the Soviet Union. The more I read, the
clearer it became that the three prevailing investigating congressional committees that were now fully active—HUAC, McCarran, and McCarthy—
were subjecting the arts, professionals, trade unionists, and educators in
America to the same thought control Jelagin described. Interestingly
enough, even though McCarthy is often associated with HUAC and its
machinations, in fact McCarthy had no direct role with HUAC. While I'm
sure he did what he could to implement as much backroom damage as possible, HUAC was an arm of the House of Representatives. McCarthy was a
senator and did his wicked damage as chairman of the senate's Government
Operations Committee and its Permanent Subcommittee on Investigations.

Akim Tamiroff, who had immigrated to the United States from Russia,
was under contract at Paramount. He had also worked with Stanislavsky
and knew Mischa well. Akim was married to Tamara Shayne, a talented
actor who played Al Jolson's mother in *The Jolson Story*. Tamara had a
lively personality and was at the center of the impressive White Russian
and Soviet émigré enclave in Hollywood that included such luminaries as
the director Lewis Milestone and the composer Sergei Rachmaninoff.

I had been teaching the Tuesday class for a month when Tamara called
me out of the blue and said, rather imperiously, "Jeff, your class must do
Michael Chekhov exercises. What Mischa demonstrates on Monday night
should be the subject of your class work on Tuesday." I was a novice teacher
and was just beginning to feel comfortable with how I was teaching, in
spite of my limited experience. Tamara had quite an intimidating presence
and was deeply involved with the Stage Society community.

I took a deep breath and composed myself. "I really don't feel qualified
to teach what Mischa is teaching," I told her. I went on to say that if I tried

to teach what Mischa was teaching it would be, at best, mechanical. I further explained that I had enormous respect and love for Mischa—and employed many of his approaches in my work as a film and stage actor. I ended my conversation with her by saying, "Tamara, I am not Mischa." There was a short silence on the other end of the phone. "Mischa is one of a kind," I continued, hoping to convince her. "I am Jeff trying to find my own center as an acting teacher. I simply can't do what you are asking."

In a huff, Tamara categorically dismissed what I said and advised me she would bring the matter up with the Board of Directors of the Stage Society. I got off the phone realizing that now even my nonpaying teaching position was threatened. After all I had been through, I just couldn't feel stressed. There were too many real troubles assailing me, and I had not been teaching long enough to feel any diminishing of my status in that profession. If I wasn't going to be a teacher, so be it.

Later in the day, Mischa called me at home. In his lovely Russian accent and kind voice he said, "Jeff, darling, Tamara is a fool. Of course you must teach the way you must teach." Then in an urgent tone, he added, "Jeff, always, always listen to your own heart."

His words instantly swept away my gloom, and his good advice stays with me still.

10

It Arrives

In June 1951 a federal marshal delivered the long-dreaded subpoena to my home. He was an amiable fellow who simply had a job to do. I was trying to come up with an idea for a radio show when the doorbell rang. As he handed me the envelope, which had "Personal and Confidential" written by hand on it, I told him, "Boy, this is very sad." He was sympathetic and not at all happy about what he had just done. After he left, I opened it. In a childish impulse, I spat on my subpoena to show my contempt of Congress. Then I called my attorney, A. L. Wirin.

I was initially ordered to appear in front of HUAC in Washington, D.C. The government would reimburse me for my airfare but no other expenses. I held the bright pink subpoena in my hand. The term "pink slip" came to mind. Why the color pink? Was the cheerful color intended to ameliorate the pain of dismissal? Was it so important a scrap of paper that it had to stand out from its paler, less effusive white and cream bureaucratic counterparts? Was the pink meant to disarm the reader? After speaking to Wirin, I showed Hope the wretched piece of paper. Our hearts sank as we again reaffirmed our determination to hang on and stay in America.

A series of telegrams ensued. The government, showing the indifference and lack of humanity that had become its trademark, changed the date and location of my appearance, time and time again, throwing what was left of the semblance of order in our life into complete and utter chaos. Finally, it was decided I should appear in Los Angeles at the Federal Building on September 21, 1951.

The date was still some weeks away, and although my acting career had essentially evaporated, it had not yet been truly demonstrated that I would be an unfriendly witness. Miraculously, right after my subpoena was delivered, two jobs materialized.

The first job starred Rochelle Hudson, who had done several successful B pictures with James Dunn. James had won an Academy Award for Best Supporting Actor in *A Tree Grows in Brooklyn*. I played Rochelle's distraught husband who kidnaps our infant daughter when she initiates divorce proceedings. It was shot in 16-millimeter film in a run-down studio on Sunset Boulevard near Van Ness Avenue. The atmosphere had none of the panache of the major studios I was accustomed to, but beggars can't be choosers. I did my own stunts. At one point I had to stride over the railing of a footbridge on the Arroyo Seco Freeway near Pasadena, clutching my swaddled infant. Cars by the hundreds zoomed under me as I made my way along the narrowest of footing, literally hanging on for dear life. Once again, art imitated life. The pilot was never screened.

The other job, as it turned out, was great fun and a notable alleviation of my troubles. I played Luke, the heavy in the original pilot of *Superman and the Mole Men,* starring George Reeves and Phyllis Coates. The producer, Barney A. Sarecky, a man with considerable guts, decided to hire me and damn the consequences. The networks must have found the pilot irresistible and made no issue about my appearance in the cast. My name, in fact, appeared prominently in all the promotional placards and photographs. Fans still write to me, praising the show as a landmark event.

During that same period, gratefully, I was able to continue to work in radio. A brave producer-director named Jerry Devine was working on a show called *This Is Your FBI*. Jerry called me in for a part. We both noted the irony. Jerry also made a special point of hiring Frances Chaney, whose husband, Ring Lardner Jr., was one of the Hollywood Ten. Ring was serving time for his contempt of Congress conviction, and though Frances had not appeared before the committee, nor had she been subpoenaed, guilt-by-marriage meant no one in Hollywood would hire her. Frances and I were delighted to see each other and very grateful for the work.

In spite of these minor distractions, HUAC still hung heavily in the air. Before my hearing, I had a troubling dream. I was on the back lot of the Hal Roach Studios, working on a film. During the lunch break, my friend Ray Spencer suddenly appeared. Ray seemed stricken. I asked him what the trouble was. He told me he was thinking of informing. I immediately became alarmed and said, "Ray, you can't do that!" I woke up full of dread and concern for Ray. I couldn't shake the feeling, and I finally called a friend who was a psychiatrist and shared my dream with him. With astonishing acuteness he said, "Jeff, there's an old saying. 'You are your own best friend." As he said those words, it immediately became clear to me that somewhere inside my psyche, I was trying to find out if I could inform to save my career. The answer was instantly clear to me. "No!" I might speculate about it in a dream, but never in real life.

How to proceed became the next order of business. The Hollywood Ten's use of the First Amendment had seriously backfired and had resulted in jail sentences. For those of us who followed them, legal counsel recommended we take the Fifth instead. Among other things, the First protects our right to free speech and religious and political beliefs. In its essence, the Fifth Amendment protects citizens from being forced to testify against themselves. Navigating between these two stellar amendments was new territory for those of us who had been subpoenaed, and the decision to avail ourselves of our Fifth Amendment right did not come all that easily. In 1950 and 1951 the Kefauver Committee, another congressional committee, was investigating the rather unsavory world of organized crime. Many crime bosses invoked the Fifth to avoid prosecution. During this time there were many unfortunate references to "hiding behind the Fifth" that had nothing do with HUAC. This gave the Fifth a very bad name.

Uncomfortable with the crime-boss association, yet unwilling to risk the complications and possible fines and jail time associated with the First, those of us who had been issued subpoenas didn't know where to turn. My attorney organized some training sessions for a group of us to discuss the challenges and discover more about what was involved with taking the Fifth. One of these gatherings was at Mike and Zelma Wilson's house in the San Fernando Valley. Mike, a dear friend and a marvelous screenwriter, ended up taking the Fifth and moving his family to France, where he continued to write spectacular screenplays under a pseudonym, including the Academy Award–winning *Bridge on the River Kwai,* which won for Best Screenplay and in many other categories. When the Oscar was handed out in 1958, Mike's name was not mentioned. The Academy gave the award to the French author Pierre Boulle, who had written the novel the film was based on. Boulle did not speak or write a word of English, but they gave him the award anyway. Mike died in 1978. In 1984 the Academy bestowed his Oscar posthumously on Zelma and his daughters.

But that night at Mike and Zelma's, we did not know what the future would bring. The training session was both difficult and bizarre. We had enjoyed many marvelous dinner parties at their home. To be sitting in their living room, filled with some of the best and brightest in Hollywood, discussing which constitutional amendment might make our lives less terrible was surreal.

Hope and I hosted a training session at our home as well. Robert Kenny, the eminent Democratic civil libertarian who had served as California's attorney general, stood in our living room as a group of extremely tense and talented men and women who had received subpoenas playacted a committee hearing while our children slept upstairs. These sessions were the oddest rehearsals I had ever been part of.

At one point, Kenny looked at all of us carefully and with great determination slowly said, "Someone has to throw himself in front of the juggernaut. I am sorry that it is you. The privilege you are invoking honorably will continue to be used dishonorably by scoundrels in the next twenty years." Pausing a moment, he said vigorously, *"HUAC will be stopped."* Kenny's wisdom and encouragement restored our faith in the Fifth, and while none of us was eager to face the committee, we at least felt certain we were taking the right course of action.

In truth, the Fifth has a very prestigious pedigree dating back to the sixteenth century and the British monarchy's cruel Star Chamber proceedings. Parliament in 1640 enacted legislation making it illegal for a witness to be forced to testify against himself. This powerful legislation made a transatlantic crossing in 1641 when the *Massachusetts Body of Liberties* proclaimed, "No man shall be forced by torture to confess any crime against himself." Historical precedent emboldened our Founding Fathers to embed this important human right in the Articles of Confederation, the precursor to our Constitution. By the time the Bill of Rights was entered as part of American law, the Fifth Amendment was well ensconced in the fabric of our judicial system and commitment to personal freedoms.

My refusal to cooperate with HUAC was not intended to uphold the American Communist Party's Democratic Front platform or indicate my support of the Soviet Union. In fact, by 1951 I no longer agreed with or believed in much of what had been a youthful exploration into hope for a better world. Whatever investigations Hope or I made into the Communist Party in the 1930s were based on our enduring belief in the importance of labor unions and the rights of the working poor. From that viewpoint, the ideals of the Communist Party looked promising and engaging. It did not take long, however, before we were both completely disenchanted by what we saw coming out of the Soviet Union. We were repelled by the Moscow Trials. We abhorred Stalin's dictatorial and ruthless tactics. Stalin wasn't a communist. He was a fascist in communist clothing. Regardless of how my political leanings might have been refined, transformed, or eroded altogether, I could not in good conscience provide HUAC with the names of well-intended social activists who had been my friends and were not subversive or conspiratorial in any way, shape, or form. I had no option but to refuse to name names.

My date with the committee turned out to be a convergence of events. After my summer session at UCLA, I decided to pursue my degree. Unfortunately, the day I was to appear in front of the committee was the same day I needed to register for fall classes at UCLA. It was also my daughter Jane's first day of kindergarten. Hope and I awoke at 5:00 a.m. to Jane's nervousness. We, along with her older sister, Evie, spent the early hours of the morning reassuring her that all would be fine. It was still barely daylight when I left my house and made my way across town to UCLA. By 7:30 a.m. I was in line to register for my freshman classes. I was thirty-seven years old and at least fifteen years older than most of the freshman in line. Dressed in my stylish Brooks Brothers seersucker suit, a silk polka-dot tie, and sunglasses to shroud my identity, I was readily mistaken for a professor. Everyone deferred to me in line. In less than an hour, I had signed up for an entire semester of freshman classes. After I'd registered, I had time to drive west to the Santa Monica Pier. I gazed out at the ocean, feeling forlorn and bereft. "What have I gotten myself into?" I wondered, gazing out to sea. The salty air I had learned to love on the *Yorktown* had little effect on my despair. Nothing could lift my mood. I had to be at the Federal Building by 10 a.m. With a heavy heart, I walked back to my car and started the drive toward downtown Los Angeles.

As I maneuvered along Sunset Boulevard, an enormous black limousine pulled up beside me. Inside were the HUAC congressmen also on their way to the Federal Building. They had spent the night at the posh Beverly Hills Hotel and now, well rested and well fed on their government stipends, I could see them talking and laughing through the darkened windows. Engaged in their own conversation of what trifles I could only imagine, they did not notice me.

HUAC's arrangement with friendly witnesses was very cut-and-dried. If you mentioned the names of one or two people who had already been mentioned—perhaps even someone who had died—and then offered up at least two fresh new names, you could avoid the blacklist. Before my appearance, I had met with A. L. Wirin and had prepared a statement that

I thought relevant to the proceedings. I was a distinguished war veteran. I shared the Presidential Unit Citation along with 3,300 other men on the *Yorktown,* and the commander in chief of the Fifth Fleet had issued a personal commendation to me that read, "By your devotion to duty and outstanding work as a member of the Photographic Unit aboard the USS *Yorktown,* you contributed materially, working under difficult conditions in the combat area, to make this record possible."

On Navy Day, October 27, 1945, a month after my honorable discharge, I received a personal citation signed by the secretary of the navy, James Forrestal, and Captain Edward Steichen, director of the Naval Photographic Institute, that read, "For outstanding achievement as a U.S. Navy motion picture Combat Photographer and for an extremely valuable contribution to the visual record of the war in the Pacific. His sequence of a Kamikaze attempt on the *Carrier Yorktown,* done in the face of grave danger, is one of the great picture sequences of the war and reflects the highest credit on Corey and the U.S. Navy Photographic Service."

I wanted the committee to know about my service to my country and included these quotes in my notes, which were tucked into my coat pocket.

Hope met me at the Federal Building. Jane and Eve were at school. Our friend Faith Kovaleski, who was a lead animator at Disney, had volunteered to miss work and babysit Emily. Hope took her seat in the audience next to Mike Wilson, who had testified the day before but was called back that day. Hope remembers a conversation she had with Mike as they sat in the tense hearing room. The two of them agreed, "Today is the day our worst fantasies come true."

I took my seat at the witness table next to A. L. Wirin. As the hearing started, I asked that the cameras be turned off—one of the only concessions the committee would allow their witnesses, friendly or otherwise. The hearings were broadcast live on the radio, and newsworthy segments were repeated over and over again throughout the day and then put on newsreels in movie theaters around the country.

In retrospect, that might have been a mistake, as there is no film documentation of my testimony, but at the time it seemed the dignified thing to do. I didn't want my face smeared across the national press. As the hearings began, I invoked my constitutional privileges under the First and Fifth amendments and also referred to Article Eighteen of the Declaration of Human Rights as passed by the General Assembly of the United Nations, which I paraphrased: "Everyone shall have the right to freedom of conscious thought and religion, the right to change his belief or religion in private or alone, in public or in community with others to so manifest his belief."

Congressman John S. Wood of Georgia, who chaired the committee, snorted, "Well, the directives of the United Nations are not as yet the law of this land." When asked by Congressman Clyde Doyle of California to provide the committee with the names of old associates, I told them, "I believe that no one can bargain for the key to my brain wherein is stored multitudinous attitudes about life, religion, politics, and art. You may try to ferret it out against my consent, but—"

At that point Congressman Donald Jackson, also of California, cut me off, saying he had heard this speech fifty times. Wirin replied, "Not this one." Congressman Doyle barked, "I didn't ask you for a stump speech." Wirin retorted, "Is that the prerogative only of Congressmen?"

If I had been allowed to speak, this is what the notes in my coat pocket would have prompted me to say. I wanted to give the committee a historic perspective on what they were doing and what had conspired throughout history to give Americans the freedoms we all shared. I wanted to tell them that in the last analysis, it was the public that was being blacklisted. Because of the committee's actions, cash-paying audiences would no longer get to see the good works and performances of those declared pariahs by HUAC. I wanted to ask them to allow me to continue to work in my craft without the threat of badgering and blacklist. I wanted to point out to them that under a system of free enterprise, an artist should not be restrained from competing freely for a career and a livelihood or have his thoughts constrained.

I also wanted to tell the committee I was not intimidated by them, and that I had great faith in the future of my country. I wanted them to know that no matter what they did to my colleagues and me, I knew their committee would not last forever and that we would have freedom in spite of them, along with a glowing, glorious American theater and cinema, and the blossoming art of television. I wanted them to know that I owed full and unqualified allegiance to my flag and to our Constitution, which has given hope and encouragement to the world. I wanted them to know that I believed loyalty is measured by deeds and devotion to one's neighbors and by active participation in civic and charitable functions, not by a devotional fetish that required the mechanical affixing of a signature to a meaningless loyalty oath. I wanted them to understand that what they were doing was unworthy of the men who committed themselves to great hazard and grief when they signed that great, all-time act of nonconformity, the Declaration of Independence. They signed for freedom. In 1951 in America, people signed loyalty oaths out of acquiescence and fear. I wanted to ask them, "How can you reconcile that?"

But they would not let me speak and refused to hear anything about my war experience or commendations or my observations about freedom. It was common for HUAC to dismiss any mention of honorable war records of those who refused to testify as simply records of Benedict Arnolds. This was utterly convenient for them, if not simply blind. The committee was done with me. Before I was summarily dismissed, however, Chairman Wood took a moment to personally attack me when he said, "If, by any action of this committee, we could be instrumental in eliminating from the field of public entertainment the views of people—particularly the youth of this country being moved by a large extent—people who decline to answer a question as to whether or not they are members of the Communist Party, it would make me extremely happy."[1]

Wood's last comment regarding the youth of our country turned out to be particularly ironic. During my twelve years of being blacklisted, I held many classes for children and volunteered my time teaching creative dramatics to inmates at the Sybil Brand Juvenile Hall and the Las Palmas School for Girls. In 1965 a Los Angeles grand jury commended my volunteer work with an official citation and thank-you. Congressman Wood would have been appalled.

But on that day I was numb. Hope and I walked out of the hearing room together. There was very little we could say, and nothing could be done to change the outcome of what had just transpired in front of us. We stepped out of the Federal Building together into the bright sunlight, despondent and holding on to each other for dear life. Hope drove home to take care of the children. I made my way to my third event of the day, at the new Studio Center at Cahuenga and Willoughby in Hollywood. Even though I was on the gray list, weeks earlier I had been cast in a television pilot dealing, ironically, with Washington movers and shakers. I was assigned the role of a distinguished senator. Ann Harding, one of the really great ladies of theater and films, was playing the leading role. Phil Brown, my friend and colleague from the Actors' Lab, was directing the pilot, and Edward Lewis was producing. The first cast reading was set for the afternoon of my hearing.

I entered the room. Not a word was said about my appearance, but I knew it had been reported throughout the day and was about to hit the afternoon papers. During the rehearsal, everything was treated as normal. Later, the assistant director distributed our call sheets for the next day and we left. Moments after I arrived home, a disconsolate Eddie Lewis called to tell me the network would not, on any terms, allow me to appear in the pilot. Eddie was a decent man and I did not fault him. The committee had the networks and advertising agencies in a panic. Even old-line studio tycoons knuckled under. As fortune would have it, years later Eddie and I did manage to work together in a marvelous movie called *Seconds,* starring Rock Hudson. But that week, it was not meant to be.

On occasion, I muse about those phantasmagoric encounters on that September day in 1951. Our friends the screenwriter Frank Tarloff and his wife, Lee, were the first visitors to our home that night. We were soon joined by a host of others. We were not a cheerful lot as we sat nibbling Italian pastries from Sarno's and drinking pots of strong, black coffee. Frank made the droll observation that it felt like we were attending our own wake. It was hard to shake the gloom. On the other hand, the other shoe had finally dropped. There would be no more ducking subpoenas, no more impending dread about appearing in front of the committee. My blacklist had officially arrived.

That weekend our neighbors Mae and Sol Babitz urged us to join them and their daughters, Eve and Miriam, at a house they had rented in Blue Jay, near Lake Arrowhead. Mae was a self-taught artist who worked with quill and ink and did beautiful drawings of old houses and buildings in Los Angeles, often just before they were torn down. Sol was a Baroque music zealot and the resident upstart of the Los Angeles music community. While he often doesn't get credit, he was the true founder of the Early Music Movement and published many tracts deploring the homogenization of Baroque music, principally by Leopold Stokowski, whose symphonic arrangements of Bach fugues and cantatas rankled Sol greatly. Sol was a close friend of the great modern composer Igor Stravinsky and the film composer Bernard Herrmann, who were often guests at the Babitzes' dinner table.

Mae and Sol's offer of a weekend sojourn away from the mayhem of Hollywood was a welcome distraction. Early Saturday morning, Hope and I put the children in the car and drove into the mountains. We cooked and ate divine food, and the Corey and Babitz girls, who were very close in age, dug in the sand and invented games all weekend long. We breathed in the clean, clear mountain air and walked along the perimeter of Lake Arrowhead, relieved to be away from HUAC-benighted Los Angeles— grateful to be living across the way from such supportive and caring neighbors.

We returned home late Sunday to the descending gloom. After getting the girls to bed, I did what I always do when I feel forlorn. I memorized a poem. It works unfailingly. I drew strength from a passage in Carl Sandburg's *The People, Yes,* "The fireborn—they go far—being at home in fire." He also wrote, "They will be tricked and sold and again sold. And go back to the nourishing earth for rootholds." During the blacklist years, whenever the tension verged on the untenable, I'd heed Sandburg's advice and take my little hand spade and do some weeding so that I could smell the brown earth and feel the nourishing hold of the earth's roots in my hands.

On Monday morning, the vicious and mean-spirited gossip columnist Mike Connelly, who was a rabid McCarthy supporter and a cohort of Hedda Hopper, went out of his way to attack Hope. In his column he identi-fied her as "the wife of Fifth Amendment Commie Jeff Corey" and sug-gested she should not be allowed to be a room mother at Cheremoya Avenue School. The ugly brutality of his comments made me quite ill. It was bad enough that I was in the limelight, shunned by my profession, but now my wife was being attacked for her good work as a caring parent. Luckily, no one at the school paid attention to Connelly's ranting, and Hope contin-ued to volunteer in our daughters' classrooms throughout their education.

On Tuesday I showed up to teach my class at the Stage Society. I was thankful the class was well attended. Gary Cooper and Pat Neal were there. Coop was very much aware of the harrowing experiences so many of us were being subjected to. He was working on *High Noon* and knew I had been up for a part in that prestigious film that was nixed by the studios because of my subpoena. Later in the year, when filming for *High Noon* was complete, Coop tried to establish a production company with my friend Carl Foreman, who had written and co-produced *High Noon.* Carl had also been summoned before the committee and had taken what was known as a diminished Fifth. Carl agreed to answer questions about his own affilia-tions but refused to implicate other people. Taking a diminished Fifth put you in peril of being held in contempt and subject to one year's imprison-ment for each refusal. Regrettably, the studios would have none of Coop's teaming up with Carl, and Carl eventually moved his family to England.

It was inevitable that the rumblings of HUAC would reach the Stage Society. Unbeknown to me, Hedda Hopper, the wicked syndicated gossip columnist and a member of the Motion Picture Alliance for the Preservation of American Ideals, had contacted the Stage Society's Board of Directors. Hopper offered them all the upholstered theater seats they could use to replace the spartan wooden seats originally installed by Mae West's manager. She informed the board the free seats would be made available only if the relationship between the Stage Society and Jeff Corey was terminated, immediately.

The next Monday night, when I arrived at the Stage Society to take Mischa's class, I was totally unaware of the witches' brew that had been stirring. At the end of Mischa's class, the playwright N. Richard Nash took my hand and began stroking my palm with his right index finger. I was completely taken aback by this strange action. Nash continued grinning.

"Jeff," he said, "don't you know what that means?"

"No, Richard," I said as I pulled my hand away. "I have no idea what that means."

"In ancient Greece," he continued, "when a citizen was excommunicated, they indicated it by putting a snail in his palm."

Nash's fondling of my hand was his metaphor for a snail. I found it gross and insulting. The next day I was officially asked to leave the Stage Society. Twenty-eight years later, Richard Erdman, who later became president of the Stage Society, wrote a feature article that appeared in the *Los Angeles Times* that said:

In 1951, we lost our entire leadership. Anthony Quinn went to Europe, J. Arthur Kennedy returned to New York, Akim Tamiroff became ill. For a brief moment we were lucky. Jeff Corey took over the acting classes and his lyric, almost messianic eloquence and energy filled the void. Then he was cut down by the House un-American Activities Committee and the scrawling of Hedda Hopper and Mike Connelly. They wrote that the Stage Society was infiltrated with lefties and Reds. Membership lists disappeared from our files and there were rumors that the entire group might go unemployed in films if "the Reds" weren't rooted out.[2]

After I left, the Stage Society continued to flourish, and many prestigious film folk joined its ranks. Eventually, the company grew too big and the powers that be began paring down the membership. They kept the stars on their roster, and the less-experienced, lesser-known actors were told there was no longer a place for them in the Stage Society's future.

One of the people asked to leave was Johnny Dutra, who had done sound effects at the Actors' Lab. Johnny was understandably upset by this turn of events and asked if I would be interested in starting my own class. I told him I was interested but wouldn't know how to promote one. I explained that I'd find it humiliating to take an ad in the trade papers. Johnny offered to organize the class himself. Within a week, eighteen potential students arrived at my house. Obviously, many of them were wary of the political taint of being associated with me. I had no way of assuring them but made it clear that no matter what, I would teach as good an acting class as I could muster.

Viola Spolin, who had been teaching acting in Hollywood since the early 1940s, graciously offered me the use of her studio, free of charge. Twelve of the eighteen showed up for the first class. After a few weeks, word got around, and our numbers increased. Emboldened by consistent class attendance, I decided it was time to rent a space of my own. I found a very small studio at the corner of Cole Avenue and Romaine Street in Hollywood, just across from the Technicolor Studio Lab. The theater was furnished with a woebegone wreck of a burgundy mohair sofa, some spindly wicker chairs, and a decrepit coffee table. In its own way, it was in the finest tradition of the best rehearsal halls.

With my acting career gone, I had officially become a teacher.

11

Cheremoya Mini-Theater

Hope and I were fortunate to have purchased our house in Hollywood at the T-shaped intersection of Cheremoya Avenue and Chula Vista Way in 1949. It was a quiet street lined with camphor and sycamore trees. The house was a generous home with a wide hallway, wainscoted dining room, kitchen, breakfast room, living room, library, and, at the end of a hallway, a music room. At the entrance, a broad stairway with a handsome mahogany railing led to a small landing, off which were four sunlit bedrooms.

In addition to Mae and Sol Babitz, we had a marvelous collection of neighbors up and down the block. Next door to our house were the Swans. Mrs. Swan was a caring educator who alarmed her superiors at the Los Angeles Board of Education by her excessively enlightened approach to teaching. She was principal of a public school in the Pico and Crescent Heights district, and her contretemps with the entrenched bureaucracy often made headlines. Just north of us lived Jan and Jose Smit. The Smits were Dutch émigrés who had been very active in the Dutch resistance. Both delightful and highly principled people, Jan risked his life when he successfully smuggled a young Jewish boy out of Holland. During the height of the committee hearings, Jan and Jose would cook breakfast together in their kitchen and show their support by serenading Hope and me with a resounding rendition of "The International," the international workers' song.

Next door to the Swans were Morgan and Mildred Cox. Morgan was an older man, a Yale graduate who majored in English literature. He had been a screenwriter and worked on many B Westerns in Hollywood. I first met Morgan in 1948, when he was the line producer on *Bagdad*, starring the beautiful and fiery Maureen O'Hara as an Arabian princess. I played her granduncle. I was thirty-four at the time, and Maureen was only a few years younger, but they wanted me for the part. Emile LaVigne, one of the great Hollywood makeup artists, lined my face with convincing wrinkles and a gray beard. The film was in a genre affectionately called "tits and sand," and the studio daringly showed just an edge more skin than the stuffy and self-righteous Hays Office would allow. The brilliant dancers Lester Horton and Bella Lewitzky were hired as choreographers. Bella and I became fast friends, and over the years as I watched her develop her craft of movement and dance, it became clear to me that Bella was truly one of the greatest artists of the twentieth century. The bootleg musical score for *Bagdad* was a hybrid of Middle Eastern music and symphonies adapted from the great Russian composer Nikolai Rimsky-Korsakov.

Morgan owned two objects that I loved and truly coveted. The first was the greatest Maurice de Vlaminck painting I have ever seen. Morgan had purchased the painting in the 1930s on the advice of a friend who owned the Hatfield Gallery at the Ambassador Hotel. It hung gloriously over his fireplace. The other item was a beautiful Ford Model A that strad-dled a platform in his garage. In the twenty-two years we lived there, he never drove it. My daughters, in particular my youngest, Emily, were always welcome in his house, especially in his library. One day he entrusted ten-year-old Emily with his first-edition copy of Louisa May Alcott's *Rose in Bloom*, which had belonged to his mother. Emily took it home and devoured it. The age of the book and the generosity of the loan made a great impression on her.

Morgan was a true curmudgeon and a delight to have in the neighbor-hood. Even after a stroke slowed his step, the cane he was obliged to use only enhanced his irascibility as he maneuvered it to underscore his pas-sionate opinions. Charles Dickens's *Bleak House* was his favorite novel, and he had read it ten times. One day he gave Hope a copy. In it he wrote, "Thank you for your consideration of me."

From the day we moved in Morgan appeared at our home, most often at dinnertime. He would sit in one of our Lincoln rocking chairs in the corner of the dining room and conduct a symposium of the day. It might be something that he read of Mark Twain, Bret Harte, or George Meredith. He always integrated it with life on Cheremoya Avenue and invariably quizzed my daughters on what they had been reading and what they were studying in school. Morgan was a militant trade unionist and was reputed to have been a firebrand at the Writers Guild of America (WGA) negotiat-ing meetings. When he died, the WGA created the Morgan Cox Service Award for individuals who give significant service to the Guild.

When I ran into the HUAC melee, Morgan was disturbed at the distress it caused our family, but he would comment ruefully, "Jeff, when Uncle Sammy asks you to answer questions, you have no option but to accommodate him." I thought it contradictory for a man who could be so lucid in his discussions about the social disintegration in *Oliver Twist* to be so insistently myopic about disintegrated values in his own backyard. Yet I loved him dearly, as did Hope and the children.

In his benevolent moods he would type out quotes from the American Transcendentalist philosopher Ralph Waldo Emerson on the art of poetry or an excerpt from a work of the nineteenth-century English novelist Anthony Trollope and insist that I read it to my class that very night. Morgan wrote an original play for Emily's Brownie troop called *The Floating Island.* Inspired by Shakespeare's *The Tempest,* it had a decent part for every girl in the troop. They performed it in my backyard theater with all the families in attendance and, of course, the playwright-director himself happily taking center stage. One morning the FBI dispatched two agents to question Morgan about his neighbor Jeff Corey. Morgan rushed to the house at the conclusion of the interview to tell me all the glowing things he had said about our family.

All this occurred concurrently with my student activities at UCLA. It was difficult being a thirty-eight-year-old college student sitting in class with seventeen-year-olds right out of high school. It had been twenty years since I'd graduated from New Utrecht High School. I felt detached from the rest of the students and the vague presence of assorted professors, and the classrooms had the stillness of a Balthus painting. The most painful part of each semester was always the first day of class, when my name was called for roll. Invariably, dozens of students would turn and stare at me, startled to hear my name. Invariably, after class a brave few souls would come up to me and whisper how much they admired how I comported myself before the committee.

As my own roster of acting students continued to grow, I began to ponder a way of converting my two-car garage into a little theater. By this point, Eve and Jane were away at school all day and Emily spent part of her day in nursery school. It would be fairly simple to use the house as my studio. The plan I envisaged could be supported by only a minuscule budget, as our finances were now extremely tight. Less than a quarter mile from our house, the Hollywood freeway was under construction. Every day, crews were filling wooden forms with concrete. Once the concrete hardened, they'd throw away mountains of plywood and two-by-fours. Early in the morning or just as dusk was falling, I'd load select pieces of cast-off lumber into my station wagon. These castoffs constituted the bulk of my building materials. With the help of some of my students, I added a six-foot extension to my garage, laid a plywood ceiling, built a little stage, and backed it up with four-by-eight-foot Masonite panels. I purchased several decrepit spotlights from a theatrical warehouse and carefully figured out how much wattage I could safely draw from the fuse box in the house without sending the entire household into darkness. The patchwork that characterized the construction of my jerry-built theater was a perfect metaphor for the juggling and adaptations we had been enduring as a family since my HUAC appearance.

My first class in my Cheremoya mini-theater included Karen Hale, the daughter of the actor Alan Hale Sr.; Kathleen O'Malley, whose father was the silent screen star Pat O'Malley; Carl Milletaire, who had been on the GI Bill at the Actors' Lab; Delia Salvi, who later got her Ph.D. in theater arts and became a full professor at UCLA. Other students were Jim Moloney; an as yet unknown Carol Burnett, who was a classmate of mine at UCLA; Herb Jacobs; and the actress Georgia Phillips. Another student was Bert Schoenberg, an attorney who brought his friend Alla Markoff, and she, in turn, brought in Polly Adler, the notorious Manhattan madam and best-selling author of *A House Is Not a Home*. Lenny Bruce's mother, Sally Marr, who ran a strip-tease academy on Santa Monica Boulevard, also joined this polyglot group, as did Diane Webber, a highly cultured young lady who did nude centerfolds years before *Playboy* gave status to that activity. And, of course, there was Johnny Dutra, who organized it all. From the start, as in all the subsequent classes I've taught over the years, I had to find a way of bringing form and purpose to what I was teaching. This lovely and highly eclectic group of men and women had faith in me.

I did everything in my power to return the favor.

12

Battalions of Trouble

My backyard studio on Cheremoya Avenue accommodated a class of twenty students. The backside of the studio was the third wall of a handball court that also served as my children's basketball court. Our backyard was quite large and contained a massive carob tree that grew an abundance of edible pods. Two avocado trees stood at attention at one end of the yard, while a wild plum tree and a pomegranate tree brought up the rear. It was a cozy, welcoming environment, and many of my students began arriving early to get their weekly basketball and handball workouts in before class.

My children enjoyed having my students at the house. Just before class each evening, students would congregate on our brick patio under the carob tree, and the girls would come out and join them in a game of handball. One of my students taught Emily how to ride a bike, and it seemed there was always some brawny young actor willing to pick up Jane or Eve and twirl them around or watch them do somersaults and cartwheels.

My classes met on Tuesday and Thursday evenings for three hours. More and more people called, interested in enrolling. Soon I was running out of space and had to start another class. It met on Monday and Wednesday evenings. Shortly after that, I added an afternoon class on Tuesday and Thursday, which gave me only a few hours to rest between the day and evening sessions. Along with that, I still had to keep up with my fifteen college units and research and write the obligatory term papers.

Years later, many of my ex-students told me how cozy it was to walk up our driveway and see Hope and the girls still lingering over our dinner table. Hope juggled everyone's schedule to accommodate my need to have dinner on the table at five. It wasn't convenient, but if I had dinner that early, it gave me a chance to see my children briefly and then go upstairs for a quick nap before my evening class. Hope was a marvelous cook and had an exquisite aesthetic. Everything she prepared was beautiful, and even in the middle of summer, with the sun still shining brightly outside, the dinner table was beautifully set, and colorful candles from a little shop on Olvera Street were always lit. Many of my students had come from broken homes and much more difficult circumstances. The sight of our family sitting down together for a meal was a foreign idea and became an example for more than one of my students to live by.

My scant income from my classes was beginning to come close to the $120 income ceiling the Veterans' Administration allowed under the GI Bill. In a letter to the VA, I happily advised them I no longer required their monthly stipend and thanked them for defraying the costs of my college tuition and textbooks.

I threw myself into teaching.

The makeup of every class was different, and I soon realized I had to find a way of bringing form and purpose to a very diverse group of students. Through my years of maneuvering, I have learned that no teacher can really transmit what he or she knows, but that a lot of good things are learned in a class where an honest effort to teach is made. In all my years of teaching, I always showed up to class determined to make that effort.

In act 4 of *Hamlet,* King Claudius, at a distressing juncture, ruefully proclaims, "Gertrude, Gertrude, when sorrows come, they come not single spies but in battalions." My classes were growing, but unbeknown to me, sorrow was rearing its head again.

On June 2, 1953, my onetime friend Lee J. Cobb made a compact with the committee to privately name names. Lee met secretly with a HUAC investigator named William A. Wheeler in Room 1117 at the Hollywood Roosevelt Hotel in Hollywood. Rumor has it he paid the committee twenty-five thousand dollars cash not to make his testimony public. It was part of a payoff system that apparently funded corrupt unions and politicians. After his meeting with Wheeler, Lee continued to see his old friends, including Hope and me. Months later, the committee double-crossed him and published his testimony in the *Congressional Record.* It was headline news that my name had been included in Lee's testimony. That day only two of my students came to class. I mustered the self-discipline to teach them.

The next morning, seven of my absentee students arrived at my home. They were a delegation sent to explain why they could no longer attend my classes. I listened patiently. They assured me they loved the class but were afraid their careers would be jeopardized if they studied with me. I understood their concerns and was not critical of them. I expressed my abhorrence of the thought control that was permeating Hollywood and deplored the panic that engulfed these young artists. I told them it made me sad to see them so fearful of incrimination. As they got up to leave, I reassured them I would have a class again on Wednesday night and that they were all welcome. We stood there silently. One after another, they began to cry. All seven of them came back to class, as did hundreds on hundreds more in the years that followed.

As my reputation grew, the same studios that would not hire me as an actor began sending their stars to work with me both in class and privately. Word got out that James Dean was sitting in on my classes along with another *East of Eden* cast member, Lois Smith, and the film's composer, Leonard Rosenman. Class regulars included Dean Stockwell, Robert Towne, Richard Chamberlain, Carole Eastman, Louise Fletcher, Robert Blake, Jack Nicholson, Nancy Werden, Julian Burton, Robert Radnitz, John Shaner, Sally Kellerman, Corey Allen, Luana Anders, Nadyne Turney, Virginia Aldridge, Jerry Reynolds, Lou Morheim, and Gene Reynolds. The median age was twenty, and all of them were still unknown. A contingent of Twentieth Century Fox contract players who were not happy with the training they were receiving at the studio came, en masse, as well. The studios liked the effect my classes were having on their actors and would eagerly pay for their lessons, even though they would not allow me to step foot on studio property, much less cast me in their films.

From the very beginning, I told my students too much talk was the death of an acting class. I asked them to bring in a scene or monologue at least once a week and underscored the importance of rehearsing outside class. Rehearsing wasn't just about learning the lines. I asked them to keep in mind the German word Max Reinhardt, the marvelous film director, used for rehearsal, *probieren,* which means "to taste or sample." I encouraged my students to use their rehearsal time to sample the richness of the play and to taste its delight.

When the scene work was presented in class, I would jot down notes. I soon learned the virtue of starting to talk even when I was not sure of what I was saying. In my role as teacher, I found, to my good fortune, that I could express a still undefined gut reaction to a performer's work and in the very process of talking it through, generally discover what I really meant to say. After a scene, I tried to describe what the actors had done and then discuss how effective or ineffective their choices had been. Then

I'd suggest alterations in context and assumptions. My purpose was to help them find some essential aspect of the scene that everyone in the audience could relate to in his or her own life experiences. I often invoked Stanislavsky's imprecation, "It is the actor's function to reveal the human condition!" I tried to frame these observations in the most honest yet positive way possible.

I was encouraged by the affirmative responses of the classes to the hands-on reworking of scenes without a lot of theoretical palaver. In an oblique way, it pleased me that my students didn't really know they were in a method class because I chose not to use those incessant phrases like "You're indicating," or "Playing the result," or "What's your action?" More important, I found there were better ways to deal with actors than giving them bad report cards.

During my freshman year at UCLA, I enrolled in a course in American history taught by Dr. Brainerd Dyer. Dyer was a very stringent lecturer. He was hooked on details and subjected us to weekly exams. To prepare, I formed a study group with three other students. Of course, they knew about the circuitous events that had brought me to their classroom and thankfully seemed to care less about my HUAC mess. Our sessions led us to good grades, and we enjoyed each other's company. On several occasions, I asked them to our home and we'd have a bite of food along with our studying.

Christmas season was upon us and I mentioned that our Chanukah-Christmas coffer was, at best, meager. Two of them said, "We're signing up with the post office for temporary holiday work. Why don't you do that, too?"

I tried to imagine delivering mail door-to-door to people who might recognize me. It would be humiliating, and I could only imagine the wretched conversations that would eventually lead to why I was delivering their mail instead of acting in a film. My college friends were emphatic. "You have nothing to be ashamed of, and you owe it to your family to earn that extra money." With a very heavy heart, I agreed to do it for my kids.

The next day I went downtown to the main post office next to Union Station and waited in line. I was standing near two young African American postal clerks. "What are you doing in this part of town, Doc?" they asked me.

A third clerk joined them, his face radiant. "Yeah, here he is. Doc, from *Home of the Brave*," he said, beaming at me.

I said, very evenly, "I want an application for temporary Christmas work."

They all laughed, "You're kidding, Doc."

I said, "Please give me the form." It seemed to take an eternity for them to ascertain that I was serious.

They gave me a form and in funereal tones told me to walk over to the basement of the Federal Building. It seemed all my roads led back to that fateful edifice. When I arrived, there was another long line. I filled out the form, signed my name, and tried not to dread the inevitable degradation. As I stood in line, more and more people recognized me. "Weren't you in *My Friend Flicka?*" or "I loved you in *The Devil and Daniel Webster,*" and "Weren't you in that picture with John Wayne, Wallace Beery, Gary Cooper, Ingrid Bergman?" and so on; I was truly wretched. As I moved slowly toward the desk, there was finally just one person ahead of me. I overheard a voice say, "Now, sign the loyalty oath here."

The application froze in my hand. I turned to the person in back of me and mumbled something about coming back later and fled the miserable basement as quickly as I could. I could not possibly have stood up to HUAC only to cave in and sign a loyalty oath. For the second time in my life, I walked out of the downtown Federal Building without a job.

My Cheremoya mini-theater became a haven for me. I was able to work privately with students during the day and hold classes during the evenings and on Saturdays. When I wasn't teaching, the girls used my mini-theater to put on plays with their friends, often inviting the entire neighborhood to see their performances. They wrote plays, made up songs, and offered shows that were inventive and charming. I soon came to believe that all children should have a mini-theater in their backyard. I only regretted that ours was the result of the blacklist.

I was pleased to learn so much from my students. They didn't just bring in the run-of-the mill scenes done in every acting class in the country. They brought in excerpts from Styron's novel *Lie Down in Darkness.* Nadyne Turney did Molly Bloom's twenty-minute soliloquy from Joyce's *Ulysses,* which had a sexual vigor and pertinence that startled us all. Sally Kellerman prepared a long monologue from Saroyan's *Beautiful People.* It was transcendent. Robert Towne brought in Elizabeth Bishop's poem "The Fish." I remember, too, Bob's simple, nonstentorian rendering of *Richard II*'s speech beginning "No matter where; of comfort no man speak." Roger Corman, a fledgling producer at the time, performed only one scene in all the months he attended class but paid close attention to Towne's work, as well as the enormous talents of his classmates Jack Nicholson and Carole Eastman, and put them to work in his films. Eastman went on to write *Five Easy Pieces,* and Towne wrote *Chinatown* and *The Last Detail;* Jack's remarkable and beautifully complex acting was showcased in the starring roles in all three.

In class, Robert Blake would generally sit next to Sally Kellerman, and together the two of them would stretch whatever items of clothing they were wearing to just below their eyes. They inevitably looked like the cartoon "Kilroy Was Here." I often pointed out to them that their presence in the room was noted even though they sometimes seemed to pretend that they were not there. I was never impatient with them. During one afternoon class, Robert did an inspired "To be or not to be." Oddly enough, Robert disappeared after his token triumph. He did the definitive Shakespearean speech with panache and then evaporated from class, something he did on and off over the many years he studied with me. He would still drop by the house, generally at dinnertime, and Hope would always ask him to join us at the table. My children found him charming and always enjoyed his company.

To supplement our income, in the summer I took a job as a counselor at Haskell's Rascals Day Camp. Our dear friend David Robison, who had also been blacklisted, worked there as well. Ollie Haskell was a Bulgarian immigrant who possessed an odd sense of chaos and fun. His camp was a clutter of disarray and delight and was filled with children from Los Angeles' most progressive families. The camp was on a fairly barren section of a twenty-acre dairy farm in the San Fernando Valley. No one there cared that I was blacklisted. My job was to pick up eight kids in the Hollywood area every morning, deliver them to camp, and then teach creative dramatics to three or four groups of children throughout the day. I earned fifty-five dollars a week, and Eve and Jane were able to attend the camp at a reduced rate, as were David's children, Paula, Deborah, and Josh.

I loved the very old barn where we held our classes and was pleased at the children's reactions to the work, but, all in all, it was uphill for me. At the end of the day, I'd deliver my load of kids back to their homes, head to our house for a quick shower and dinner, take a short nap, and then go teach my regular evening class. I spent a hot, dusty summer hanging out with marvelous kids, but it was a far cry from what I wanted to be doing and was sometimes a difficult reminder of just how far I had veered from my chosen path.

I had already packed work into every minute of the day and night, so when the producer George Boroff offered me the lead in a production of the Irish play *Danger, Men Working*, it didn't seem practical to accept his offer. It was a play the distinguished stage designer Mordecai Gorelik and George had optioned after they had seen it at the Edinburgh Festival in Scotland. Nonetheless, against my better judgment, I succumbed to the offer. The raw hurt of the blacklist and my exclusion from the Stage Society had left me so artistically wanting that it suddenly felt easy to modify my day to fit in rehearsal time.

Mordecai, or Max, as we liked to call him, directed the piece himself. Max had designed most of the Group Theatre's sets and had written a scholarly tome called *New Theatres for Old*. He was not a great talker, and his median look could be described as severe, but I trusted him. He had a good eye, he didn't like to intrude, and he was willing to assist me when requested. During the first week of rehearsal, two actors dropped out because they were uneasy about the potential incrimination of being associated with me. Max and George, to their credit, brushed aside their exits and asked me to recommend actors to replace them. I suggested two of my students, Kathleen O'Malley and John Alderson. *Danger, Men Working* received respectable reviews. When John Houseman saw John's performance, he cast him in *Julius Caesar* at MGM. A number of other actors in the production also got work in the industry, but I was still considered an untouchable. No one would hire me. It was painful to ruminate over my entrapment in the blacklist nightmare. Was this truly the termination of a twenty-year acting career?

It seemed that it was.

13

The Act of Teaching

Over my decades of teaching, I have conceived various exercises, or études, that reveal the choices and multiplicity of meanings that are available to an actor who wishes to go beyond the literal words of a script. A script is a powerful and imaginative resource, but the words themselves do not tell the story. I often use improvisation in my classes, but it is always with the intent of further discovery rather than to rehash the plot, which is so often the case in other classes. Rehashing spins wheels and paralyzes the story into one or two options. Improvisation, when used with imagination, ignites the actor's mind and allows him to explore the unexpected and vibrant depths of the plot. Most, if not all, of my études intentionally laden actors with a detailed plot and then let them improvise without a single reference to that plot. This allows actors to explore the script without being unnecessarily burdened by the thematic tenor of a story. By throwing out the literal meaning of the film or play, we can search for the rich and unexpected undercurrents that are always part of the human condition.

In 1995, when I was on the faculty of the American Film Institute, Jack Nicholson spoke to a large meeting of the fellows and faculty members. Jack spoke with great affection about his years in my class and the charms of my mini-theater on Cheremoya Avenue. He also proclaimed that he was the best improviser he knew. At the conclusion of the evening, I thanked Jack for his fresh and insightful comments on acting and improvisation. Jack turned to Hope and said, "Doesn't he know it was Jeff speaking through me all evening?" It was a delicious tribute, and I was grateful for the compliment.

This exploration is vital for the actor, but the undercurrent discovered through the examination of improvisation also has a place in our everyday lives. Very little of what we say is literal. There is always a suggestion of unspoken emotion in any conversation. We say to a new girlfriend, "I love you," but underneath is the nagging concern about commitment. We go to work, determined to speak up at a meeting, and then allow ourselves to be intimidated by the antics of a fellow worker; we end up saying something we don't necessarily mean or saying what we mean without conviction or enthusiasm. All these undercurrents and mixed emotions affect our behavior and are the stuff that everyday life is made of. These undercurrents and mixed emotions dramatically influence an actor's performance, and anyone who has sat through a dull presentation of a brilliantly written play can attest to the importance of this investigation.

At the start of any class, I really don't know what is going to happen. You can't re-create what is going to happen from what happened in a previous class. It is always unique. I don't know what the scenes are going to be and where the work will take us. I can only listen and then, through accessing my knowledge, experience, and instinct, take the class where it needs to go.

The discipline involved in improvisation is to articulate the implications of the plot for people caught in a miasma of events. My études are designed to encourage actors to speak the subtext while making no verbal reference to the story at all. This process was aptly described in an interview with Robert Towne in John Brady's book *The Craft of the Screenwriter.* In it Towne relates:

Corey had an exercise in which he would take a scene from, say, *Three Men on a Horse,* which is a farce, and he would say, "OK, you're a junkie, and you're trying to sell this guy some dope." In other words, the situation that he would give would be totally contrary to the text, and it was the task of the actors, through their interpretation of the various bits of business they could come up with, to suggest the real situation through lines that had no bearing on the situation. When you see that for three years running, when you are asked for improvisations in which you are given a situation and told that you must talk about everything but the situation to advance the action, you soon see the power of dealing obliquely or elliptically with situations, because most people rarely confront things head-on. They're afraid to. I think that most people try to be accommodating in life, but in the back of their accommodation is suppressed fear or anger or both. What happens in a dramatic situation is that it surfaces. And it shouldn't surface too easily, or it's not realistic.[1]

During those early years of teaching in my backyard theater, I knew I might run into a zoning problem. Technically, I was running a business in a residential area. The city was well aware of this. I paid for my Los Angeles business license for seven years, and my address was clearly printed on the license, so it was never an underground enterprise. Every year the local fire station would send two or three firemen to examine my backyard to look for fire hazards. On at least three occasions I spotted the inspectors walking around my backyard while I was teaching. Fortunately, they never noticed us or, if they did, kindly ignored the class in session. But in 1958 the zoning commission contacted me and informed me I was in violation. I believe a rather conservative neighbor across the street, who, despite the overall friendly tenor of the block, had never spoken to either Hope or me, filed a complaint with the city. The commission generously gave me three months to relocate my enterprise. It turned out to be a blessing in disguise.

Shortly after the production of *Danger, Men Working*, George Boroff had purchased the Circle Theater on Vine Street in Hollywood. He rented the space to me at a very good price, and I moved my classes there. I installed a lighting system and designed and constructed an array of movable platforms that could be set up to accommodate any given scene. I continued to use my backyard studio for interviews and private work and a series of informal drill sessions. The drill sessions were weekend gatherings where students from any class could go over problems they had encountered with a scene. It was a wonderful way to continue to explore the work and allowed students from all my classes to interact and engage in the process together. We invented a range of impromptu études for problems, and the extra sessions gave the classes an added excitement and dimension that had not emerged before my move.

I found my appointment book from 1955. It exhausts me to look at those daily logs. While much of my day was given to working with people privately, I also dedicated a portion of my time to interviewing potential students. After my HUAC appearance, I received a number of death threats and numerous hate calls. Often very ugly hate mail would arrive at our door. Hope and I changed our phone to an unlisted number. We didn't want our children to inadvertently pick up one of these calls, and we always went through the mail before the children got home from school. If prospective students had the wherewithal to track down my unlisted phone number, I felt I owed them the respect of interviewing them in person. I did not accept everyone I met with in my classes, but meeting one-on-one seemed the best way to maintain the high caliber of students needed to keep the classes exciting and engaging.

I charged $25 a month for a biweekly, three-hour class. This fee included the weekend drill sessions. I charged $5 an hour for private sessions. My private students included my own students who wanted help with a particular problem and a host of young up-and-coming stars the Hollywood studios sent to me to work on a particular role.

My day began at 8:00 a.m., even before my children left for school, and ended four nights a week at 10:30 p.m. at the close of a three-hour evening class. I took half an hour for lunch and then resumed seeing people privately until 4:30 p.m., when I would come in for half an hour with my children and a bite to eat. When I was no longer teaching at home, I had to leave for my new studio by 7:00 p.m. I worked mornings, afternoons, and evenings and at one time taught sixteen three-hour classes a week. It was a difficult schedule and meant being away from my family four nights a week and much of Saturday. I rarely attended my daughters' school open houses or teacher conferences, or sat in the audience when they performed in a school play. The blacklist had not only affected my career. It had turned my family life upside down. But teaching had become my profession, and I took it seriously and with commitment.

I look back at the extraordinary assemblage of young and talented artists who came to those early classes and know that the success of these classes was a marginal gift that helped lift up my spirits. Sadly, it was all transpiring in the benighted environment of the blacklist, and there were also periods of great despair. On one summer afternoon, at a time when I could in no way afford an evaporative air cooler in my studio, I fell asleep while preparing for class. I woke up in the hot and humid room and lay there in a stupor. For a moment, I didn't know where I was. Suddenly, the harrowing events of the first years of the blacklist ran through my mind like a phantasmagoric montage. In my life, I have rarely been that disconsolate. I suddenly thought of a passage from a Shaw play in which the daughter says to her father, "Oh, father, I am so unhappy," and her father retorts snappily, "Read a good book. Read *King Lear.*"

Still in a stupor, I reached for my copy of the *Cambridge Complete Works of Shakespeare* and flipped it open to a random page. On the very top of the page I had selected, I read the line "Othello's occupation's gone."

There was no controlling me. I have never before or since wept so profusely.

14

Refining the Approach

Overall, during my years as a college student I related well with the faculty members in the Theater Arts Department at UCLA. My fellow students knew who I was and most, if not all, had seen movies I had been in. On more than one occasion I was a student in a class that used a film I had costarred in to illustrate fine American acting. I learned to get used to these uncomfortable encounters, and, by and large, professors and students alike treated me with the utmost respect. I was particularly gratified that Dr. Ralph Freud, the chairman of the Theater Arts Department, allowed me to design my own curriculum. As part of my degree in Theater Arts, however, I had to take a film survey class. Our last assignment was to do a paper on *Home of the Brave*. I honestly don't remember what I wrote, but I got an A.

After receiving my B.A. in theater arts in 1955, I started to collect material for my master's thesis about the British actor Richard Mansfield. A professor named Eddie Hearn who was in charge of stagecraft in the Theater Arts Department wanted to meet with me. Eddie was a wonderful guy. "Jeff," he said, "if you're going to get your master's, you need to do some technical work."

I asked him what he thought I should do. He suggested I do some stage lighting. I said, "I worked with Milton Smith. He wrote the definitive book on lighting." Eddie thought for a moment and said, "Well, I guess that takes care of that." He paused for another long second and then said, "What would you say if I asked you to take this broom and sweep from my office to Royce Hall?" I grinned at Eddie and said, "In the kindliest voice possible, I'd tell you to go fuck yourself." We both laughed. Eddie assigned me to the publicity staff, where I wrote releases about UCLA's production of *Romeo and Juliet*.

I soon realized I really had no time to pursue a master's degree properly. I was tired. My teaching schedule combined with all the preparation I did for my own classes ate up all my time, and, as it was, I barely saw my family. Mid-semester, I called Dr. Freud and told him I had run out of energy. I thanked him for the years of serendipity and bid farewell to my college days. It was now time for me to concentrate, full-time, on teaching.

There's an old aphorism, "Nothing is really lost, there's just something on top of it." I've come across outlines for practically every class session from 1951 to 1955. I am impressed with my self-discipline, and I must say those files triggered an array of names of hundreds on hundreds of students, past and present. I realize that my detailed preparations, however commendable, were also the result of an unremitting panic that made me think, "I've got to prepare; I don't know enough."

In truth, I needed the classes not only for financial sustenance but also for the measure of creative ballast they afforded me. My hope was to keep my ship on an even keel. To do that, I had to keep my classes interesting. The études I continued to develop kept my students engaged and prevented me from being set adrift as a teacher.

A year after I started teaching, I had an enlightening experience that defined my approach to teaching for the rest of my career. The house was quiet and I was alone in my backyard theater with some time and my wonderful blackboard that I used in class to boldly spell out many of the principles that guided my lessons. I was determined to devote the entire afternoon to quietly assessing what I was doing right, identifying areas of confusion, and sorting out how I could find ways to simplify my approach to teaching.

I had posted as many placards as my studio walls could contain with precepts such as Mark Twain's "Courage is resistance to fear, mastery of fear—not absence of fear"; John Howard Lawson's maxim, "Drama cannot deal with people whose wills are atrophied"; and Stanislavsky's description of overused mannerisms as "the despotism of acquired habits." I erased my blackboard and reached for a fresh piece of chalk. I wanted to coin a new catchphrase that would encompass my mode of teaching. With eyes shut, I deliberately tried to clear away all extraneous thoughts and impulses. "Go blank," I said to myself. After a time, with my eyes still closed, I inscribed these words on the blackboard, "Teach *people*, not things."

It was deliverance!

I had a list of all the people in my classes on four separate sheets of paper—a list of at least seventy actors. I shut my eyes again and waved my right hand around and around and then brought my finger down on a single name. I decided that the work for all the classes for the following month would be in relation to that randomly selected student's needs and attributes. As it turned out, it was not just luck or happenstance. The problem to be explored that pertained to a single student invariably applied to every student in the class.

From then on, that became my procedure every month for the succeeding years, all based on the good fortune of that vital phrase, "Teach *people,* not things."

15

Treading Water

By 1955 the success of my acting classes was bruited about. High-powered entrepreneurs came to me with a proposal calculated to bring in a quarter of a million dollars a year. Their extravagant plan was for me to write a correspondence course wherein I would describe acting exercises that people could do by themselves or in groups. A new lesson would be forthcoming every week. The enthusiastic promoters of this plan proposed to advertise in movie magazines and weekly tabloids and include the list of all the successful actors, screenwriters, and directors who had studied with me. I simply could not imagine it, and no amount of money could persuade me from that position. Hope heartily agreed. I politely told them "No" on all counts. They were bewildered by my refusal.

Shortly after that, Mammon, the great god of commercial acquisitiveness, appeared again in the form of a man I had known as a production manager in a remake of Robert L. Stevenson's *Kidnapped*. He said he knew how to get me off the blacklist. He was involved with a film called *Invasion U.S.A.*, and there was a part in it for me as a university professor who discovers an international plot to invade America and destroy our system of government. He wanted to know if he could he send me the script? I said, "Yes," rather gingerly.

It was drivel. The character he wanted me to play faces the audience and, in a long harangue borrowed from HUAC and the McCarthy and McCarran committees, alerts the public to the imminent invasion of the country. In spite of his promises that he could put me in front of a camera again, I couldn't, in conscience, avail myself of this grotesque gambit to "clear myself" before the American public. I politely said, "No, thank you."

Not too long after that, a producer for CBS, Bill Anderson, called and said he wanted me to play Leon Trotsky in a teleplay about Trotsky's last years before his assassination in Mexico City. I told him I would be very interested but reminded him of my blacklist status with the networks. Bill assured me it would work out and sent me the script. I liked it very much and told him to please feel it out with the powers that be.

The next day, I got a call from a top CBS attorney, who asked me to meet with him at his office. After a few introductory niceties, he removed some papers from a manila envelope. "I see, Jeff, that you are still an unregenerate radical," he said.

I sat there and honestly couldn't think of anything of a radical nature that could be attributed to me. I was too busy trying to make do for my family at the most minimal level. I sat there, staring at him in silence. Shuffling more papers, he referred to his notes. "I understand you read a poem at a luncheon honoring the playwright John Howard Lawson when he was released from the federal penitentiary after serving time for contempt of Congress."

I frankly had no recollection of such a luncheon, nor could I think of what possible poem I would have selected. I knew John, and while I would have been honored to be present at such a lively event, it had never happened. Before I could tell him so, he moved on to another topic.

"Further," he advised me, "you shared a platform with Linus Pauling at the First Unitarian Church." That I happily acknowledged. Pauling was an amazing man and a renowned scientist who had won the Nobel Prize in Chemistry in 1954. At the event the lawyer referred to, I read a passage from Thomas Paine's *American Crisis*. Published from 1776 to 1783, *The American Crisis* was a series of propaganda pamphlets that aided and abetted the ideals of the American Revolution. The passage I read began, "These are the times that try men's souls." I told him I had much cause to identify with Paine's sentiments.

He sorted through a few more papers without saying a word, but there seemed to be no more references to me in his dossier. "Well, thanks for dropping by, Jeff," he said, and that concluded our meeting. Apparently, he was looking for me to be actively remorseful or apologize in some way for the Pauling event. Bill called me later that afternoon and told me the legal department would not clear me for work. Sadly, I was not surprised.

In another attempt to break through the clutter of the studio bureaucracy, one of my ex-students, the film director Irvin Kershner, and the great cinematographer Haskell Wexler had a fine script about a struggling farmer in the Midwest. They wanted me to play the lead. They were sure it would work out. But to no avail. The investors were reluctant to have me in the film. They were sure it would jeopardize the project. Haskell was very upset when he had to break the news to me. By this time I was quite inured to rejection, and, rather than being despondent, I found myself comforting Haskell instead.

Though I couldn't work in film, the stage still had a bit of room for me. In 1958 I was cast as the lawyer Alfieri in Lamont Johnson's production of Arthur Miller's *A View from the Bridge* at the prestigious La Jolla Playhouse. The Playhouse was founded by Gregory Peck, Dorothy McGuire, and Mel Ferrer in 1947 and had a stellar reputation. Sherman Marks was our director, and apparently no one involved cared about my blacklisting.

I recommended my student Rita Moreno for the role of Catherine. Martin Balsam played Eddie; Stephen Joyce took on the role of Rodolpho; Bob Gist was his brother, Marco; and Mary Carver played Eddie's wife, Beatrice. It was a marvelous cast. On opening night, Hope brought our daughter Evie backstage before the performance. Evie had seen me rehearse at the Actors' Lab when she was six or seven years old, but now she was fifteen and was well aware of what the blacklist had done to my career. She had not seen me act since she was a very little girl.

There was a spacious foyer that led to our dressing rooms. Everyone in the cast happened to be gathered there when Evie and Hope appeared. Evie looked at me with total love and burst into tears. I embraced her for a long time. The cast, well aware of the circumstances, slipped quietly away to their respective dressing rooms and, as they told me later, had a good cry.

Later that year, I received a call from Steve McQueen. We had never met, but he knew who I was. Steve gently complained that he had had a "heck of a time" trying to get my phone number. When he asked casting people how he could get in touch with me, he was told I was "unavailable." Steve wanted to know if that was true. I assured him I was indeed available but that didn't mean anyone in the industry would hire me. He was genuinely surprised. Steve was in the heyday of his success in *Wanted Dead or Alive* and told me that he had no idea such a policy existed. I was amazed by his innocence and astonished that in only seven years a new generation of actors could be so oblivious to the blacklist. "I watched your movies when I was growing up," he said. "I want you to play a role in our next episode and I'm going to do something about it."

His attitude was admirable, and I hoped, for his sake as well as mine—and the whole frightened industry—that he would have the power to break through. A week later he called me back and told me with great anger and frustration that he had been unable to move the studio heads. He deplored their "lack of guts" and assured me his producers would have loved to use me. Seven years after that, Steve and I acted together in *The Cincinnati Kid* at MGM. I played Hoban, a pool hall wheeler-dealer and quasi manager of the Kid. Neither of us ever brought up the failed attempt to get me that role, but we had a great time working on the film together.

Remarkably, Steve was not the only one who was unaware of my black-listing. One day in 1959, the legendary Lucille Ball called out of the blue. I did not know Lucy personally, but she knew me as an actor and heard that I had been teaching. She had started a workshop at Desilu Productions for talented young actors. She asked if she could attend one of my classes. I was surprised by this. "Lucy, how could you possibly find time for a class with your hectic schedule?" I asked. She assured me she would work it out.

Then she asked me how things were going. "Have you been doing a lot of film work, Jeff?"

"Lucy," I replied, "I haven't done any work in film in eight years."

"How come?" she asked. There was genuine innocence in her voice.

"Lucy, I've been blacklisted," I answered.

There was a very long pause. Finally, and with an unexpected poignancy, she said, "Maybe you're lucky, Jeff."

I have no idea what prompted her comment. I knew Lucy had made remarkable progress in the studio world. She and her husband at that time, Desi Arnaz, had broken all kinds of barriers; most important, Lucy had become a producer of her own show. From my position, it was difficult to fathom being grateful for unemployment.

I said, "Call me when you're ready, Lucy."

She never did, but years later her daughter, Lucie, interviewed me for her syndicated radio show. I relayed my conversation with her mother. She was very moved and, I presumed, understood a great deal more clearly than I did the import of her mother's poignant statement about my luck.

Lucy had not been a communist, but in 1951 she had been summoned by HUAC to explain why she had signed a petition to put the communist Bernadette Doyle's name on the California ballot for secretary of state. Apparently, HUAC was not above scanning any and all documents for evidence of treasonous behavior. Lucy's grandfather had been a strong union supporter of Doyle, and as she explained to HUAC, she adored him and did everything she could to accommodate his wishes. He had asked her to sign the perfectly legitimate and legal petition. Doyle, incidentally, ran a good third in that election, garnering over a quarter of a million votes. The committee accepted Lucy's testimony—it was genuine—and allowed her to keep working, which was a boon for us all. But it did point out that even the all-American action of signing a lawful petition was up for grabs with the committee.

During the early years of my teaching, Hope and I would see old friends at social gatherings. Many of them had been untouched by the blacklist, but they were caring people. By and large we were never socially ostracized, but when you cease seeing people in the workplace there is a concomitant lessening of social contact. At several parties I found it almost unbearable to hear people crowing about film deals they were involved with or amusing situations that transpired on the set or the witticisms uttered while watching dailies. This kind of shoptalk made me feel invisible.

On the brighter side, friends not stigmatized by the blacklist would bring my daughters splendid hand-me-downs. I often suspected they were new purchases made to appear used. Often, delicious meals would appear out of thin air or bags of groceries were left because someone had "over-shopped." Our doctor dropped his fees, as did our pediatrician, dentist, and optometrist. Emily was put on scholarship at a wonderful local nursery school, arranged in part by the marvelous First Amendment expert and lawyer Stanley Fleishman, and his wife, Doris. We solicited none of this. People were kind and supportive out of the goodness of their hearts.

It made all the difference in the world.

16

The Doors Open

During the blacklist years, Hope and I did not have passports. In the midst of McCarthyism, the government had required applicants to sign an affidavit regarding past or present membership in the Communist Party, which we, of course, would not do. A psychoanalyst named Dr. Walter Briehl, who was a pioneer in group therapy, along with the artist Rockwell Kent, took the government to court, and in 1958 the Supreme Court overturned that regulation. In 1959 Hope and I applied for and received our passports. In 1960 we signed up for a Los Angeles County Museum of Art tour of Europe. We asked Hope's father and stepmother to stay with the children, and off we went. We landed in Paris and for thirty-seven blissful days wandered France, Germany, Italy, and Great Britain. It was liberating to possess a passport and delicious finally to be able to visit all the great architecture and museums Hope and I were so familiar with but had never seen in person.

Just before we left for Europe, a very reputable talent agent named Robert Raison contacted me and said he'd like to represent me. His gut feeling was that the film industry had just about "had it" with HUAC, McCarthy, and the unpalatable right-wing clearance operations. Raison offered to get in touch with studio casting directors and advise them I was available for roles. It took a year for one of those roles to materialize, and when it did, it did not go unnoticed. On January 6, 1961, the *Hollywood Reporter*'s headline read, "Jeff Corey Comeback," with a lead article that stated, "Jeff Corey goes before the cameras today for the first time in 10 years. The actor who hasn't appeared in film or on TV in over a decade—since being named in connection with the House Un-American Activities Committee probes, has been signed for a co-starring role along with Telly Savalas in *The Antidote* segment of Desilu's *The Untouchables* series. Corey, represented by Bob Raison in the deal, has been conducting acting classes for the past decade."[1]

It was not work for a major film studio, but it was my first on-camera role since the blacklist. When I arrived on the set, some of the older crew members greeted me simply with "How are you, Jeff? Been working lately?" There was no indication at all that anyone was aware of my predicament or what I'd been doing since 1951. I played the part of a pharmacist who is used by some slick underworld figures. When I was called to rehearse the first scene for the camera, it was as though I'd never been away. When the assistant director called, "Camera rolling," followed by "Action," I felt totally at ease. I was fortunate that through my decade of teaching, at almost every class session, some problem would arise that could be best clarified by investing the moment with some shift in meaning and assumption. My connection to those moments, unbeknown to me, had kept my acting skills alive and well and immediately accessible.

The press was interested in my return, and I felt obliged to speak out. I had only broken into television and still hadn't been allowed on a legitimate studio lot for a film, so I was aware of my fragile position. When Bob Thomas, a levelheaded reporter from the Associated Press, and Murray Schumach of the *New York Times* both approached me, I didn't hesitate to say my piece about the committee. I knew it meant I might find myself out of work again, but after all my family and I had been through, I didn't want to be silent about it. Thomas's headline read, "Jeff Corey Returns from Shadowy Exile." Schumach's headline was "TV Role for Actor Blacklisted in '50." Both articles were published and syndicated across the country. As I imagined, this stirred up a new pot of fear. Robert Raison called and told me everyone he spoke to at the studios was now too afraid to hire me.

In 1960 Ray Stark, the head of the recently formed Seven Arts production company, had asked me to work with Nancy Kwan on a screen test for *The World of Suzie Wong*. Nancy was talented and beautiful, and she played a pivotal role in the acceptance of Asian actors in Hollywood. The film was a great success. A few months after my appearance on *The Untouchables*, Ray asked if I could find space for Nancy in one of my classes. One day during a break she told me she would have to miss class for the summer because Ray wanted her in London to prepare for a film called *The Main Attraction*. She was to star with Pat Boone. At the time, Pat was one of the most successful pop singers in America. I was pleased for her and said jokingly, "Tell Ray I'd like to come along and work with you." Nancy looked at me and said, quite seriously, "I'll do that."

My remark was an aside really, but Ray called that afternoon. "I hear you'd like to come along and work with Nancy in London," he said. "Can you leave on Saturday?" Without hesitation, without even talking to Hope, I said, "Yes."

I called Leonard Nimoy and asked him to take over my classes. Lenny was a smart, intuitive actor, and he had been in my class for a number of years. I knew my students would be in good hands with him at the helm.

Branson O'Casey, who was a relative of the great Irish playwright Sean O'Casey, found me a spacious flat in St. John's Wood in northwest London, diagonally across from the London Zoo, in Regent's Park. I flew out on Saturday, and Hope, Evie, Jane, and Emily joined me shortly after. Ray lent me his Bentley and chauffeur to pick them up at Heathrow Airport. The luxurious, chauffeur-driven car enchanted my daughters.

Our first stop was at Chiswick Mall to have afternoon tea with our friends Phil and Ginny Brown. Phil, an actor, and Ginny, an artist, had left Hollywood in the 1950s to escape the committee and had established a very good life in London. They had transformed a World War I Canadian Coast Guard cutter into a marvelous houseboat that was permanently docked on the Thames River. They lived quite comfortably there with their two boys, Kevin and Jed. There were swans floating on the water and a private garden on the riverbank that was in full bloom. It was a perfect introduction for my children to the delights of London. My daughters, raised to have an inclusive social consciousness, insisted we invite our chauffeur in for tea. He refused immediately, looking both shocked and a bit grateful. My children, undaunted, took tea and biscuits out to him.

Nancy Kwan had sublet Peter Sellers's flat, and she and I spent several hours each day there, working on her role. My children spent the summer exploring London, visiting museums, and learning everything that could be learned about high tea. It was a marvelous, relaxed time for all, and while I was not working as an actor, my paycheck came from a bona fide production company. At the end of the summer, we returned to Los Angeles and I started teaching again.

It was easy to step back into my classes. After the exhilaration of *The Untouchables* and the deliciousness of helping Nancy prepare for *The Main Attraction* in London, however, I wondered if I'd ever work for a major studio again.

17

England

Pre-production began on *The Main Attraction* in early spring of 1962. Ray asked me to return to England to work with Pat and Nancy in London and then travel with the company to its Austrian location as dialogue coach. It meant moving to London for four months. Hope and I discussed it and immediately agreed it was the right thing to do. Eve, now in college, would stay in Los Angeles. We found a school in London that would take Jane and Emily, midyear. Within weeks, both girls were enrolled in Mrs. Hugh-Jones's Tutorial School in Hammersmith. Mrs. Hugh-Jones was delighted that Janie had already read most of Thomas Hardy, and Emily, a voracious reader, had read Dickens and Alcott.

A former student of mine, the English director Alan Cooke, was moving out of his flat at 17 Camden Hill Square in Notting Hill and invited us for dinner to meet his landlords, Adrian and Pamela Terrell. The Terrells were delightful. They lived in the basement and main floor with their two young girls. Pam was pregnant with their third child. Two young women shared a picturesque garret on the fifth floor. The two floors in between were available. We hit it off immediately, and my family moved in the next day. Our flat had a spectacular view of the London skyline, and, in fact, in the 1800s the great English painter J. M. W. Turner had a friend who lived in what was now Hope's and my bedroom. Turner was known as the "painter of light" and was revered for his stunning oils and watercolors of the London sky, many of them apparently painted from our flat window. My family was equally enthralled by the view.

The Main Attraction was written by John Patrick, who was best known for writing the play *The Hasty Heart*. The delightful and creative Daniel Petrie was to direct. Dan and I took long walks around Green Park and Pall Mall, talking about the script and how he envisioned the characters. In *The Main Attraction,* Pat Boone was to play a cynical, hard-drinking, chain-smoking libertine. Up until this time, Pat's roles had been happy-go-lucky, spirited young men who would occasionally sing sweet ballads to equally lighthearted young women who joined him in close harmony. Our task was to find a way for him to believably play his role without altering his very agreeable, genuine disposition. It was a heady experience for Pat to playact an utterly amoral man.

There was so much pleasure in being involved with a film and shooting schedules. Pat and I worked together on the set and sometimes after hours, into the evening. We had wonderful discussions. We talked a great deal about many aspects of our lives. I never consciously censored myself, but oddly enough, we never talked about the blacklist. Pat was a great storyteller. I loved his tales of fishing with his grandfather in Tennessee and his family ties to Daniel Boone. Pat's speech was marked by rich southern colloquialisms. We often discussed religion. I told him that I was a struggling agnostic. That was good enough for him, and he didn't try to proselytize me. We disagreed about certain interpretations of the good book. I thought the phrase "Thy will be done" did not mean abject compliance but rather a prayer that God's will for a better world is what we must actively strive for. Pat's interpretation was more literal.

It was hard for Pat to keep up with my Yeshiva training: I appeared to know more about the Bible than he did. I never put down his beliefs, but I did, on one occasion, suggest his religion was a little pallid. He said, "I'm never going to discuss religion with you again." And he didn't. But we did continue to talk about everything else under the sun and enjoyed ourselves very much in the process.

I had an additional function for Seven Arts. Ray Stark asked me to see every play that time allowed and report to him on the play's quality and the names of any outstanding performers on the off chance there was something he should option or there was an unknown actor he could "discover." He set up a special expense account for that delectable extracurricular activity. London was having a wonderful season. Hope and I saw the opening nights of *Luther* with Albert Finney, and *Cherry Orchard* with John Gielgud and Dame Peggy Ashcroft. We took the children to see Vanessa Redgrave in *As You Like It* at the Royal Shakespeare Company. We saw *Chips with Everything*, and *The Kitchen*. In Chichester, we saw *Uncle Vanya* with Lawrence Olivier, Michael Redgrave, Sybil Thorndike, Joan Plowright, Lewis Casson, and Joan Greenwood. We took Emily and her friend Denise Leader to box seats at the original production of *Oliver*. Jane and Emily were both delighted by the satirical humor of *Beyond the Fringe*. We also saw Anthony Newley's *Stop the World—I Want to Get Off* and a production of *Lady Chatterley's Lover* starring Jeanne Moody and directed by Alan Cooke. Alan and Jeanne had met in my class in Los Angeles a few years earlier, and it was wonderful to see them do such fine work together. It was delightful to be immersed in so much exciting, excellent theater.

As *The Main Attraction* continued production, my family traveled with me to the location in the Austrian Alps above Innsbruck, where scenes from *The Main Attraction* would be shot. It was an idyllic setting, picturesque and full of charm, and the mountain vistas were stunning. Hope, Jane, and Emily explored Innsbruck and spent time on the location set with me. It was important for the girls to see their father, if not in front of the camera, at least being respected for his opinions about another actor's performance. Dan Petrie showed me the utmost deference, and I think that made an impression on my children as well.

When the shooting was over, we returned to England briefly and then left for California. It was quite emotional for me to leave London. It had been a happy, happy time. We had spent four and a half months there, and every moment seemed enchanted. Back in Los Angeles, Ray put me on a retainer for one more year. We didn't sign a contract. We shook hands on the deal. As I got up to leave his office, Ray said, "The thing I like about you, Jeff, is you never bullshit me." I appreciated the comment and my year and a half working with Seven Arts brought me closer to feeling as if I belonged in the industry.

Fortunately, it was only the beginning.

18

Breaking Down the List

Joe Strick, whom I had known at the Actors' Lab, decided to get into film production. He wasn't interested in a run-of-the-mill Hollywood project. He had seen Jean Genet's very successful off-Broadway production of *The Balcony* and had negotiated with Genet's agent in London to acquire the screen rights. Peter Falk was hired to play the Chief of Police, Kent Smith the General, Ruby Dee the Thief, Shelley Winters Madame Irma, and Lee Grant was Carmen. Joe called and asked if I'd be interested in playing the Bishop. Just like that. No auditioning for the role. Fait accompli! While it wasn't a major studio production, it was nonetheless a film, and it was wonderful to be asked. Joe needed an actor for the role of Roger. I immediately suggested Leonard Nimoy. Leonard was perfect for the part. Ben Maddow had made a skilled screen adaptation of the play, and Joe was ready to start production. Ben had originally taken the Fifth and then changed his mind and offered the committee names. I remembered him as a quiet, sensitive man, but whenever we were on the set together, he turned garrulous and talked nonstop, as if somehow he could avoid a disagreeable conversation if he bantered wildly enough. His fears were truly unfounded. I was grateful to be working again, and putting him on the spot or trying to shame him for what he had done was as far from my mind as possible.

After *The Balcony,* my next film role finally put me back on a major studio lot. Oddly enough, this came about because of Pat Boone's determination. Pat was contracted to do one more film for Ray Stark, called *The Yellow Canary.* During preproduction, Pat came to the house several times a week and we'd go over the script. He was playing an arrogant pop singer who gets involved in a bizarre murder-kidnapping. During our rehearsals, I would read all the other parts. There were a few scenes with an interesting character named Joe, a custodian of a sort, and one day Pat said, "You really ought to play this part."

"It will never happen," I said.

"Why not?" he asked.

"The legal department at Twentieth Century Fox won't allow it," I said.

It was the first time in the many months of being close to Pat that I broached the subject of the blacklist. I explained why Fox wouldn't hire me. Pat stopped for a moment and, looking as serious as I had ever seen him, said, "I'll talk to them." The next day Pat arrived at my front door chanting, "We did it! We did it!"

Pat had pushed all the way up through the studio ranks, and at one point had even threatened to walk off the film if they didn't hire me. They relented. And as he said, he had done it. I was cleared to do a major studio feature. As his words began to sink in, I became very aware that something momentous was happening. Pat Boone had just informed me my black-listing was officially over.

I like to tell this story because so often we make unfounded general-izations about good people whose worldviews are not congruent with ours. There was a lot about life that Pat and I disagreed on. Yet we also had a trusting relationship. I told him many things about myself that were of a personal nature, and he to me. As it turned out, we had infinitely more in common than otherwise. Pat assessed my worth as a friend and fellow actor without being disconcerted by my reputed left-wing past. In the end, the conservative, wholesome, all-American, Christian, sweet-song singer, "do-gooder" Pat Boone turned my career in Hollywood around. I was very grateful and am still for what Pat did. After Pat left, I went into the house to tell Hope. We hugged each other with delight and spent the better part of the day in a delicious trance.

I was no longer a displaced person. It took a few days for the reality to set in. The realization that the dark cloud that had been hanging over my head for twelve years had suddenly blown away was exhilarating. I realized that, in spite of my success as a teacher, in spite of my optimism and per-severance under fire, the blacklist had weighed very heavily on me. It was a delight to have it finally gone. I was calmer and more patient with the children. I'm sure I became a better husband. And probably even a better teacher.

In the wake of my good news, I applied for membership in the Academy of Motion Picture Arts and Sciences, and I received a very warm letter of welcome. Soon after that, I received a roster of the approximately three thousand members in the actors' division of the Academy who qualified for the annual election to the Actors' Nominating Committee. Each member was asked to check ten names on the list. The ten members receiving the most votes were put on the Nominating Committee. To my surprise, I was selected as one of the top ten. It was particularly pleasing for me to have been chosen by my peers for this committee, and I was selected for this honor five years in a row. While I believe the vote was truly given out of respect for my work as an actor and a teacher, I also think it was a way for members to voice their discomfort with the political restrictions that had injured the Academy in the fifties. My presence on the Nominating Committee was a resounding statement that the blacklist was finally over.

After my five-year stint, I was appointed to the Executive Committee of the Actors' Branch of the Motion Picture Academy. It was an eight-year appointment, but through some bureaucratic slipup several of us, myself included, served for eleven years. I felt a particular pride when the Academy awarded Charlie Chaplin his long-overdue Oscar. Chaplin had been so maligned by HUAC that he had fled to Europe, and the great inventor of early film and comedy had not set foot on American soil since then. His return was part of the overall healing and further vindication of us all.

Kathleen Nolan, who was president of the Screen Actors Guild (SAG) in the late 1970s, asked if I would fill out the term of a board member who was leaving the area for an extended period. I gladly accepted. It felt like another validation of my sorely overlooked curriculum vitae. I served out my term on the SAG board and was asked to run for reelection by the SAG Nominating Committee. We were at a board meeting late one night when the vote tally came in. Of a slate of several dozen names, my vote was far ahead of the next-highest vote. I mention this only to suggest that, again, the large vote for me was a reflection of how strongly many actors felt about Hollywood's twelve-year submission to McCarthyism.

I could once again enjoy my role as an actor, only now I had the role of teacher under my belt as well. The old freelance pattern began to envelop me. Once you get the heady feeling of working in films and then encounter the arid periods of little or no work, you feel as if you've fallen down the rabbit hole. Actors often have to go through periods of doubt and self-incrimination. Sometimes it has nothing to do with reality. Anthony Quinn, who was working nonstop at the time, told me he went bonkers if he didn't have at least three films lined up. George Sidney, one of the great directors of the golden age of MGM, told me that when Laurence Olivier found out that Greta Garbo chose John Gilbert over him for the costarring role in *Queen Christina,* he was convinced his career was over. David Niven once confided to me that he always believed his latest film would be his last.

When I was working with Gary Cooper in Michael Curtiz's *Bright Leaf,* Coop introduced me to Gertrude Lawrence. Gertrude was filming *The Glass Menagerie* on the set next to ours. Irving Rapper was directing. Sometimes during my breaks, I'd wander over to *The Glass Menagerie* soundstage. One afternoon, I was standing behind a mock window when I suddenly heard a muted voice next to me ask, "Do you know Mr. Rapper?" I turned and there was Gertrude, tears streaming down her cheeks. "There's no pleasing him," she said sadly. "I am totally lost. I'll never work again." Gertrude was one of the truly great actors of the century. She was beautiful, willowy, and multifaceted, and here she was drenched in self-doubt, sobbing her heart out to a fellow actor she had just met. I tried to console her as much as I could and reassured her that her performances were always enchanting and that I looked forward to seeing her in many more roles.

It is not uncommon for the most successful performers to feel this trepidation. Vernon Scott of UPI interviewed me during the filming of "The Land of the Free," part of a series, *From Sea to Shining Sea,* directed by Leo Penn. I played the role of General Andrew Jackson. Off the record I told him, "I look back at a very good career and I've been unemployed through most of it." Vernon is an honorable columnist, but he couldn't resist headlining that quote. It is a sentiment that is well comprehended by my film and theater colleagues. The blacklist certainly presented extenuating circumstances to what was already a difficult row for an actor to hoe. Regardless, I was happy to be acting again, whether onstage or onscreen, and in spite of the downtime, it truly felt second nature and right to be back.

There were so many new actors who had arrived on the scene in Hollywood during the 1950s that I might have met but for the blacklist. When I resumed working, most of them were acquainted with the black-and-white films I had been in, and I even sensed that some of them were envious of that experience. One evening I met George C. Scott at a party in Malibu. George pointed his finger directly at me and exclaimed, "Blinky Franklin!"—referring to the part of the dope addict I had played in *The Killers.* Many actors whom I have met on the set for the first time invariably comment about having seen me in an "old" film when they were growing up. They attached an alluring patina to the vintage medium. When I met the legendary superstar Richard Burton on the set of *The Wild Geese,* no introduction was necessary. He had seen so many of my old films, first as a youth in Wales and later on the "telly." He knew all about me and was nothing but gracious. When I met the wonderfully talented Peter O'Toole on the set of *Creator,* he regally bowed from the waist and said, "I am awed!" I do not require this kind of tribute but confess I don't mind it, particularly in light of the large hole left in my career by the blacklist.

During those years, sometimes in the morning, I'd have to wake up and realign my thinking. I was no longer a blacklisted actor with a great teaching career.

I was, indeed, an actor again.

19

Coming Home

After *The Yellow Canary,* my status in the industry began to feel secure, and the twelve-year-old blacklisting slowly faded into an odd and hard-to-believe background. I was once again part of the shaky mainstream profession, which never did run smoothly for freelance actors even in the best of times.

I was hired as the wino in *Lady in a Cage,* starring Olivia de Havilland. Ann Sothern played my hooker friend. The director, Walter Grauman, and the writer, Luther Davis, had cast six of the seven important roles but had not yet found an actor for the role of the Skid Row bum. The casting directors, Lynn Stalmaster and Jim Lister, were frantically searching for someone to fill the role. The story I was told is that Jim ran into "Nicky" Persoff on the Paramount lot and asked him if he could suggest someone for the part. Nicky knew the script well and apparently without hesitation said, "Yes, Curt Conway." To further clarify Curt's identity, he told Jim, "You know Curt; he teaches acting in town." Jim heard the word "teaches" and immediately thought of me. He called and asked if I could come to Paramount to meet with Luther and Walter. I was cast on the spot and sent to a one o'clock table reading of the script. That's how chancy casting is in Hollywood.

A few months after we finished filming *Lady in a Cage,* Ann Sothern called and asked if she could come work with me on a play she was rehearsing called *God Bless Our Bank.* We set up a time and started to go through the script. Whenever I do preparatory work with an actor, I read the roles of all the other characters. In one part of the play Ann had a conversation with a character named Sandy MacGiver, a native Scotsman.

Ann liked my Scottish burr, and when they were reading actors for the role of MacGiver in New York, she kept telling the director, Ezra Stone, "Jeff does it better." She stubbornly refused to go along with any of the East

Coast candidates. Finally, Ann called and asked if I would go to New York to do the role. The play was going to have a summer stock tour of the Eastern Seaboard and then, if successful, a Broadway run. Ann arranged a top salary for me as well as luxury accommodations while we rehearsed in New York. I was delighted.

God Bless Our Bank was written by Mac Benoff. Mac had cozied up to HUAC when subpoenaed. Naturally, he was at our rehearsals. Mac and I were always polite but remote, and we never discussed our respective behaviors under fire. I enjoyed twitting him about the character I was playing. One day, tongue in cheek, I mentioned how much I applauded my character's sober, ultraconservative view of the world. Mac really forgot whom he was talking to when he asked, "Jeff, how can you think that way? I thought you were a liberal."

Summer stock was a marvelous way to spend a summer, moving from town to town with an entire troupe of actors. It reminded me of my early days on the road with Clare Tree Major and Leslie Howard. Hope and the girls came out to travel with me. Emily and Jane often volunteered as ushers at the various theaters where we performed. Roland Winters, the great doyen of early movies, was also in the cast. My daughters were enchanted by his stories of Hollywood.

When we arrived in Westport, Connecticut, Mac brought in Abe Burrows, another cooperative HUAC witness, as a "play doctor." Now that I was working again, these encounters with people who had chosen a different path seemed inevitable and were always uncomfortable. Abe and I engaged in a few monosyllabic exchanges, but a dark cloud of unutterable subtext hovered over us. Not much could be done to help the play. Audiences laughed at the one-liners, but *God Bless Our Bank* did not deliver much of a punch in spite of the efforts of a very dedicated cast. Alas, it did not go to New York, but it was a lovely way to spend the summer and gave me a bit of a break from teaching. As had become our pattern, Leonard Nimoy took over my classes while I was gone.

In early spring of 1964, I did Arthur Penn's *Mickey One* with Warren Beatty and spent an exciting month in Chicago. It was immediately followed by a segment of the television drama *Doctors and Nurses,* which was filmed in New York. Shortly after that, I received a telegram from Robert Siodmak, who had directed me in Hemingway's *The Killers.* Robert asked me to come to Berlin to play Abraham Lincoln in a screen adaptation of Karl May's novel *Treasure of the Aztec,* or *Der Schatz Aztecan,* as it was known in German. My good friend the blacklisted writer Paul Jarrico had written the screenplay.

This was twenty-five years before the fall of the Berlin wall. I flew to Tempelhof Airport in West Berlin and was met there by a host of journalists and a battery of photographers. Someone on the production staff knew how to garner publicity. Out of nowhere, a rather pathetic-looking hairpiece emerged, and someone stuck it awkwardly on my chin to make me look like Lincoln. That evening an absurd photograph of me appeared in the Berlin newspapers under a banner headline that read, "Abraham Lincoln hast zu Berlin Gekommen," loosely translated, "Abraham Lincoln has come to Berlin." I was horrified. I looked more like the cartoon character Alley Oop than Lincoln.

The next morning, when I arrived at the studio in Spandau, the dreaded hairpiece emerged once again. I marched over to Robert with the gawky beard in my hand and said, "This absolutely won't do." I dug into my pocket and produced an American five-dollar bill. Right in the center was an etching of the Civil War photographer Matthew Brady's photo of Lincoln with a marvelous beard. As Robert gazed at Lincoln and then back to my hand holding the ratty hairpiece, he laughed and said, "Good God, you're absolutely right." He led me to a very skilled makeup artist and handed him my five-dollar bill. I gladly gave it up to the cause as he went to work constructing me a beautiful and very realistic Lincolnesque beard.

On my first day off from shooting, I went through the cold and rather intimidating Checkpoint Charlie into East Germany and walked the short distance to Bertolt Brecht's Berliner Ensemble at the Theater am Schiffbauerdamm. I introduced myself as an American actor and teacher. A woman named Frau Killian immediately invited me to watch a rehearsal of Brecht's adaptation of Shakespeare's *Coriolanus*.

There was a triumvirate of directors sitting at three desks on a mobile platform in the middle of the orchestra pit. I watched as Ekkehard Schall, Brecht's son-in-law, struggled with his leather Coriolanus tunic. It was sewn so tightly that he was having trouble lifting his arms. Someone called for help, and the remarkable Helene Weigel appeared. Helene was Brecht's widow and was one of the great actors of the century. She walked onstage with a needle and thread protruding from her mouth and a handy pocketknife in one hand and scissors in the other. In one determined tug, she ripped the seam, resewed the costume, and announced that Coriolanus could now gesture all he wished. It was hard to imagine any American actor of her stature taking on such a pedestrian task with equal grace or equanimity. Her practical presence and dedication to her task were a sight to behold.

I had been advised in West Germany that tickets were absolutely unattainable for all performances of the Berliner Ensemble. In spite of that, Frau Killian kindly provided me with a complimentary ticket for that evening's performance of the *Die Dreigroschenoper (The Threepenny Opera)* as well as a ticket for *Arturo Ui* the following night. I was delighted.

I had first seen *The Threepenny Opera* in New York in 1937 starring Burgess Meredith and then, over the years, several other productions in the States. It was a thrill to see Brecht's own production. The greater theater adventure for me, however, was *Arturo Ui*. Brecht's didactic theater approach encouraged actors to set up a face-to-face relationship with the audience, as though to say, "Watch this and learn something!" The production was intoxicating, and his players presented wonderfully wrought, stylized performances that left the entire audience, including me, mesmerized.

Shortly after my return to the United States, I got a call from Martin Ransohoff, who was producing *The Cincinnati Kid,* starring Steve McQueen and Ann-Margret. Ann-Margret was a fine actor, but the studio was still wary of her teen-idol image. Ransohoff heard that Frank Capra had hired me to work with Annie when she was preparing for her role in *Pocketful of Miracles* with Bette Davis. When the film finished, Annie continued to work with me for her roles in *Kitten with a Whip* and William Inge's *Bus Riley's Back in Town*. Ransohoff asked if I'd work with her on *The Cincinnati Kid*. He also asked if I'd be interested in playing the role of Hoban, Steve McQueen's card-playing mentor. I was delighted and said yes to both offers.

The Cincinnati Kid was my longest stretch of work on any film. My friend the former blacklisted writer Ring Lardner Jr. had written the script and Sam Peckinpah was set to direct. I don't know the details of what happened, but after the first few weeks of filming, Peckinpah and Ransohoff had a terrible falling-out, and Peckinpah was fired. Ransohoff kept the entire cast and crew on payroll while the directorial reins were handed over to Norman Jewison. Norman reshot everything Peckinpah had filmed, greatly lengthening our production schedule.

Principal shooting was on the main set, which represented a posh New Orleans hotel suite where a dozen of the greatest poker players in the country sat around the table, competing for the big money. Joan Blondell played the card-dealing Lady Fingers. Joan and I, having plenty of motion picture savvy between us, knew that for weeks to come, if we were not careful, we would be required to stay on the set for the sake of continuity. During the rehearsal for the first shot, Joan and I quietly removed ourselves from the central poker-playing area and settled into a little alcove to the left of the set. We watched the poker game from there. No one seemed to mind our decision. I even asked Norman if my character could occasionally use a pair of binoculars to follow the game from our remote location. Luckily, he thought it was a great idea, and Joan and I were spared the role of "extra." Poor Annie was placed directly behind Edward G. Robinson and Steve McQueen. As a result, she had to sit there as background for nearly 90 percent of the poker game footage, which took weeks to shoot. Joan and I, on the other hand, when we weren't directly in the shot, could sneak off and play a game of Scrabble or catch up on our reading.

The cast of *The Cincinnati Kid* was populated by a host of wonderful actors, including Karl Malden, Tuesday Weld, Jack Weston, and the great singer Cab Calloway. One day when we had some free time on the set, I told Annie about Cab Calloway's celebrated panache in the 1930s at the popular Cotton Club and his inimitable style of scat singing. I asked Cab if he would sing "St. James Infirmary" for her. That wonderful man graciously provided us with the momentous song, a cappella, his voice ringing throughout the soundstage. Annie, who had her own original manner of presenting a song, watched and listened to the one-of-a-kind Cab Calloway with delight and awe.

When *The Cincinnati Kid* finished filming, Annie and I segued almost immediately into *Once a Thief,* starring Alain Delon and Jack Palance. Again, I was hired to work with her on the role and play a police officer by the name of Lieutenant Kebner. Ralph Nelson, who had toured with me in Leslie Howard's *Hamlet,* was the director. We spent many weeks shooting at night on location around Fisherman's Wharf in San Francisco. It was a wonderful time, and the shooting schedule gave me ample time to visit my daughters Eve and Jane, who were both attending UC Berkeley. During the editing of *Once a Thief,* Ralph wrote a note to me thanking me for the work I did with Annie and praising the performance I was able to help her deliver. In the note he described showing Margaret Booth, the chief editor at MGM, the raw draft of the movie: "The rough assemblage of the film proved a startling surprise to Margaret. As the lights came up, she was reaching for a handkerchief, a rare gesture for a tough critic such as she."

My return to acting continued to bring with it a delicious connection to a roster of talented actors, writers, directors, producers, and all the marvelous support staff that accompany a film, from the grips to the gaffers to wardrobe to the teamsters who drive the trucks. One of my most exciting shoots was the three-month filming of the Western author Louis L'Amour's *Catlow*, directed by Sam Wanamaker. Sam had moved to London during the blacklist, and during his British residency he was responsible for initiating and completing the reconstruction of Shakespeare's Globe Theatre on its original site. *Catlow* starred Yul Brynner and Richard Crenna. Leonard Nimoy and I costarred.

Hope traveled with me to Spain. The cast and crew stayed at the beautiful Aguadulce Hotel, not far from the port city of Almeria, which had been ruled for a long time by benign Moroccan administrators. The view of the Mediterranean Sea from our hotel window was like a Raoul Dufy watercolor seascape.

Yul was the master of hyperbole. He was most facile role-player I ever encountered and a marvelous liar whose fabrications turned out to be the equal of truth. He could be imperious, threatening, and, in a sudden alteration of mood, a simple man of the people. Yul claimed to know everything, and if his comments lacked credibility, he was not deterred.

In particular, Yul knew how to take care of himself. On the *Catlow* set, he made a series of unreasonable demands, including the requirement that the most expensive limousine made by Mercedes Benz be at his disposal for the entire shoot. He traveled in that sleek, gray behemoth to all our location sites. Yul also insisted that Euan Lloyd, the film's producer, pay for the entire top floor of the Aguadulce Hotel for his entourage, which included his daughter and her tutor, his wife Jacqueline, and his personal secretary. His daughter left for France a few days after shooting began, but the third floor remained Yul's domain. He would accept no other trailer on the location site but his own Rolls-Royce-driven caravan, which had to be transported from his wife's home in Normandy, over the Pyrenees, and down to the southeasternmost area in Spain.

Yul played the leader of an outlaw gang, and I played Merridew, his second in command. Nine or ten former matadors were recruited to play the other brigands. Yul held court wherever he was, and no matter the conversation, he had the definitive say-so. If the subject was sailing on the

Mediterranean, he'd offer encyclopedic details on the types of sailing vessel used in the area, the weather patterns and hazardous winds, and how to maneuver a particular craft. One day at a Sunday brunch at the hotel, Hope idly asked Yul a question about a matador everyone was talking about who was to appear in Barcelona the following day. Yul instantly rose up and for over an hour illustrated the different approaches of Dominguín, Manolete, El Cordobés, and the Mexican Procuna, four of the world's most notable bullfighters. In no time at all, the people in the restaurant formed a circle around him as Yul held forth about every nuance and strategy that characterized his list of toreadors.

I couldn't get over the exceptionality of Yul. I admired his carefully wrought characters. His performance as General Bounine in *Anastasia* with Ingrid Bergman and Helen Hayes was powerfully centered. I use that term purposely because in a preface Yul wrote for Michael Chekhov's book *To the Actor: On the Technique of Acting,* he ascribes his success as an actor to Mischa's tutelage. It was something I could easily relate to.

Two years after *Catlow,* I directed a segment of the *King and I* television series that starred Yul and Samantha Eggar. A consummate professional, Yul did not denigrate television at all and cooperated on getting optimum quality in his new venture. After he was diagnosed with lung cancer, Yul made a poignant antismoking film that was released after his death. In it he says, "Now that I'm gone I tell you, don't smoke. Whatever you do, just don't smoke."

I was touched by his gallantry. It was Yul *himself,* not the role-player.

20

Manila

In the early spring of 1968, I flew to Manila to work on a film called *Impasse,* starring Burt Reynolds and Anne Francis. It was not a great script, but the part included a trip to the Orient, so I agreed to do it. I had been in the Philippines once before, in 1945, when the USS *Yorktown* dropped anchor off Tacloban. It was at the height of the War in the Pacific, and two U.S. Navy Seabees were assigned to guard me as I photographed Osmeña Park, the navy's wartime recreation center, and then the island of Leyte, where I took photos of several small villages that only two weeks earlier had been under Japanese occupation.

On the flight to the Philippines more than twenty years later, our plane carrying the cast and key crew members for *Impasse* stopped on Wake Island to refuel. Early in the war, U.S. Marines on Wake Island had fought as bravely as they could against an overwhelming Japanese naval and landing force. Those who survived were taken as POWs and put into forced labor. The *Yorktown* raided Wake Island, but it took over two years of brutal fighting before the Japanese garrison surrendered. Now, in 1968, the feeble lights on the landing strip at Wake Island looked ominous. We refueled in the eerie light and arrived in Manila the next morning. My hotel room provided a clear view of the Island of Corregidor across Manila Bay.

Anyone who had served in the Pacific in World War II would feel a connection with Wake Island and Corregidor. Corregidor was where General Douglas MacArthur turned over his command to Lieutenant General Jonathan Wainwright, who had no choice but to surrender his half-starved, besieged troops to the Japanese. His troops had been holed up in the Malinta Tunnel, where an understaffed, undersupplied medical team strove to attend to the wounded. Wainwright sent a tristful farewell message to President Roosevelt on May 6, 1943, saying, "With profound regret and with the continued pride in my gallant troops, I go to meet the Japanese commander. Good-bye, Mr. President."

I made inquiries about visiting Corregidor and was told there was no public access. The only way to get to Corregidor was by means of the Philippine Coast Guard. Anne Francis and I had a day off, and we asked the public relations man on the film if he could make contact with the coast guard. A Philippine naval officer agreed to take us to Corregidor on a hydrofoil cutter.

The crew cautioned us that the area was still strewn with live World War II ammunition—aerial bombs that had not detonated and five-, eight-, and sixteen-inch shells from naval vessels that had failed to explode. We were told the old barracks remained as they were before the Japanese surrender in 1945.

Anne and I left our hydrofoil in silence, taking great care where and how we stepped on the bumpy ground. In a few moments, we came across the Malinta Tunnel, which once contained our wounded. We had been warned we might hear the spectral wails of the beleaguered American boys. As Anne and I stood alone in this vast crypt, it was sepulchral, to say the least.

We left the tunnel and walked quite a distance to the demolished American barracks that had been taken over by pillaging Japanese troops in early 1942. It occurred to me that some of these barracks and large gun emplacements had probably been targeted by the *Yorktown*, and that many of the shells lying on the ground might have been from my ship. The barrack we entered was frozen in time. Its interior was cluttered with broken cots, torn straw mattresses, shoes piled in phantasmagoric heaps over a crazy array of tattered soldiers' gear, toothbrushes, combs, shoehorns, eyeglasses, pens and pencils, writing paper, and empty bottles with Japanese writing on the labels. I felt, in a small way, that we were intruding, but, then again, these enemy souls were on the other side of a destructive military venture. I was not there as a trophy hunter.

Anne and I began walking over the live ammo area. We saw no actual signs indicating danger below the huge gun emplacements, so we heedlessly went on. We plodded through thick underbrush, constantly clearing a path for ourselves. Suddenly, we heard the piercing, whistling scream of a descending aerial bomb—the same sound heard in so many World War II films. It went on for about thirty seconds. We waited, paralyzed. The end explosion never happened. Anne and I, shaken and without speaking, quickly made our way back to the pier.

Ten years later Anne and I worked together again in an episode of *Banjo Hackett*. We agreed we both heard that ghostly interlude and concluded we had shared a moment of total, transient detachment from reality—a passing hysteria that made us both hear an aerial bomb that wasn't there. Or we clearly heard the ghost of such an event.

I will truly never know.

21

The Greater Connections

I must confess that after more than half a century of films, I can still be starstruck when I work with a truly great artist. My dear friend the director Ken Annakin hired me for a role in *Paper Tiger*, starring David Niven and the great Japanese actor Toshiro Mifune. I knew David socially and was delighted to have an opportunity to work with him. He truly was one of the classiest men I have ever met.

I had never met Toshiro Mifune but was very familiar with his work in Akira Kurosawa's *Rashomon, Red Beard,* and *Throne of Blood*—all spectacular films. Toshiro spoke very little English, so he always traveled with a translator. This time around, his translator was Miko Taka, an ex-student of mine. When Miko learned I had a role in the film, she asked the producer, Euan Lloyd, if I could record Toshiro's dialogue in English so that he could learn his part that way. On a sunny spring day, I sat in my backyard in Studio City and recorded the great master's dialogue, employing as much as I could of Toshiro's arresting mode of speech and his compact stresses and cadences. I sent the tape off to Tokyo a few weeks before we began shooting.

When I arrived in Kuala Lumpur, Miko introduced me to Toshiro, who bowed regally and said, in the most compelling, basso profundo voice I have ever heard, "My teacha." Miko told me he was grateful for my recording and was particularly aware of the sounds of the songbirds from my garden in the background of the tape. I was touched by the grace of this masterful actor, whose forte was enacting thunderous samurai chieftains but who had such a delicate ear that he noted the birds chirping in my backyard.

Hope and I had met Jean and Dido Renoir at Floyd and Betty Crosby's house on Sycamore Avenue in the Hollywood Hills. Floyd was a marvelous cinematographer who won an Academy Award for his work on Robert Flaherty's film *Tabu*. Jean was the son of the great Impressionist painter Pierre-Auguste Renoir and was a wonderful filmmaker in his own right. Jean's films *Grand Illusion* and *The Rules of the Game* remain staples of history of film classes around the world. Flaherty, Jean, and Floyd were great friends and respected each other as artists. Together they formed a highly gifted and imaginative triad.

At the outbreak of World War II, Jean made the decision to remain in France, hoping to continue to produce and direct, but when Nazi forces took control of his country in 1940, his plans were derailed. Dreading the prospect of being asked to make propaganda films for the Nazis, Jean and Dido knew it was time to leave. Flaherty, who was a pioneer of the documentary film movement and made his mark in 1922 with the release of *Nanook of the North,* spent months working with French officials to secure the necessary visas. Finally, Jean and Dido were allowed to travel to the United States. Within months of his arrival, Jean was directing movies for major studios in Hollywood, including *Swamp Water, The Southerner,* and *This Land Is Mine,* starring Charles Laughton. Bertolt Brecht, also on the run from the Nazis, served on the sets as Jean's consultant.

Hope and I were delighted to be invited to lovely evenings with the Renoirs at their mountain villa off Coldwater Canyon in Beverly Hills. The house was tasteful in every way, and I must say it was impossible not to be bowled over by Jean's collection of works by Camille Pissarro, Paul Cézanne, Henri Matisse, and other of his father's contemporaries scattered throughout the house. It was particularly moving to see *Jean as a Huntsman,* the father's beautiful portrait of his son as a young boy, hanging in the hallway. Jean and Dido were marvelous good fun, and the conversation at the dinner table was always stupendous.

Hope and I invited the Renoirs to spend a weekend with us at our country home in Ojai. The Crosbys joined us for dinner, and the next day we all hiked along the lovely Matilija Creek in Los Padres National Forest. As we walked along the rocky bank, the rapids took a turn in the stream. Jean stood silent for a moment, staring at a massive bluish-purple protruding rock and proclaimed, "We are looking at a Courbet!" He spoke from firsthand experience.

One evening around the dinner table the film *The Sound of Music,* which had just been released, became the topic of discussion. I laughed and quoted the *New Yorker* critic Pauline Kael's acerbic observation that the film was "sugar-coated" and "not for diabetics." My daughter Emily shyly remarked that she'd rather enjoyed it. Jean, with gusto, declared, "I thought it was absolutely charming." Jean laughed and then said, "Nothing is better than sitting in a dark theater and having all your troubles swept away for a few hours. It makes life bearable."

His comment certainly made my daughter feel vindicated, and I must say, forced me to take a step back from my own cynicism about the film. Over the years I've thought about what Jean said, and I am grateful this magnificent and exemplary filmmaker shook me off my skeptic's limb. He was right. While there is plenty of room for movies to shake us up in the most intellectual and profound ways possible, we must not forget that film is also for entertainment. The great Preston Sturges knew this when he made *Sullivan's Travels*. Steven Spielberg knew this when he made *ET*. An hour or so of a good comedy or a heartwarming saga is not only sweet; perhaps it is even necessary.

Even for diabetics.

22

Celebrity versus Acting

It was never my intention to create movie stars or celebrities through my teaching. I never liked to see anyone fail, but my students' trajectories to stardom or starving artist were not as essential to me as the quality of work they did and what they learned along the way. I filled my classes with men and women who were curious about acting, regardless of their profession or expertise. In fact, in addition to many struggling young actors, my classes were often populated by doctors, nurses, lawyers, and men and women from all walks of life who just wanted to learn. I loved teaching these varied personalities, and they often brought unusually exciting scene work into class, enhanced by their unique perspectives and professional stances.

Shortly after *The Yellow Canary,* Ray Stark was planning a Broadway musical about his mother-in-law, the gifted singer-comedian Fanny Brice. Fanny was the darling of the Ziegfeld Follies, a box-office draw in motion pictures, and a hilarious Baby Snooks on the radio. The musical was called *Funny Girl.* Isobel Lennart had written the libretto, Jule Styne had composed the music, and Bob Merrill had written the lyrics.

Ray asked me to work with a number of gifted but relatively unknown actors and wanted to know which one I thought would be suitable for the leading role of Fanny. I gave him my honest appraisal. After seeing quite a few candidates, he sent a young performer named Barbra Streisand. At the time, I had no idea of her remarkable talents as a singer, but after our first meeting, I called Ray and told him he had found his Fanny Brice.

Barbra and I did some subsequent work at my studio, and on one occasion she looked at her watch and said with great urgency, "Can I call a taxi? I have an appointment with Jule Styne at the Beverly Hills Hotel and he'll kill me if I'm late." I told her I had an errand to run in that direction and offered to give her a lift. En route she asked me who was in my classes.

I politely replied, "I don't like to name-drop." Her abrupt response was "I wouldn't be impressed anyway!"

As it turned out, Barbra's friend Sheree North had been a student of mine for many years. Sheree and Barbra had worked together on Broadway in David Merrick's *I Can Get It for You Wholesale,* written by Harold Rome and Jerome Weidman. I believe that is where Barbra met her first husband, Elliott Gould, who was also in the cast. Barbra had a rather minor role of a secretary but had a show-stopping number called "Miss Marmelstein" that brought down the house each night.

When Sheree learned Barbra was working with me, she eagerly called her and asked, "How do you like working with Jeff?" Barbra responded, "I don't know about this psychological stuff." I didn't take offense. It was pure Streisand and honest.

Barbra invited Hope and me to the Ambassador Hotel's posh Coconut Grove to hear her debut California performance. We were delighted to accept her invitation and were given the very best seats. Milton Berle and Danny Thomas were her warm-up acts. Barbra's physical presence onstage was impressive. She graciously paid tribute to the composers and lyricists before singing each song. The audience was enchanted.

When we went backstage to congratulate her, Barbra complained that it was a lousy audience and that they all "sat on their hands." We told her how much we had loved her performance, and, as for the audience she had criticized, I assured her its response was effusive.

Barbra really is one of the few people who came to study with me who had such a focused sense of who she was and what she wanted that trying to push her into further investigation of a role was truly unnecessary. Barbra was clearly Barbra. We worked together only briefly, but I was glad she was able to find ways to take hold of the role of Fanny Brice and make it very much and uniquely her own.

Every four years, right after the winter and summer Olympics, Norman Brokaw, a top executive at the William Morris Agency, arranged for me to teach his new gold medalist clients. This included the ice skater Dorothy Hamill; the decathlon champions Rafer Johnson, Bruce Jenner, and Bob Mathias; the triple gold medal winner for track and field Flo-Jo Joyner; the pole vaulter Bob Seagren; and the swimmer Mark Spitz, who broke seven world records and garnered seven gold medals in the 1972 summer Olympics in Munich, Germany. I always enjoyed working with these stellar Olympians, even though whatever training they did with me usually facilitated their appearance in commercials rather than launching an acting career. Regardless, I was happy to do what I could to help these impressive men and women find ease and purpose in front of a camera, even if it was only to sell Wheaties.

Along with Olympians, the football stars Frank Gifford, Mike Henry, Bernie Casey, Jack Ging, and Fred Williamson all studied with me, as did the boxer Ken Norton. Interestingly enough, most of these great professional competitors had an aptitude for acting and the arts. Fred Williamson produced, directed, and starred in his own spaghetti Westerns in Italy and went on to have a solid career as an actor. Bernie Casey did a fair amount of film acting and became quite a competent painter. He had his first show at the Ankrum Gallery on La Cienega Boulevard. Mike Henry starred in a few Tarzan movies and went on to have a decent career as an actor as well.

At one time in the mid-1960s, I was pulled into a plot to help the marvelous Dodger pitchers Sandy Koufax and Don Drysdale negotiate a raise with the team's owners, Walter O'Malley and James and Dearie Mulvey. Sandy, Don, and the home office were at an impasse over their contracts, and these two stellar players announced to the press they were on strike. In response, the Dodger owners dug their feet in. There would be no raise. Period.

Buzz Kulik, who had directed *The Yellow Canary*, had come up through the ranks directing cameras for televised games at Yankee Stadium and knew Sandy and Don well. Buzz invited me to be part of a televised press conference with Sandy and Don. In the middle of the conference, in front of an audience of syndicated sportswriters from around the world, Buzz announced that I was working with Sandy and Don to prepare them for roles in his upcoming film, *Warning Shot*. A member of the press asked me how I felt about this holdup strategy. I replied that I had been a Dodger fan since the Ebbets Field days in Brooklyn, and I'd like Sandy and Don to play next season. But if they chose instead to embark on an acting career, I would be happy to teach them. Both men came to study with me privately, and it was marvelous to work with them. They were smart, talented, and very much engaged in the work at hand. There is no way to ascertain whether their maneuver helped them get the deal they wanted, but soon after the press conference, the Dodgers gave them both the contracts they were hoping for.

Pat Riley, who in the late 1970s was the radio broadcaster for the Los

Angeles Lakers, came to study with me. He worked zealously with his scene partners and seemed to enjoy the acting process. One day in 1979 Pat told me he couldn't make class the following week because of a contretemps between Magic Johnson and the Lakers head coach, Paul Westhead. Pat had been asked to be the interim coach while the Lakers organization interviewed a list of prospective candidates for the job. He didn't think he could coach the team and continue class. The Lakers, under the neophyte Pat Riley, soundly beat all their competing visitors that week and the next, and Pat was elevated from radio broadcaster to assistant coach of the Lakers' trophy-winning team. I was extremely pleased for him, even though the time demands of his new position made it impossible for him to return to class.

I have always believed that the lure of acting for sports icons was an attempt to find a way to be competitive without having to experience the physical hardships and strains of competition. I was happy to help them explore the competitive inner world of the artist without the pulled tendons or broken ribs.

On the other end of the spectrum, I was often the acting teacher of choice for the children of Hollywood megastars. I imagine one of the reasons was that both parents and children knew there would be a kind of clarity and honesty in my teaching. Though I was sensitive to the fact that Hollywood—and the public at large—would probably hold them to a higher standard, I would never treat these students as special or beyond hard work.

I always found it touching when a parent called and, without any push of celebrity or brouhaha, would in the most simple and loving parental voice possible ask me how his or her son or daughter was doing. I never revealed any personal aspects of the work being done in class, but it often turned out that these children were every bit as talented as their mothers and fathers. Most of them had a true love of the craft.

When Tina Sinatra was studying with me, Frank would often call to check in. He was in the middle of the Rat Pack madness, and his public persona was quite unsettling. Yet when he called to ask about Tina, he could have been any father in the world at a parent-teacher conference, anxiously wanting to know how his kid was doing.

From time to time, I'd bump into Carl Reiner at the old Motion Picture Academy on Melrose Avenue. Carl's son Rob and his soon-to-be wife, Penny Marshall, were both attending my classes. We'd chat about all sorts of things going on in Hollywood and the world, and then Carl would invariably ask for a report on how Rob was doing in class.

I would assure him Rob was talented and doing great work. Frequently in our conservations, Carl would wince and say, "I deplore nepotism, otherwise I'd help him." My answer, every time it came up, was to point out how many families, from R. H. Macy of Macy's Department Store to the entire Rockefeller clan, enlarged their dynasties through nepotism. I encouraged him to help Rob where he could. I reassured him that while it was noble of him to be concerned, nepotism was only wrong if the family member being supported couldn't carry his or her weight and didn't deserve the job.

Carl called me out of the blue one day and said CBS was interested in hiring Rob for the role of the son-in-law in Carroll O'Connor's new series, *All in the Family.*

"Do you think Rob is up to it?" he asked.

"Absolutely," I said.

I shared with him the fact that a few days earlier Rob had brought a scene into class from Saul Levitt's *Andersonville Trial.*

"Rob was brilliant!" I told him. "The network would be lucky to have him."

Of course Rob got the job, and for the next nine seasons he epitomized the young liberal who could go face-to-face with Archie Bunker's redneck, conservative ethnocentrism.

Regardless of where you come from or what your background is, a true love of acting and the courage and curiosity to explore what that means in its most intricate detail are what make a good actor.

Celebrity has nothing to do with it.

23

Innocents Abroad

Nine years before the fall of the Berlin wall, the Screen Actors Guild arranged for a delegation of its members to visit actors in East Germany. I was invited to be part of the group. Our contingent included four SAG executive board members, Joseph Ruskin, Daryl Anderson, my ex-student G. D. Spradlin, and me. Additional delegates were the actors Bert Freed and Susan Hunt and the costume designer Marianna Elliott.

We arrived in East Berlin in May 1981 and settled into our compact but very comfortable hotel rooms. Early the next morning, G. D. joined me on a long walk through rows of newly built, government-owned apartment houses. G. D. had been a successful attorney and entrepreneur in Oklahoma City and at one time had run for mayor. He had sailed all over the world with his family and finally, determined to be an actor, had amassed some excellent screen credits. To our surprise, East Berlin was quite attractive; it had broad, imposing boulevards and many, many green parks. The chestnuts and lilacs on the famous avenue Unter der Linden were in bloom.

The East German government had prepared a detailed itinerary for us that included visits with theater and film personnel, graphic artists, opera and dance companies, museums, civic leaders, collective farms, and government-supported recreation spas for workers on holiday.

The first evening we were invited to the principal theater in East Berlin to see Gerhart Hauptmann's *The Beaver Coat*. We saw a superb performance by an actor who sported a walrus mustache in the role of the Janitor. At the third curtain call, that actor, in a sweeping gesture, pulled off the walrus mustache, removed his janitor's hat, and the beautiful tresses of the company's leading lady cascaded down to her waist. Backstage, we met with the cast. There was a young man who played an office clerk and we particularly admired his characterization. He modestly thanked us and, in whispers, told us that his fellow actors rarely surprise him and he wished he could enjoy the freedom of actors in the West.

In Karl-Marx-Stadt we saw a well-mounted production of Bertolt Brecht's *Mother Courage*. The older actors seemed tenured and too much in the groove. Conversely, when we went to a performance of the Berliner Ensemble, the marvelous theater company founded by Brecht and his wife Helene Weigel, it was the older actors who were inventive, playful, and refreshing. They seemed to embody Brecht's maxim that actors should always be "astonished" as the events of the play transpire. In Berlin we met with actors who had been trained in East Germany's principal acting academy. Besides acting, they were taught speech, gymnastics, modern dance and ballet techniques, singing, the history of theater, and world plays in German translation. Two young apprentices performed the Biff and Happy scene in the first act of Arthur Miller's *Death of a Salesman*. They playacted two tormented American losers drifting in an unfeeling capitalistic environment. It was an intriguing, if not a badly distorted, interpretation of *Death of a Salesman* and fascinating to watch.

A man named Bernhard was assigned co-leader of our group. He was to acquaint us with the political and social history of the towns and villages on our itinerary. Bernhard grew up in a family of strong trade unionists and antifascists. When Hitler started his blitzkrieg against Poland, Bernhard was cashiered, against his will and political beliefs, into the Nazi army. He was with the German occupation forces in Belgium but figured out a way to get captured by the British. Bernhard knew English and was sent to England to work with British intelligence until the end of the war. He was a lovely and interesting man.

Bernhard drove us through the steep U-turn roads that went through the town of Jena, the glass and optical center of the world. From there we made our way to the National Gallery of East Germany in Dresden. In Potsdam we visited the old UFA studios, which had a connection with Universal Studios in pre-Nazi days. The background footage they used from *S.O.S. Iceberg* for *Mutiny in the Arctic* had been shot there.

The next day, Bernhard took us on the short ride to the once-lovely beech forest near Buchenwald. The top of the hill had been deforested to erect hundreds of horrible barracks for concentration camp internees. It was appalling to see the 180-degree vista of verdant forests just beyond the murderous campsite. We met with the director of the Buchenwald Museum, who walked with us through the crematoria. While tears normally come easily to me, this was not so at Buchenwald. I absolutely could not cry. None of us could cry. We just walked together in complete silence. The director led us into the medical lab where Nazi surgeons used children for their morbid experiments. Susan Hunt finally let out a shattering "Oh, no!" and began to weep. That cued us all, and the entire SAG delegation broke into sobs and wept profusely. Joseph Ruskin, Bert Freed, and I gathered wild cowslips and clover and laid them on the ground. We wept as we said Kaddish, the Jewish prayer for the dead.

When we returned to our bus, a quiet moroseness set in. After about ten minutes of driving in utter silence, Bernhard pulled over to the side of the road. He took out a concertina and started playing Earl Robinson's "I Dreamed I Saw Joe Hill Last Night," its lyrics written by my friend the poet Alfred Hayes. The song was written in support of the labor movement in America in the 1930s. Those of us who knew the song joined in. He then went on to "Michael, Row the Boat Ashore." Everyone knew that. It was followed by "I've Been Working on the Railroad," "America the Beautiful," and a collection of songs by Stephen Foster, Rodgers and Hammerstein, and Irving Berlin. By the time we returned to our hotel later that evening, we were in better spirits, thanks to Bernhard's impromptu performance. Back at the hotel, I had the strongest impulse to see if the kitchen was still open. It was. I prevailed on one of the cooks to give us the ingredients for old-fashioned chocolate ice cream sodas. He graciously came up with chocolate syrup, ice cream, and seltzer water for all. Admittedly, it was a strange nightcap on a very disturbing day, but it helped sooth our nerves.

The next morning we met with more of the political and cultural hierarchy. I was proud of the way our group discussed our reactions to what we had seen so far. We observed that the subsidized training and guaranteed employment of their professional actors were compelling. We also told them, however, that in America we have crafted distinguished theater through the tenacity and talent of actors, writers, and directors who eagerly freelance their way upward in an unstable yet independent profession.

They asked about my experiences with HUAC. I spoke honestly about the value of political freedom of speech and assured them that while I thoroughly objected to the machinations of HUAC, I remained deeply loyal to my country and was grateful to live there. Our parting words, as we made a farewell toast, was to hope that theater in their country as well as our own would be forever free of the heavy hand of censorship and loyalty oaths. Certainly, there was nothing in my time there that made me feel that communism would have been a better choice. The people we met were lovely, and the artists we spent time with were committed to their craft as much as any one of my students or member of our SAG delegation.

Art thrives in the oddest of circumstances. Sadly, too often, it has to do so under the stress and strains of struggle. Our East German friends did it under the eye of an oppressive government that also gave them beautiful theaters and a monthly stipend. My American friends did it within the context of tremendous creative freedom but often at the expense of making a living and having to perform in makeshift neighborhood theaters that could barely pay the rent each month.

Would that someday there will be a meeting of the minds and that governments all around the globe will elegantly support the arts without a thought to stepping on their creative toes.

24

Exits and Entrances

Along with the reboot of my career in film in the 1960s, I had the good fortune to return to acting on the stage as well. My former student Gordon Davidson was the founding artistic director of the Mark Taper Forum in downtown Los Angeles. Gordon directed the American premiere of *In the Matter of J. Robert Oppenheimer,* Heinar Kipphardt's dramatic account of the Atomic Energy Commission's hearing in 1954 that branded Oppenheimer as a security risk. He cast me along with my friends Bert Freed and John Randolph. Johnny had also been blacklisted, and Bert was a political progressive who, later in his life, did admirable work on behalf of actors as a trustee for the Screen Actors Guild Pension and Health Plans. Backstage on opening night, the three of us tried to imagine what Congressmen Wood and Thomas would think of our success in public. The show ran to rave reviews and was a great joy to do.

A few years later I played the part I had always wanted to play, King Lear, at the Venture Theatre in Beverly, Massachusetts. When I was preparing for the role, I discussed the part with my brother-in-law, Dr. Paul Siegel, a renowned scholar who had written several reputable books and articles on Shakespeare. I described for him what Lear's relationship with his wife was before she passed away. I even speculated about the cause of her death. Paul looked at me with a pained expression and said, "Jeff, there is no internal evidence about the existence of the monarch's wife."

Understandably, Paul, as an academic, took the writing literally. As an actor, I had the luxury of stepping outside the confines of the lines. In truth, there is no backstory, but that does not preclude an actor from inventing or assuming one in order to flesh out Lear's character, which is exactly what I did. William Henry III, the Pulitzer Prize–winning critic for the *Boston Globe,* kindly wrote of my performance, "In the part Charles Lamb called unplayable, he is magnificent."[1]

The following year Gordon asked me to play Polonius in a production of *Hamlet* at the Mark Taper Forum starring Stacy Keach. Kitty Winn played Ophelia and Salome Jens played Gertrude. Polonius is often portrayed as a foolish windbag. I made a conscious choice to play him as an experienced political hand who knew the score. Smokey Robinson, the marvelous Motown singer, was studying with me at the time. He and his wife came to see the play. Afterward he came to my dressing room and said, "Jeff, you were making up that shit." His wife told me he kept saying that to her throughout the entire performance. My dialogue came out so easily that Smokey could not believe I was speaking lines I had memorized. I assured him it was the Bard of Avon's dialogue, not mine. What I tried to do with Polonius's speeches was in no way an attempt to make it overtly or obviously colloquial. I always found iambic pentameter easy to deal with, particularly when it contains the most inspired writing in the language. I was merely trying to connect to the humanity I imagined Polonius had; that made sense to me and, ultimately, made sense to the audience.

My return to the stage reinforced my love of the theater and the deep gratitude I felt for those early days in New York and then later in Los Angeles at the Actors' Lab. I encourage my students to do as much stage work as they possibly can, and I have seen some marvelous performances emerge from the ramshackle storefront theaters that line the "Great White Way" of the ninety-nine-seat, Equity-waiver houses that work so hard to keep theater alive in Los Angeles. An interesting side note: the reason they called Broadway the "Great White Way" was because it was one of the first streets in the United States to be lit by electric lights.

Theater is always ahead of its time.

25

The Past as Prologue

Antonio, Prospero's usurping brother in Shakespeare's *The Tempest,* sincerely repents his evil past, and when his moral sensibilities are restored he says to his comrades, "The past is prologue." All through the writing of this modest chronicle, Antonio's cryptic phrase kept coming to mind. To me it suggests that there are periods of time that are terminated but not necessarily concluded. They are not marked with finality. The past hangs in and maintains itself as new ventures transpire.

Our past is, indeed, prologue. The future doesn't filter out what I choose to remember. The point, of course, is to let the past live but not to live in the past. This is true in life, and it is true in the development of a character as you act.

The blacklist had its hold on my life. Its reach was long and lasted many years. It was an honor and a joy to return to film in the 1960s and watch as my career as an actor was firmly reestablished. But there is no way of knowing what might have been if I had been allowed to continue in my chosen profession uninterrupted. I can only conclude that my very solid and successful career as a film actor before 1951 would have continued unabated if not for the blacklist.

Over the years the stigma of the blacklist has become an honor, and many of the leading organizations that supported the blacklist so long ago have deeply and publicly regretted that position. In 1999 the *Los Angeles Times* published a list of the one hundred most important events of the twentieth century, events that affected the city's social and artistic climate. Item fifty-one was *Red Channels: The Report of Communist Influence in Radio and Television,* published in June 1950. About this suspect report the *LA Times* wrote, "An offspring of a publication titled 'Counterattack,' this handy guide to 'Commies' cited as traitors 151 of Hollywood's biggest, best and brightest. Along with the House Committee on Un-American

Activities, Sen. Joseph McCarthy and other demagogues of the time, 'Red Channels' set the tone for a witch hunt that would destroy lives and careers and have a scarring impact on the way ideas were presented and business conducted in TV for years to come."[1]

In September 1997 *Screen Actor Magazine* announced that the Screen Actors Guild (SAG), along with the Directors Guild of America (DGA), the Writers Guild of America (WGA), and the American Federation of Television and Radio Artists (AFTRA), would be sponsoring an evening honoring the fiftieth anniversary of the Hollywood Ten's appearance before HUAC. In the announcement SAG wrote, "While the stories and pain of the era are still vivid in the minds and hearts of our older members and their friends and family, many young people—perhaps many reading this article—don't even know what the blacklist was all about or that the entertainment Guilds were heavily pressured to 'eliminate subversives' and very sadly succumbed to the paranoia of the time. . . . The event will commemorate those who lived through it while educating the new generation of professionals and performers in Hollywood of the tragic happenings of the blacklist era."

AFTRA published a similar statement that said, "Senator Joseph McCarthy begins his 'witch-hunt' as the publication of *Red Channels* makes sweeping, unverified accusations of Communism in the entertainment industry. Torn by internal politics and conflicts, AFTRA failed to oppose the infamous blacklist. It is the saddest chapter in the union's history."

During the second round of Hollywood HUAC hearings, SAG and AFTRA did, in fact, expel all its members who invoked the Fifth Amendment. That ruling has since been nullified, and those who were expelled had their memberships reinstated, myself included.

At one time I thought that the blacklist would never end, so the unsolicited apologies from AFTRA, SAG, the DGA, and the WGA were profoundly gratifying. Later, the Alliance of Motion Picture and Television Producers Association also expressed its remorse for structuring the blacklist. To its credit, of all the unions, only Actors' Equity publicly combated blacklisting from its onset and did not prevent its members from appearing onstage.

An adjunct professor named Max Lamb taught a graduate course at the University of Southern California (USC) on the history of film. As part of his discourse, he discussed Michael Wilson, Adrian Scott, Dalton

Trumbo, Ring Lardner Jr., and Waldo Salt—all blacklisted writers who had used pseudonyms or had writer friends front for them in the 1950s. Lamb's students were appalled by what they learned and decided it was time to honor those who had stood up to the Hollywood blacklist. They drew up a proposal to build a memorial park honoring the men and women who were blacklisted during the 1950s. The USC Board of Regents approved their plan and gave them a garden area at USC's Fisher Art Gallery. Jenny Holzer, recognized as one of the most innovative sculptors of the century, was selected to design the site. The park stands today as a poignant reminder of what was.

I understood but did not quite agree with my friend Dalton Trumbo's statement, "We were all victims." The friendly witnesses who mentioned the names of actors, directors, screenwriters, and producers buttressed HUAC with self-serving testimony that provided fuel for the committee's reckless machinations. I barely knew many of the people who named names, but on the other hand, an equal number had once been good friends. This made their actions doubly painful.

I never snubbed Larry Parks after he named names, but I thought what he did was destructive, and, in the end, it didn't save his career. While I was appalled by his submission to HUAC, I understood his pain. We knew through the grapevine that though his wife, Betty Garrett, remained loyal to him, she had not wanted him to do it. It was strange that when the news of Larry's death was broadcast on the radio in 1975, Hope and I felt compelled to visit Betty at their home off Laurel Canyon and to talk to their sons, Andrew and Garrett. Before the blacklist, Betty and Larry had been very good friends. Our children played together, and in 1948 Betty, Larry, Hope, and I had been part of a group of parents that founded the Canyon School, a cooperative nursery school in Hollywood that all our children attended. After Larry gave names to the committee, Hope and I couldn't imagine sharing a workday with Larry and Betty, which was required by the cooperative format. Instead, we sent Emily to a nursery school in San Vicente Park in West Hollywood. We hadn't spoken to Betty since Larry testified. After his death, Hope and I renewed our friendship with Betty, and I know we all regretted the years we lost and the time we weren't able to spend together.

I've heard all sorts of gossip about what transpired in the families of cooperating witnesses. I've directly encountered young people whose parents mentioned me. I attach no stigma to these children. When work began again for me, I had professional connections with many sons and daughters of informers, and quite a number of them, bravely, came to study with me. Only in one instance did a discussion ensue, and my intent, if anything, was to comfort this young person, never to condemn her.

In the early 1980s I did a segment of *Today's FBI* starring my ex-student Mike Connors. Julie Cobb, Lee J. Cobb's daughter, and I were guest stars. In the evening, after our day of filming, Julie was appearing in a revival production of *Waiting for Lefty* at the Company of Angels Theatre in Hollywood that was produced by my daughter Emily. Julie was a lovely actor, and Emily had no qualms whatsoever working with her. I don't believe the two of them ever felt the need to speak about the blacklist, but fate seems to have had a vote in whether Julie and I would talk about it. On the second day of shooting Julie and I had finished a scene, and the crew had moved on to another location. We found ourselves alone in an empty barn in Lancaster. "I guess we have a lot to say to each other," Julie said.

Julie told me that her father mentioned HUAC to her on only two occasions. Oddly enough, the first time was when he told her that I had snubbed him on the Universal lot. The next occasion was when he said, "You cannot imagine what it was like, Julie, to have every arm of the government zero in on you." I looked at Julie and said, as kindly as I could, "You cannot imagine how exhilarating it was to tell every arm of the government that you refuse to play the 'toady' for them when they do evil things to good people."

I assured her I didn't hate Lee. I shared with her the fact that a few years earlier I had visited him backstage in New York when he was in *King Lear,* and I was glad I had. I told him he had given a wonderful performance. He said, "You can't think that I'm wonderful. How can you? I am nothing. I am disgusting."

I also told Julie that when Dan O'Herlihy and I were filming a pilot called *Banjo Hackett,* for some reason I cannot remember we had been bad-mouthing Lee and perceiving what we thought was the diminution of his talent. It was idle and needless gossip. At the end of the day, I got into my car at the Columbia Studio Ranch in Burbank and turned on the ignition. The radio announced that Lee J. Cobb had been declared dead on arrival at a North Hollywood hospital. Like a possessed man, I heard myself say to the radio, "I forgive you, Lee."

I was puzzled by what I had spontaneously uttered. Why did I forgive Lee yet feel no such sentiment when I read the obituaries of other informers? Perhaps the answer came over twenty years later when I read this excerpt from Faith Hubley's interview in Patrick McGilligan and Paul Buhle's wonderful book about the blacklist, *Tender Comrades*. In it she says, "When I worked on *Twelve Angry Men* as a script clerk, I would be on the set with Lee J. Cobb. I had been at Cobb's studio as a student, and we had a very deep relationship; I babysat for him and his wife, Helen, when he went into the Army, and I stayed with her. And on the set Lee would look at me and burst into tears and say, 'How can you sit there looking at me? Who ever thought that I would be this disgusting person and you would be watching me?' So [director] Sidney Lumet and Henry Fonda would say, 'Take that script and go hide!' There was no pleasure in that."[2]

It is commendable that in 1984 Julie produced and directed a production of Arthur Miller's *The Crucible* at the Company of Angels, a play dealing with the parallel aspects of the Salem witch trials and the McCarthy era. *The Crucible* dramatizes in particular the characters who stood steadfast and those who cravenly named names to save their hides.

I made the choice I made for a variety of reasons and have always been profoundly grateful that my decision to not name names is something my children and grandchildren are proud of. The burden carried by children of the men and women who informed, in almost every instance, is too great.

As for Hope and myself, we have reason to look back with pride at how we maintained ourselves during those trying years. Our intention was not to shield our children from the factual details of our limbo status in the movie marketplace but to make sure there was uplift, spirit, and movement in the life they were about. I was not going to let HUAC intrude on their childhoods.

Shortly after I was blacklisted, Hope and I decided to take the children camping. Our first trip was to Yosemite National Park. We had three folding canvas cots and a wide mattress that just fit into our Plymouth Suburban, the first all-steel-body station wagon. Hope and little Emily slept in the Plymouth. Evie, Jane, and I froze on our war surplus cots. In spite of the blacklist, I wanted my children to see America. I wanted them to understand what an astonishing country they were living in. As we sat around our little campfire at night, I'd read them Thomas Jefferson or Tom Paine or have a go at the good Duke's speech in *As You Like It*, which begins:

Now, my co-mates and brothers in exile,
Hath not old custom made this life more sweet
Than that of painted pomp? Are not these woods
More free from peril than the envious court?
Here feel we but the penalty of Adam,
The seasons' difference, as the icy fang
And churlish chiding of the winter's wind,
Which, when it bites and blows upon my body,
Even till I shrink with cold, I smile and say,
"This is no flattery. These are counsellors
That feelingly persuade me what I am."

I don't know how absorbing my woodland recitations were to my children, but they meant a lot to me—particularly the phrase "brothers in exile," which led me to think of so many of my friends and their families who had left their homes during what my friend Dalton Trumbo called the "time of the toad," to raise their children in France, in England, and in Mexico. My wish to take my children to wilderness havens was not to get away from it all but a desire to return to the soil. Shakespeare's good Duke expounds on the very same theme in *As You Like It* when he says:

And this our life, exempt from public haunt,
Finds tongues in trees, books in the running brooks,
Sermons in stones, and good in everything.
I would not change it.

Over the years, Shakespeare has been a good friend and companion. On other camping trips, when the children were tucked into their sleeping bags, I would sing them "Under the Greenwood Tree," "Blow, Blow, Thou Winter Wind," "O Mistress Mine," "Hark, Hark, the Lark," and other random sylvan ditties. I think the kids indulged me somewhat, but I know they enjoyed those forest nocturnes. Years later, I sang the same songs to their children.

With the passing of the Freedom of Information Act in 1966, I asked the FBI for whatever data they had on me. They advised me there were not enough trained personnel to handle the many requests, and I was given a number. After a three-year wait, an eighty-two-page surveillance sheet, most of it blacked out, was delivered to me.

The report is filled with details that, to my mind, make absolutely no sense. An early entry in the report included some gossip that in 1950, on the set of Johnny Paxton's *Fourteen Hours,* I gave a fellow actor a newspaper clipping about the war in Korea and suggested that he show it to others in the cast. I have no memory of doing that and can't imagine, even if I had, how it might have been construed as subversive. It also said I played Abe Lincoln in *Abe Lincoln in Illinois* at the Actors' Lab, which was not only true but an honor. Another entry, from November 20, 1952, revealed an item in the *Hollywood Reporter* that again went after Hope: "Jeff Corey is 'attacking' at the grade school level now. His wife is running for committees at the Cheremoya School P.T.A."

A detailed entry in the dossier correctly asserts that on August 23, 1953, I read a passage from Mark Twain's *The Mysterious Stranger* in which the author dealt with futuristic witch hunts in rural America. It also reveals that I appeared in a dramatic presentation of the Lincoln-Douglas debate at Will Geer's home in Topanga Canyon. Another reference correctly states that I was featured in a dramatic skit entitled *The Trail of William Penn,* in which I played the Quaker leader. The report also includes a fairly accurate account of my talk with two FBI agents who came to our house in early 1955.

What is not mentioned is the music- and literature-filled hootenannies at the Geers' home. Anne Revere, Paul Revere's descendant, and Gale Sondergaard (both Oscar recipients and both blacklisted actors) frequently joined Will, his wife, Herta Ware, Hope, and me around a roaring pit fire, where we read excerpts from Walt Whitman, Ralph Waldo Emerson, Henry David Thoreau, Thomas Jefferson, and Mark Twain. Occasionally, Pete Seeger, Woody Guthrie, and Earl Robinson would drop by to provide glorious music. We drew a fairly good number of people to these rustic recitals. In 1971, after Will made his comeback from the blacklist in the role of Grandpa on the long-running television series *The Waltons,* Will and Herta's property became home to Theatricum Botanicum, a delightful open-air performance space that is still doing exciting work today.

More disturbingly, I had spent my blacklisted years believing that three actors had given my name to HUAC: Marc Lawrence, Lee J. Cobb, and Paul Marion. Upon perusing the many pages of my FBI file and the vividly blacked-out pages, I found that the FBI spoke to hundreds of people about my family and me over a rather long period. I will never know who these blacked-out names belong to, what they said about me, or if what they said was true. But I do know for certain that the Hollywood blacklist, like any form of censorship, did not seek the truth. It sought to substantiate a particular point of view. In doing so, it became, instead, the very propaganda HUAC said it wanted to fight against.

In an entry dated June 1955, my FBI file states that my name should be cleared from the security list and that I was not a threat to the United States. In addition, it reported that I was not informant material. This judicious opinion, tucked away in a file cabinet, did nothing to alleviate the conditions of my blacklisting. Even though the FBI cleared me to work again in films, it took Hollywood another seven years to get the message.

Whenever I am invited to speak about the blacklist, I try to frame my personal story with the history of censorship in the Western world. Actors have always been fair game for despots. The Greek word for actor is *hypokrites*. It means one who pretends what she or he is not. In Rome actors were degraded slaves without legal or religious rights. In the epilogue to Plautus's *The Casket* the audience is told, "The actor who has made mistakes will get a beating. The one who hasn't will get a drink." During the reign of Elizabeth I, the statute of 1572 stated that all players had to be licensed by at least two justices of the peace or receive the same punishment meted out to rogues and vagabonds. It is estimated that an average of 72,000 rogues and vagabonds were hung annually in prison courtyards during this time, and certainly some, if not many, were actors. It is also appropriate to tell audiences that even the president of Yale University warned his nineteenth-century students, "To indulge a taste for play-going means nothing more nor less than the loss of that most valuable treasure, the immortal soul."[3]

There is an astonishing analogy to the Hollywood blacklist and the actions of informers in the rise of surreptitious theater in England in 1621. Leslie Hotson, in *The Commonwealth and Restoration Stage*, writes, "Just how far the government winked at the surreptitious performances is hard to say. But to judge by the large number of raids which occurred only because the actors were betrayed (often by jealous members of their own profession), one would say that the actors were safer from the soldiers than they were from themselves; and that the routs happened only often enough to appease the Puritan die-hards."[4]

When I resumed working in the industry, I had a few days' work in an adaptation of F. Scott Fitzgerald's *The Last Tycoon*. I met with the producer, John Houseman, and the director, Elia "Gadge" Kazan. I had known Gadge in New York but had not seen him since he had appeared in front of HUAC and had informed on his friends and colleagues at the Group Theatre. Gadge and I talked guardedly when we met. As I was leaving his office, he put his arm around me and, as was Gadge's wont, sighed deeply and said, "Oh, Jeff, we're just a couple of survivors."

I muttered, audibly, "Not on the same raft."

After I returned to acting, I encountered a number of men and women who had informed. Often they were working as producers or writers on films or television shows I was guest-starring in. I never intentionally snubbed anyone, but when we would meet, our conversations would invariably be rather low-key and detached. They never looked me in the eye, focusing instead on something far away on the set. I cannot speak to what their discomfort level was, but it appeared to me that the shame of informing hung over their lives like a dark, brooding cloud that never went away. There was nothing in me that wanted to make it worse for them, but on the other hand, I wasn't about to tell them what they did was okay. It wasn't.

In the film *Getting Straight* I played an ultraconservative chairman of a graduate school program who is the nemesis of a hippie activist graduate student played by Elliott Gould. The film also starred Candice Bergen and was directed by Richard Rush. It was filmed on location in Eugene, Oregon. The hotel we stayed at had an excellent dining room where I frequently ate breakfast and dinner. Unfailingly, one of the other cast members, Irene Tedrow, would ask if she could join me. I reluctantly invited her to sit with me, but it always was uncomfortable. I had reason to dislike her.

Through the nearly ten-year existence of the Actors' Lab, during which there had been over eighty-five productions, countless seminars, and hundreds of well-attended classes under the GI Bill, Irene and her husband, William Kent, were great supporters. They attended every production and nearly all our events. Everyone at the Lab was very pleased when Irene volunteered to serve on our Executive Committee. We were equally pleased when she appeared in many of the Lab's productions, which often got her work in Hollywood. And why not? The Lab was a marvelous showcase for all of us, and we were always thrilled when one of our own was hired.

But in 1948 Irene revealed at a public hearing that she had been spying on the Actors' Lab over a span of years at the behest of the California Senate Fact-Finding Subcommittee on Un-American Activities and its chairman, State Senator Jack Tenney. Everyone at the Lab, including myself, was shocked. We had been sorely misled by her words and actions. Instead of being a supportive member of our community, Irene had been a spy. She told the committee the Actors' Lab was subversive in its choice of plays, directors, and teachers, and, as a result, my own livelihood was threatened and three of my dearest friends were brought down. It is one thing to get backed into a corner and inform. That still may not be an ideal or pretty choice, but at least in most cases, I imagine, it was probably not premeditated for months or years on end. Irene's behavior was calculated and completely self-serving.

What purpose did it serve for her to sit with me in that dining room and make small talk? Did she think our superficial verbal exchanges indicated my acceptance or approval of her behavior? I endured our meals with as much grace as possible, but I could not possibly offer the absolution I believe she was looking for.

The director Edward Dmytryk, who had done his time in federal prison as one of the Hollywood Ten and then opted to clear himself before HUAC so he could resume work in the industry, named names and earned his employment eligibility. Like the informers who preceded him, he became persona non grata to his old friends and associates, including Hope and me. I don't know how much unease it caused him, but in the mid-1960s, after I had done a succession of films at Paramount, Eddie's secretary called me and said, "Mr. Dmytryk wants to know if you could meet with him at his office at your convenience?" I assumed he wanted to talk to me about one of his forthcoming features and didn't see why I should absent myself from a role I might wish to take. "Why blacklist yourself?" I thought ruefully. A time was set for our meeting at his office on the Paramount lot.

Eddie, as I remembered him, was not a very talkative man, but when we met that day he was a chatterbox. He went on and on about the old days in Hollywood, the great stars like Garbo, Carole Lombard, Clark Gable, and Charlie Laughton. Then he suddenly segued into the evils of the "casting couch" and how offensive he found it that young starlets were often forced to have sex with directors or producers to land a role. I could only nod intermittently, not being able to—or wanting to—get a word in edgewise. Finally, after more than half an hour of his rambling, I said: "Eddie, I've got a class to teach tonight. I'm not sure why you made this appointment. Did you want to talk to me about a role in your upcoming film?"

"Oh, no!" he exclaimed emphatically. "There are only cameo roles and the contract people are committed to them."

"Then why did you want to see me?" I asked.

He turned very serious. "What did you have to do to start working again, Jeff?"

"I just sweated it out, Eddie."

I'm certain that was not the answer he was looking for. He had wasted my time in hopes of a mea culpa I could not offer. I muttered something about having to leave and then, without shaking his hand, left as quickly as I could.

Paul Marion, a radio actor who on occasion found work in film, got the green light from HUAC in 1951 to pursue his career after mentioning the obligatory number of names, including mine. Paul was the third person, after Marc Lawrence and Lee J. Cobb, to offer me up to HUAC. I don't think Paul found much work after that in spite of his nod from the committee, and a few years later he became an agent. A student of mine, John Hackett, was one of his clients. He and Paul were driving to a studio appointment, and in the course of their conversation Paul learned that Johnny was attending my class. Paul almost insistently remarked, "Jeff's life must be awful now."

Johnny told him to the contrary, "Not at all. Jeff's in great spirits and seems to enjoy his family and his new career as a teacher."

Paul persisted: "No, no. He must be devastated."

Johnny told me he carefully turned the conversation away from my mental state as quickly as he could. I wondered what good it would do for Paul to think of me as ruined and defeated. Paul was married to Elinor Brand, Millen Brand's daughter. Millen was a lovely writer whose novel *The Outward Room*, published in 1937, was among the first to explore mental breakdown in fiction. Millen took the Fifth before the McCarran Committee. I can hardly fathom what domestic chaos transpired during Thanksgiving dinners after Paul chose to name names.

Of all the informers' sentiments, the actor Sterling Hayden's remorse was Olympian. In his book *Wanderer*, he berated himself unsparingly. In reference to his HUAC appearance he wrote, "Today, in the United States of America, the way to loyalty is this—down the muddy informer's trail. . . . Few stoolies have played this hall who were better prepared than I."[5]

When I was still a student at UCLA, one evening Hope and I walked to Pickwick Bookstore at Hollywood and Highland. I was looking over

Jeff (*seated*) at the Feagin School, New York, 1932.

Jeff as Rosencrantz (*third from right*) on tour with Leslie Howard in *Hamlet,* 1937.

Jeff and Hope on Woodrow Wilson Drive in the Hollywood Hills, 1940.

Hope Victorson the year she met Jeff, 1938.

Myrna Loy, Melvyn Douglas, Jeff, and Greta Granstedt in *Third Finger, Left Hand*, 1940.

Roddy McDowall and Jeff in *My Friend Flicka*, 1943.

Jeff as Tom Sharp in *The Devil and Daniel Webster*, 1941.

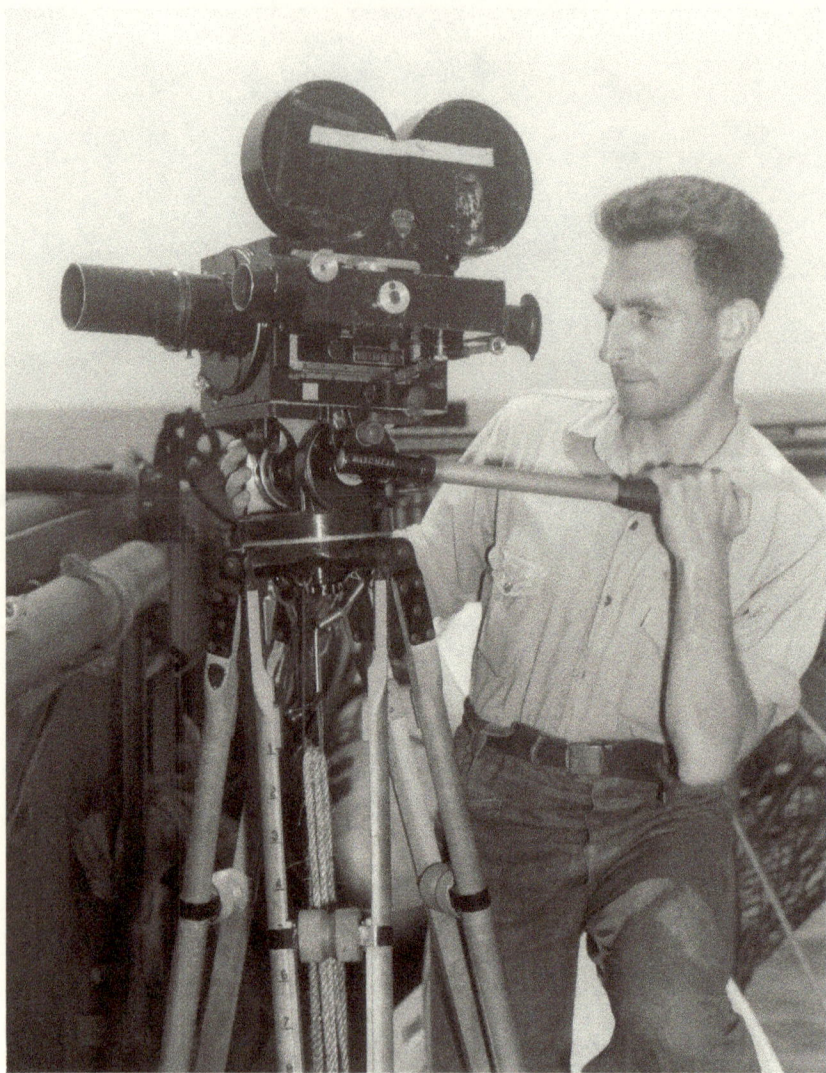

Photo First Mate Jeff Corey, USS *Yorktown,* somewhere in the Pacific, 1944.

Happy Hour on the USS *Yorktown:* Jeff is entertaining the troops alongside Chaplin Leaning and the *Yorktown* band, somewhere in the Pacific, 1944.

Burt Lancaster, Jeff, and Edmund O'Brien in *The Killers,* 1946.

Jeff in *Brute Force*, 1947.

Jeff and Ingrid Bergman in *Joan of Arc*, 1948.

John Wayne and Jeff in *Wake of the Red Witch*, 1948.

Jeff in *Abe Lincoln in Illinois* at the Actors' Lab, Hollywood, 1949.

Morris Carnovsky, Jeff, and two unidentified backstage visitors during a performance of *Abe Lincoln in Illinois* at the Actors' Lab, Hollywood, 1949.

Jeff and James Edwards in *Home of the Brave*, 1949.

Jeff in *Bagdad*, 1949.

Jack Carson, Jeff, Gary Cooper, and Lauren Bacall in *Bright Leaf*, 1950.

Jeff and George Reeves in *Superman and the Mole Men*, 1951.

Los Angeles Examiner
Wed., April 25, 1951   Sec. I—5

2 More Hollywood Witnesses Refuse Answers at Red Quiz

WASHINGTON, April 24—Two more Hollywood witnesses today refused to tell the House Un-American Activities Committee whether they ever were Communists.

Actor Morris Carnovsky and Agent George Willner declined to answer on the grounds of possible self-incrimination.

They followed Actor Marc Lawrence on the stand. Lawrence admitted he was once a Communist Party member.

Willner said he thought the committee "smells," and 53-year-old Carnovsky called committee questioning "a n unwarranted prying into the most secret and sacred areas of a man's thought."

Their appearance was in marked contrast to that of Lawrence.

Lawrence said curiosity—"I'm a curious kind of a schmoe"—led him to sign a party card in 1938.

Lawrence named screen Actor Lionel Stander as "the guy who introduced me in the party line."

The fast talking character actor testified that, after he came to Hollywood in 1938, Stander told him to go to classes at which Communists made speeches.

"These guys confused me, they gave me a headache," Lawrence testified. "After about 12 of these meetings, I left."

First, however, he said he signed a card at the request of someone—using a name he picked out of a newspaper and has since forgotten.

Stander is to be heard later.

LISTS MEMBERS—

At the indoctrination meetings —Lawrence called them "cause parties"—he testified he met Lester Cole, Standler, Producer Robert Rossen and Writer Richard Collins, an admitted Communist, earlier had identified Rossen and Cole as party members.

Lawrence said that later, in his party cell, were J. Edward Bromberg, Writer Gordon Kahn. Cole —will identified earlier as party members—and Standler.

Lawrence said Stander told him to go to the classes—"got to know the flames more."

"I liked to investigate and find out—I was a curious kind of a schmoe," Lawrence told the committee. "I'm the kind of guy who listens to speeches. I got involved that way. I found this was a great mistake, an unholy mistake, a very destructive thing."

Lawrence said he quit his Communist associations in 1939 but resumed them in 1944 who nly was asked to do a war benefit play by the Actors' Laboratory.

But, he told the committee earnestly, "I never considered myself a Communist."

'KIDS AT LAB—

At Actors' Laboratory Lawrence said, he attended about 12 or more party meetings "only because I was working with the lab and because they discussed actors' problems."

At these meetings, Lawrence testified, he met or saw Carnovsky, Bromberg, John Howard Lawson, previously identified as the party's Hollywood leader, an actor named Jeff Corey, Actress Karen Morley and "the kids at the lab."

He recalled a meeting at Miss Morley's home attended by Actors Larry Parks, Sterling

ADMITS IT—After relating that he twice became a member of Red cells, Actor Marc Lawrence, 41, declared before House probers his participation in the party was an "unholy mistake."
—International News Soundphoto.

Hayden, Ann Revere, Howard Da Silva and Lloyd Gough.

"Hayden made a speech, other guys made big speeches. It was very exciting," Lawrence said.

Miss Morley is one of nine witnesses for whom the committee is seeking arrest warrants to enforce appearance before the committee in its investigation of Communist influence in Hollywood.

Hayden, Collins and Parks have testified they were Communists but left the party. Lawrence said he parted for keeps with the Communist party in 1946.

MORRIS CARNOVSKY
Balks at Questions
—Associated Press Telephoto.

JEFF COREY
Named as Red

PE Pays $175,000 for Rails Removal

Payment of $175,000 was made in the city yesterday by Pacific Electric Railway to cover the cost of removing 12 miles of rails from the city streets on which rail service has been discontinued.

The payment was required under the terms of the company's franchise.

T. L. Wagenboth, PE general manager, presented checks amounting to that sum to City Treasurer Leon V. McArdle.

LIONEL STANDER
Termed a Party Member
—Los Angeles Examiner photo.

J. EDWARD BROMBERG
Labeled a Communist

CLASS OF SERVICE

This is a full-rate Telegram or Cablegram unless its deferred character is indicated by a suitable symbol above or preceding the address.

WESTERN
UNION

1201

SYMBOLS

DL=Day Letter
NL=Night Letter
LT=Int'l Letter Telegram
VLT=Int'l Victory Ltr.

W. P. MARSHALL, PRESIDENT

The filing time shown in the date line on telegrams and day letters is STANDARD TIME at point of origin. Time of receipt is STANDARD TIME at point of destination

LA155 SSA400   1951 JUL 22 PM 2 40

L HDA076 NL PD=HOLLYWOOD CALIF 22=

JEFF COREY=

1973 CHEREMOYA HOLLYWOOD CALIF=

THIS IS TO ADVISE THAT YOUR APPEARANCE BEFORE THE COMMITTEE
ON UN-AMERICAN ACTIVITIES HAS BEEN POSTPONED. IN
ACCORDANCE WITH THE SUBPENA WITH WHICH YOU HAVE BEEN
SERVED YOU ARE HEREBY DIRECTED TO APPEAR BEFORE THE
COMMITTEE ON UN-AMERICAN ACTIVITIES ON AUGUST 15, 1951,
AT 10:00 A.M. WASHINGTON D.C.=
:JOHN S WOOD CHAIRMAN=

THE COMPANY WILL APPRECIATE SUGGESTIONS FROM ITS PATRONS CONCERNING ITS SERVICE

Telegram postponing Jeff's HUAC appearance, July 1951.

CLASS OF SERVICE

This is a full-rate Telegram or Cablegram unless its deferred character is indicated by a suitable symbol above or preceding the address.

WESTERN
UNION

1201

SYMBOLS

DL=Day Letter
NL=Night Letter
LT=Int'l Letter Telegram
VLT=Int'l Victory Ltr.

W. P. MARSHALL, PRESIDENT

The filing time shown in the date line on telegrams and day letters is STANDARD TIME at point of origin. Time of receipt is STANDARD TIME at point of destination

LA596   1951 AUG 8 PM 5 33

L HDA003-227 GOVT NL PD=HOLLYWOOD CALIF 8=

JEFF COREY=

DLR 1973 CHEREMOYA HOLLYWOOD CALIF=

THIS IS TO ADVISE THAT YOUR APPEARANCE BEFORE THE COMMITTEE
BY UN-AMERICAN ACTIVITIES HAS BEEN POSTPONED. IN ACCORDANCE
WITH THE SUBPOENA WITH WHICH YOU HAVE BEEN SERVED YOU ARE
HEREBY DIRECTED TO APPEAR BEFORE THE COMMITTEE ON
UN-AMERICAN ACTIVITIES ON SEPTEMBER 5, 1951, AT 10:00 A.M.,
ROOM 518, FEDERAL BLDG., LOS ANGELES, CALIFORNIA=
:JOHN S WOOD CHAIRMAN=

THE COMPANY WILL APPRECIATE SUGGESTIONS FROM ITS PATRONS CONCERNING ITS SERVICE

Telegram postponing Jeff's HUAC appearance, August 1951.

The filing time shown in the date line on telegrams and day letters is STANDARD TIME at point of origin. Time of receipt is STANDARD TIME at point of destination

I A339   1951 NOV 28 AM 11 44

L.HDA002-195 PD=HOLLYWOOD CALIF 28 1108A=

JEFF COREY=

:DONT FONE 1973 CHEREMOYA HOLLYWOOD CALIF=

.THIS IS TO ADVISE THAT YOUR APPEARANCE BEFORE THE COMMITTEE
ON UN-AMERICAN ACTIVITIES HAS BEEN POSTPONED. IN ACCORDANCE
WITH THE SUBPOENA WITH WHICH YOU HAVE BEEN SERVED YOU ARE
HEREBY DIRECTED TO APPEAR BEFORE THE COMMITTEE ON UN-AMERICAN
ACTIVITIES ON SEPTEMBER 17, 1951, AT 9:30 A.M., ROOM 518,
FEDERAL BLDG. , LOS ANGELES, CALIFORNIA=
JOHN S WOOD CHAIRMAN=

Telegram postponing Jeff's HUAC appearance, August 28, 1951.

Jeff with his lawyer, A. L. Wirin, before the House Un-American Activities Committee (HUAC), Los Angeles Federal Building, September 21, 1951. (*Bettmann/Getty Images. Reprinted with permission.*)

spotlight and exposure theme.
     annals of Amer.Acad.Pol
     KEY TO MY BRAIN science..Hoover..
Fifth amendment..First amdt.
 Star chamber hearings...
  Founding fathers closer to
     it..against harassment.
Appaling misconceptions to
     public by committee..
Constitution and civil
     rights must be defended
     particularly in crisis..
     if not good in crisis..whe
Jeffersonn fought for four ye
     years. He anticipated this
     kind of inquisition.
NO POLIT EXPERT - NO APOLOGIST FORUSSR
     INDEPENDENT THINKER   NO RED BAITER
Nonconformist, unpopular opin
became popular..jefferson
most maligned man in generat
ion..No president as villifie
by press as Lincoln..FDR clos
second..But alien and sdtion
law opponents were elected
John Llilburne elected ToPar.
     - - - -

To infer is to deny const.
Implies nothing..sinews flil
 Neither lat us be slanderd many
By false occurata (ambrose - disloyal cost

Notes on index card number 1, folded into Jeff's coat pocket for his appearance before HUAC, September 21, 1951.

sequence of kamikaze attempt
..great comabt sequence...
valuable contribution to vis
regard..reflects highest crdt
to Corey and photoservice...
***
Thespis...Polit. Bullying
Actors horsewhipped
Middleton Jailed..
Lincoln..Jeff.Springfield..
Actors in bootleg shows..
some of greatest actors of
day..Cockpit..Hope..
Roman holidays..human dignity
Theater has few dozen talen
this comm.blacklists over
hundred in one day...
****

Audience blacklisted
When you qualify freedom...
many nations have lost
their liberty...

Polk resolution...precomiit.
What GI wants to go in..
Pearl Harbor...
***

Grey list if not blacklist..

Notes on index card number 2, folded into Jeff's coat pocket for his appearance before HUAC, September 21, 1951.

Jeff, Jane, Eve, Hope, and Emily, March 1951.

The Corey family, Jane, Emily, Eve, Hope, and Jeff, on the front porch at 1973 Cheremoya Avenue, Hollywood, 1954.

Hope and Jeff on their European tour, 1960.

Jeff returns to work, 1961.

In Film Again

Jeff Corey, once one of Hollywood's busiest actors, has just finished his first film work in 10 years in a segment of "The Untouchables." His exile was the result of his refusal to testify before the House unAmerican Activities Committee.

Dear Jeff:

It's raining again, and we wonder if it will ever
end. I put Pat and Euan Loyd on the plane Sat. night &
he said he would contact you and offer any help he could
in arranging terms for "Deathwatch". I am thrilled with the
possibility that you may be able to x swing it. I got a very
short but encouraging note from Rosica Colin, and I imagine
you've been it in touch with her by now. Hope to hear from you
soon with some terms for consideration.

I think I have finally been able to stimulate some more
scene work in the classes. It was a hard pull. It seems there
is a pronounced fear of failure. Am still very high on the idea
of conducting a scene class when you return, and would like
to know your reaction.
Latest deposit was $571.25 on March 16.
Ed Rowen and Kim Hamilton are in "The Blacks" at the Ivar.
It got excellent revues.
I have been interspersing classes on character along with
vXXXXX various other exercises such as conflict, goal,
XXXXX obstacle, effecting change etc. Worked last week on
metaphor with very exciting results. This week we're working
on physiological diseases and disabilities.

The most exciting results have come from working on what
I am referring to more and more as the "classic" form of the
acting experience.... The actor-character has a need which
is richly motivated and personal.... he runs into obstacles
which he tries to overcome or effect change in, and he has
emotional experiences as a result. When the experience hits
him he makes his choices as to how to play it. I told a
story about a child who is given a dozen blocks which
unbeknownst to him, are not square. He is told to stack them,
(his Goal) , and they keep falling. First perhaps he finds it
amusing, and eventually he will probably be wild with frustration
The impact of the idea lies in the fact that the child did
not set out to be happy or sad, but to DO something. At
this point our old friend Aristotle helps immensely. (The
quotation at the back of the studio).

I assume that the work continues to go well, and I also imagine
it is somewhat frustrating to watch actors work without being
able to actually direct. ..(some day soon you will, I'm sure).

Must go now to teach my peers in the Tues. P.M. group. Really
nice people, and working well too.
Will write again soon. Regards and love to your family from
all here.

Letter to Jeff from Leonard Nimoy, 1962.

Jeff in the "O.B.I.T." episode of *The Outer Limits,* 1963.

Jeff, Steve McQueen, and Ann-Margret in *The Cincinnati Kid*, 1965.

Jeff at Paramount Studios, 1966.

Sandy Koufax, David Janssen, Don Drysdale, and Jeff at a televised press conference, 1966. (*Photo by Art Rogers, copyright © 1966 the* Los Angeles Times. *Reprinted with permission.*)

Jeff and Scott Wilson in *In Cold Blood*, 1967.

Jeff and Henry Fonda in *The Boston Strangler*, 1968.

Jeff and Glen Campbell in *True Grit*, 1969.

Jeff in *Beneath the Planet of the Apes*, 1970.

Dustin Hoffman, Jeff, and the director Arthur Penn on the set of *Little Big Man*, 1970.

Yul Brynner and Jeff in *Catlow*, 1971.

Jeff in *Catlow,* 1971.

Jeff as Polonius in *Hamlet* at the
Mark Taper Forum, 1974.

Jeff, Leonard Nimoy, and William Shatner in "The Cloud Minders" episode of *Star Trek,* 1969.

Paul Newman, Jeff, and Robert Redford in *Butch Cassidy and the Sundance Kid,* 1969.

Jack Nicholson
and Jeff, 1990.

Wallace Shawn
and Jeff in
Twelve Angry Men
at the New Mercury
Theatre, 1993.
(Photo by
Matthew Modine.)

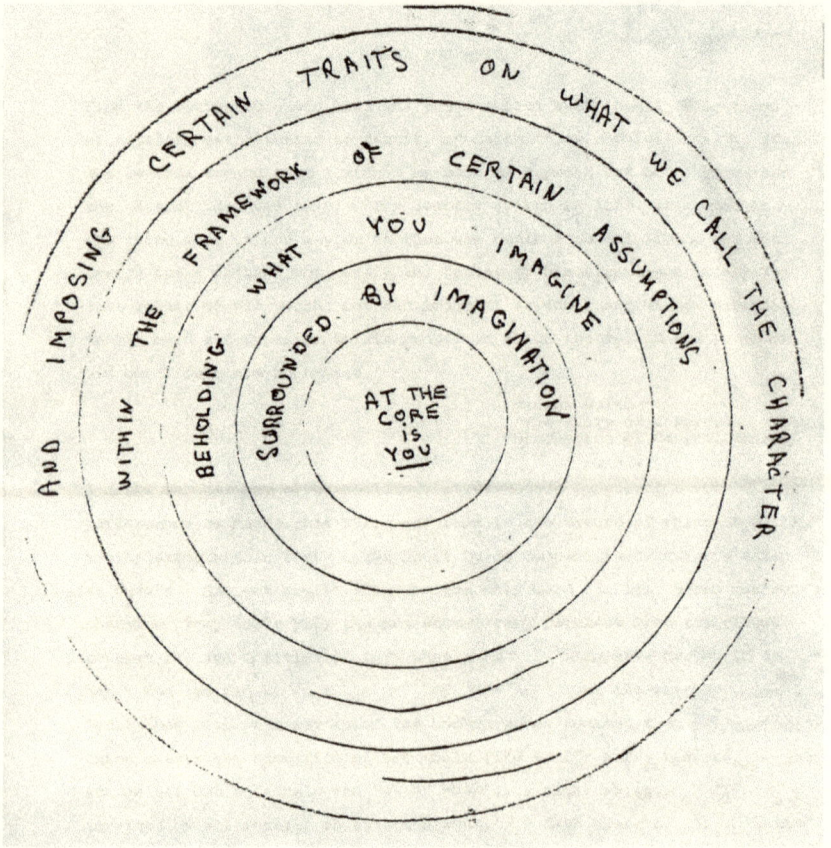

Jeff's circular theory of the actor's process (handed out to all his students).

some film books, and out of nowhere a grunting voice said, "Hello, Jeff." I looked up. It was Sterling.

"Hi, Sterling," I said as I thought to myself, "It's bold of him to reach out to me," and, clearly, he was the more uncomfortable. We chitchatted about his upcoming voyage around the world, and he mentioned he was looking for a cameraman to take with him. I suggested Jack Ferrucci, who was the brightest kid in my film class at UCLA. I gave Sterling his phone number. A week later, Jack called to tell me Sterling had hired him.

"It was the oddest thing," he said. "The first thing Sterling said to me was, 'Well, I was surprised that Jeff would even talk to me.'" Then he said Sterling went into an endless rant about what a shit he was and what a great guy Jeff Corey was. He told Jack, "I wish I had Jeff's balls. I wish I had his guts."

It did take balls and guts to stand up to the committee, but that's not what got us through. Integrity isn't a sticky wicket, and during the dark days of the blacklist, there wasn't a lot of wiggle room between right and wrong. In fact, the sides were drawn fairly clearly. If Hollywood and Congress had stood up to McCarthy and outed him for the self-aggrandizing liar that he was, our country would have charted a dramatically different course. But people were afraid, and fear makes good people lose their ballast, especially if fierce winds are blowing in their direction. I do not hold a grudge against those who informed; however, I do not take their actions lightly. I cherished my career. I had worked long and hard for it. But nothing in my nature could have made me name names. They didn't pull my nails out. They didn't crucify me. They just asked me to do something I simply could not do.

The men who oversaw the blacklist—Joseph McCarthy, Roy Cohn, J. Edgar Hoover, the committee heads and their staff—used patriotic rhetoric to their advantage. They were, in fact, not patriots. They were mean-spirited and out only for themselves. In all the years they did their dirty work, there were no genuine plots revealed to overthrow the government or any person singled out in Hollywood who legitimately intended to cause America's moral or political downfall. The only thing they succeeded at was destroying people's lives. It was the worst of America. Not our best, and we should do everything in our power to expose anyone in the political arena today who acts in such a shameful and duplicitous way.

When I look back at the years since my blacklist ended, I think my original scorn and disdain have been tempered with a kind of murky pity for the cooperative witnesses. On our side, the blacklistees and their children became an extended family. These friendships have lasted into the third generation, and we have the remarkable good fortune to be able to get together and enjoy this large family of friends, children, and now grandchildren as they talk and continue to enjoy life together.

Over the years, I have read eulogies for the poet Eddie Rolfe, who fought with the Abraham Lincoln Brigade in Spain, for my friend Mike Wilson at the old Motion Picture Academy Theater on Melrose Avenue, and twenty years later at Mike's home in Ojai for his wife, Zelma. The First Unitarian Church was the platform for eulogies for Dalton Trumbo and Waldo Salt. The Unitarian minister Stephen Fritchman's memorial drew a full house at the Mark Taper Forum.

In 1975, the year before Dalton Trumbo died, he finally received his Oscar for *The Brave One*, which he had written under an assumed name during the blacklist. In 1993 the Academy posthumously awarded his widow, Cleo, the Oscar for *Roman Holiday*, also written under an assumed name in the early stages of the blacklist. Mike Wilson received posthumous Oscars for *The Bridge on the River Kwai* and *Lawrence of Arabia*. His writing partner on *The Bridge on the River Kwai*, my friend Carl Foreman, received his award posthumously. The writer Ben Barzman was awarded the French *Ordre des Artes et des Lettres* from the French consulate for the distinguished films he wrote and coproduced during his long exile in France.

Our home in Studio City was used for a memorial for the playwright and screenwriter and my closest friend, David Robison. A few years later, when David's wife, Naomi, died, there was a celebration of her life at the Malibu home of her brother, the playwright Jerome Lawrence. Hope and I both spoke of our lifelong joy in knowing Naomi. We were all deeply saddened by the death of Paul Jarrico in 1997, the day after a tribute to blacklistees by the Writers, Directors, and Screen Actors Guilds and AFTRA. On that redeeming evening Kevin Spacey played Paul in a staged reading of Paul's testimony before HUAC. The following afternoon, Paul and Ring Lardner Jr. were honored at a lunch by the Writers Guild. On the drive back to his home in Ojai, Paul fell asleep at the wheel, and his car crashed into a tree just south of Camarillo in Ventura County. The memorial for Paul took place at the Writers Guild Theater.

A year and a half later, my friend the screenwriter Frank Tarloff, who won the Academy Award for *Father Goose* once his blacklisting was over, was diagnosed with lung cancer. As his condition worsened, Frank, a comedy writer to the end, devised a plan for a memorial event at the Mulholland Tennis Club at which he would be present as honored guest and could witness the forthcoming tributes. Unfortunately, his condition deteriorated and his memorial was preempted by his death on June 25, 1999.

I heartily endorse the trenchant observation made by the singer Lee Hayes, the onetime itinerant preacher who later became a balladeer and composer with Pete Seeger and The Weavers. At a concert at Carnegie Hall, many years after the blacklist, Hayes said, "If it wasn't for the honor of it, I would just as soon not have been blacklisted at all!" My sentiments, exactly.

Many good men and women, all deeply principled people, experienced great disruption in their personal and professional lives because of the tyranny of the blacklist. Yet, in spite of the storm, they still landed on their feet. Their past is truly prologue.

Even though the Hollywood studios refused to hire me for over twelve years, I never felt like a pariah. I had a wonderful wife, wonderful children, and wonderful friends who supported us, unconditionally. I'm proud of the way I lived my life and conducted my relationships. It's rewarding simply to be alive and be able to respond to this texture of living.

Teaching others to act was a response to circumstances beyond my control and an adjunct to my own lifelong study of the craft. In response to queries about which method I embrace, I always hold tight to the great nineteenth-century actor Joseph Jefferson's wise postulate, "Every artist must be the head of his or her academy."

I offer as well that we must all be the heads of our own lives. Acts of kindness and integrity, and the courage to stand up and say, "No," when all social pressures insist on the contrary, are the only way the world will change for the better. Being able to live with ourselves is truly a life well lived. The actor who is true to himself delivers a consistently great performance.

The blacklist is relevant today in that it is the standard of what to fight against. We must never lower the bar of truth and human decency. The blacklist was something to endure with as much grace as possible.

While I appreciate that after all these years standing up to HUAC is now viewed as a badge of honor, I hate it when people say, "Oh, Jeff, you're such a survivor."

I did more than survive. I lived a life.

Part II

How to Act

Not knowing when the dawn will come I open every door.
—*Emily Dickinson*

26

Infernal Methodists

I wince when I am asked the tiresome question "Are you a Method teacher?" I think to myself, "Poor Stanislavsky. Peace unto his ashes!" To qualify as a teacher of the Stanislavsky system would require me to reincarnate as Stanislavsky himself.

During the 1950s the poor, victimized Stanislavsky Method was too frequently equated with mumbling, slurred speech, and inaudibility. It also manifested itself as a dreadful narcissism on stage. Brooks Atkinson of the *New York Times,* the doyen of stage critics during Broadway's golden age, bemoaned the fact that theaters were filled with "too many performers who seemed to be acting for each other rather than for their audience." Brooks went on to speculate this was because actors spent an enormous amount of time showing their colleagues how well they could incorporate the techniques learned in their acting classes into their roles—rather than playing the role itself. The bad actor indulges his techniques. The great actor honors them and does everything he can to fight against them.

In 1946 the Actors' Lab initiated a series of seminars to discuss the Stanislavsky Method as understood by the Group Theatre and the Actors' Lab's own classes. I looked over my notes from one of those gatherings. The topic was "Playing an Action." My friend Art Smith of the Group Theatre led the session. At one point, Morris Carnovsky, the brilliant actor and a founder of the Method-oriented Group, spoke of his own excitement in fathoming the "right action." He told the class he always preferred to start acting first and then, when his rehearsal efforts crested, find the idea. He went on to say, "Everybody comes to a 'spine' or main action in their own way. It need not be arrived at by means of cerebration, and I am beginning to think that these things are discovered in the heat of battle. On the basis of my own experience, I would say that the action frequently comes last, and when it does, it illuminates everything because it is tied up with everything."

Art Smith's retort amused me then as it does now. "With greatest respect to Morris," he replied, "there are very great dangers in what he says—inspiring as it is."

To me, both approaches—either before or after—are equally valid, and it is important to understand that no matter how interesting a particular credo might be, an actor must bring his own instincts and ability to discern to the task of preparing for a role. When I was a young actor in New York, the Method was God. Yet it turns out that even that hallowed way of thinking was the result of chance. In a 1922 interview with the theater critic from the *Wall Street Journal*, Stanislavsky described how an actor must define his role in little "bits." In the maestro's thick Russian accent, the word came out "beats," and from that moment on the Method was misunderstood in America. As wrong as it is, generations of young actors still continue to talk about "beats," entirely missing the great maestro's point.

I fell prey to it myself. As a young actor, I diligently adhered to my understanding of the Method. For every role I played, I would run lines across the page and identify the beats at every turn of conversation as an almost religious ritual. Even as I deconstructed my roles into as many beats as I could muster I had the great fortune to be surrounded by wise men like Julie Dassin and Bud Bohnen, who joshed me out of my own obsessive attempt to be truthful on stage. Taking their suggestion to heart that it would be wiser to explore a diverse set of possibilities within a role, I was grateful to read Stanislavsky's admonition: "There are actors who no sooner try to do something than they are immediately checked by the fear of a false note. Such excessive feeling for truth may paralyze the will."

I was equally grateful to discover Yevgeny Vakhtangov's sage remark, "An inordinate search for psychological truth always leads to a psychological hernia." Vakhtangov had been a student of Stanislavsky's and was cofounder of the great Moscow Art Theater. His observation helped free me from a lifetime of unnecessary searching for meaning in a role that was probably never there and equally as likely detrimental to my performance.

Over time, and the more I relied on my own creative instincts, I grew weary of all the conscientious notes I wrote on my scripts in regard to beats and all the other techniques I thought would serve my performances. As I became more experienced and began to trust my intuition, I was able to unify my thoughts into a central theme. I learned to connect every shift in plot as cogent to the ruling idea. In fact, Stanislavsky's idea of "bits" was more relevant to me than the proverbial, misconstrued "beats."

In Nikolaï Gorchakov's book *Stanislavsky Directs,* he quotes Stanislavsky as saying, "There is no actual *method* yet; there are only a number of basic principles and exercises I suggest an actor practice in order to train himself to become a master artist."[1]

There is no denying the remarkable discoveries outlined in *My Life in Art* and *An Actor Prepares;* however, it is critical to understand that Stanislavsky never intended it as immutable truth or methodology. It was a system he updated, adapted, and revised with each new play and with each new set of actors.

It's rather exciting to note a complete change of subject that might prompt some actors to draw that predictable horizontal line across the page indicating a new beat and then say to himself, "No, it is not a new beat. My character is filibustering!" The awareness that a character might be making tidy conversation in the script but, in terms of subtext, is at complete war with himself makes for a very interesting action.

"Taking a moment" is another phrase used by the Group Theatre. This doesn't mean to calm yourself, although that would not be an unwise thing to do before beginning a performance. When you take a moment, you determine where you are coming from, what has transpired up to that moment, and what you expect will happen. Further, you figure out whom you anticipate meeting and whether the meeting will be easy, difficult, joyous, or any number of other scenarios. Whether a scene begins with two or three or more people in a dining room or a clearing in the forest, a medieval dungeon or a flophouse, when the actor "takes a moment," he must be attentive to the place and the people in it. There is a virtue in intelligently coming into the scene rather than just walking in. The Danish philosopher Søren Kierkegaard described a power and presence in the German actor Friedrich Beckmann, who played with the Königstäter Theatre troupe in Berlin, when he wrote:

He paints the scenery for himself as well as any painter could. . . . He not only can walk but he can *come walking.* This ability to "come walking" is a very different thing, and by this stroke of

genius Beckmann improvises the scenic environment. He not
only can represent a wandering apprentice lad, he can come walking like him, and in such a way that one sees the whole thing:
through the dust of the highway one espies a smiling village, hears
its subdued din, sees the footpath which winds yonder down to
the pond. . . . He is capable of coming on the stage with the street-
urchins following him—who one does not see. . . . [He] has no
need of street-urchins or painted scenery. . . . Every . . . actor must
have a voice which is audible from behind the scenes.[2]

Technique is also a word not to be trusted. The director-producer
Arthur Hopkins, who produced John Barrymore's notable *Hamlet*, was
suspicious of the word *technique* when he wrote, "Technique is substitut-
ing effect for cause. Technique is dependence on externals. Externals
develop into tricks. Tricks are the pitfall of art. The director can free the
actor from dependence on tricks by helping him cultivate authority
through clear perception of the characters, by faith in his own inner
resources."[3]

One can learn from these inspired practitioners and theoreticians of
the past and present and then go on to discover one's own voice. Joseph
Jefferson, the most successful and admired American actor of the nineteenth century, wrote, "Many instructors in the dramatic art fall into the
error of teaching too much. The pupil should first be allowed to exhibit his
quality, and so teach the teacher what to teach. This course would answer
the double purpose of first revealing how much the pupil is capable of
learning, and, what is still more important, of permitting him to display
his powers untrammeled. Whereas, if the master begins by pounding his
dogmas into the student, the latter becomes environed by a foreign influence which, if repugnant to his nature, may smother his ability."[4]

The word pedagogy is almost always used pejoratively, implying an
authoritarian or pedantic approach. But pedagogy at its best is an art, and
Jefferson's perception would serve teachers well in any educational arena.

There is no doubt in my mind that Stanislavsky's most important contribution to the art of acting was to insist that the emotional color of a
scene was not the actor's overt concern. One is not called on to *show* happiness or grief or puzzlement. The actor's job is to perceive the problem
and do something to alleviate it. Showing the audience his perception of
the problem—and then implementing the solution—leads to good acting.

This is not a new concept. Hundreds of years before Stanislavsky published his ideas, the ancient Greek philosopher Aristotle insightfully observed, "Happiness and misery are not states of being, but forms of activity; the end for which we live is some form of activity, not the realization of a moral quality. Men are better or worse, according to their moral bent; but they become happy or miserable in their actual deeds. In a play, consequently, the agents do not perform for the sake of representing their individual dispositions; rather, the display of moral character is included as subsidiary to the things that are done."[5]

The great American writer F. Scott Fitzgerald died before he completed *The Last Tycoon*. In his notes for the book, the last thing he wrote before his death, in large capital letters, was "CHARACTER IS ACTION." Defining the theme of the play opens up a range of exploration for the actors, writer, and director. It is exciting to experience how disparate choices and shifts of rhythm and mood can be linked to a strong, unifying theme.

Phrases such as "the spine of the play," "the central theme," "the clear objective," "the motivation," and "the action" confuse the actor. These words loom over his head like a litany, and in the attempt to discover things in an ordained way, an actor risks forgoing his own intuitiveness, something that must never happen. It is an actor's intuition and ability to embrace his good instincts that deliver great performances.

When I teach, I try to eschew technique as a topic of discourse. There is no single definition of technique, and the more strategies an actor makes available to himself, the better his performance will be. To achieve this, an actor must go outside his comfort zone and explore new ideas. It is not enough to be single-minded. Great performances come out of the most unexpected places. Technique is the fuel that allows an actor to pioneer a route through those remarkable, untamed territories.

When thinking about technique, and in particular the Method, it is wise to remember Stanislavsky's advice about the system he developed. "Create your own method. . . . Don't depend slavishly on mine. Make up something that will work for you! But keep breaking traditions, I beg you."[6]

27

Hooks, Lines, and Other Sinkers

Something I call hooks are all around us and we use them every day, whether we are aware of them or not. Hooks in our private lives can be ideas that drive our actions or obsessive thoughts that infiltrate the things we do. Hooks are not necessarily negative, although they can be. They can point us to success, streamline our actions, and help define how we feel about any given event in our lives.

For the actor, it is eminently helpful to find a central hook that prevails over every twist and turn, contradiction, affirmation, and all other aspects of a role. While I choose to call it a hook, what it really is is a prevailing attribute that either prompts the character into action or paralyzes him, depending on the circumstances. While a hook is not arbitrary—it must be connected in some way to the character's circumstances—hooks can be illuminatingly random and creative and serve as an anchor for an entire performance. Stanislavsky once quoted a riverboat captain who, when asked by a passenger, "How do you avoid the rocks and shoals and sharp turns of the rapids?" simply replied, "I stay in the mid-channel." Hooks are the mid-channel you discover to keep yourself safe from the rocky shores of the plot and the dialogue.

A hook can be a private thought or an action, or it can be displayed publicly, for all to see. Jane Fonda worked with me on the role of Gloria in *They Shoot Horses, Don't They?* The film is about one of the many dance marathon competitions that were held during the Great Depression. The couple who could stay on the dance floor for the longest period without collapsing won a cash prize. Often, marathons would go on for days. In the film, Gloria is steeped in an unremitting gloom and equates her impaired existence to that of an injured filly. She is prompted to destroy herself because, as she observes, "They shoot horses, don't they?" The challenge of the role was to find a way for Jane to make her performance active and engaging for a character who was terminally depressed and flat.

Jane and I came up with a strong, unifying hook that she could access, at will, throughout the entire film. We decided that while Gloria knew she was trapped inside the gloom of the marathon dance hall, somewhere inside she believed there was something beyond the confines of the marathon that could mitigate her circumstances. The set they built for the film had a glass roof. One of the panes was broken. Jane and I decided that during the shooting of the film, the only place Gloria would ever focus on was beyond that pane of broken glass and into the hope and possibility that existed outside the marathon madness.

As she danced, her eyes looked up through the skylight, searching for the distant, unknown force that might relieve her. Even when her scenes involved face-to-face exchanges with other characters, Jane never totally focused on the other actor's face. Everything in front of her was a blur except for what was slightly beyond her reach. Audiences were not distracted by this action—nor were they even aware of it—but the hook had force within Jane's own internal logic and helped her achieve a magical, Academy Award–nominated performance.

During the height of the blacklist, in 1959, one of Hollywood's most notable leading men, Kirk Douglas, and his producer, Edward Lewis, tried to make arrangements for me to work on the set of *Spartacus* as dialogue director. Kirk had boldly hired my friend Dalton Trumbo, the blacklisted screenwriter, to write the script. I was eager to serve in that capacity for many reasons. The cast was made up of an eminent galaxy of stars such as Charles Laughton, Laurence Olivier, and Peter Ustinov, and I knew Trumbo's script would be magnificent. But, alas and alack, the timid production heads at Universal Studios were fearful lest my political presence on the lot jeopardize the movie. They were probably shaken enough by Trumbo's presence and were not willing to take another risk. Nonetheless, Kirk was determined to work with me privately. Over the years of work as an actor, Kirk's tendency with a role was to plunge immediately into the physical action of the traditional movie hero pattern—something he did brilliantly in Stanley Kramer's film *Champion*. As we began to work together on his role for *Spartacus,* I pointed out to Kirk that this character was different. Spartacus had been a slave all his life and had risen to lead a rebellion against the Romans. The driving hook for Spartacus couldn't be his external strength and physicality. It had to be a much more internal, thoughtful issue. As a slave, Spartacus could not relieve his bladder without permission. He could make no decisions on his own. Now, as the leader of an entire people, suddenly his free will determined everything. Working together on his role, we decided that every decision Kirk would make had to be filtered through the newfound cacophony of choice—foreign as it was to him. To support this thinking, I found a scholarly article that speculated that the reason Moses spent forty years in the desert was that he did not want that last generation of a four-hundred-year lineage of slavery, including himself, to be the founding fathers of "the land flowing with milk and honey." He wanted men and women who had lived free to bring their sensibilities to the task. Kirk integrated this logic into his work on *Spartacus*. Again, it was a hook only he and I knew about, but it gave an insightful depth and dimension to his spectacular performance.

The process of discovering a hook requires that an actor open his mind to an idea and let the guiding images come in, even if they feel strange and unexpected. My first important role after the war was in *The Killers*. I played a cheap crook, and in one scene one of the characters says to me, "I hear you carry a monkey on your back." The phrase used for junkies was an apt description. I decided to find out how a drug addict might behave. It was postwar America, and the country was relatively clean. I visited my local police precinct and hospital emergency room to see if I could discover behavior patterns common to drug addicts. No one could help me.

One day the producer of the film, Mark Hellinger, and I were discussing my part. Mark had been an old-time Broadway columnist and was quite a man of the world. I asked him how he thought a junkie might behave. He didn't know, either, but suggested I twitch my right shoulder on occasion and blink my eyes at the same time. To support this hook he changed my character's name in the script to Blinky. When we began filming, I used the double tic sparingly and only when I thought it judicious. For many years after that, actors from all over the country thanked me for illustrating so clearly the prototype of how a real drug addict behaved. In fact, it was really only a hook that Mark and I invented on the spot that I was able to use throughout my entire performance.

After I was cast as the wino in *Lady in a Cage*, Ann Sothern and I decided we wanted to explore Los Angeles' Skid Row to learn more. In an odd turn of events, Ann insisted we ride there in her chauffeur-driven Rolls-Royce. With her elegant car safely parked around the corner and out of sight, Ann and I wandered the streets. The forlorn streetwalkers who wobbled hither and yon, seemingly without purpose, paid great attention to the decrepit canvas shopping bags they clutched to their sides. "I've got to get one of those bags," Ann said. We found several of them at Grand Central Market just a few blocks from Skid Row. It was Ann's conclusion that everything they possessed was contained in those threadbare shopping bags. It is likely that she was correct.

We also watched the unfocused movement of the transients and noticed that the winos' trousers all seemed more frayed on the right side than the left, possibly from sleeping in the streets and doorways. Some of them walked like sailors trying to stabilize their sea legs on level ground. Many walked in a spastic, convoluted manner. I surmised that because of the lack of public restrooms and the inherent lack of coordination of boozers, they were inefficient at the simple act of urinating. It was logical to assume, sadly, that the poor drifters urinated down their legs and all had acute diaper rash from the moisture. Hence, the strange walk that kept their filthy trousers from irritating their badly chafed limbs. I consciously found a walk for my wino as a physical hook that mimicked what I had seen on the streets.

On the first day of shooting *Little Big Man,* Dustin Hoffman was preparing the scene where he is drunk, broke, and mourning the slaughter of the Indian tribe that adopted him. The set was a frontier town with railroad tracks running through the main drag. The crew was preparing powerful rain effects, and Dusty was supposed to wallow in the mud in front of the town saloon, singing a song. We had met only that morning, and he had been nice enough to say, "Are you real?" when we were introduced. Dusty had been a student at the Pasadena Playhouse and his teacher, Barney Brown, would often introduce an acting exercise and describe it as "something he saw Jeff Corey do in his classes."

Out of the blue, Dusty asked me if I knew a song from the period. I immediately began to sing the beautiful nineteenth-century Irish ballad "Green Grow the Lilacs," which was sung by American soldiers who were cashiered into the war against Mexico in 1848 and died in large numbers, not as much in combat as from typhoid and malaria. The lyrics go:

Green grow the lilacs all sparkling with dew,
I'm lonely, my darling, since parting with you,
And by our next meeting I hope to make true,
And change the green lilacs to the red, white, and blue.

As the scene started, Dusty sang the song with drunken gusto, flapping his arms and rolling in the muddy slosh. It was spectacular, and they printed the first take. In the editing process, the composer, John Hammond, cut out Dusty's singing and overdubbed it with his own musical composition, but many months later, in an interview in *Esquire* magazine, Dusty told the reporter that when he heard the lyrics to "Green Grow the Lilacs," the entire idea for his character unfolded and served him throughout the entire film.

My mentioning that song was by chance. It was Dusty's remarkable creative talents that led him to contrive a hook out of that wonderful, woeful ballad.

28

True Grit

Hiring me in the role of Tom Chaney in *True Grit* was a classic case of creative casting. The first time we met for a read-through of the script, the director, Henry Hathaway, told me, "Before Maggie Roberts wrote the script, I read the novel and on page one I read that Tom Chaney, the villain, was 'a short man with cruel features . . . about twenty-five years of age,' and just like that, I got a flash of you in my head. I called Hal Wallis and said, 'I want Jeff Corey for the part of Tom Chaney.'" The fact that I am not a short man and was close to fifty-four years old at the time was irrelevant and spoke to Henry's enormous and wonderful imagination. For whatever reason, I was how Henry saw the part.

Henry was a fiery director who had a well-earned reputation for yelling at his actors to get a scene. He was a master of film noir and the Western genre and had made a name for himself in Hollywood directing Randolph Scott, John Wayne, and Gary Cooper in multiple films. In spite of his hot temperament, Henry and I always got along. Just before I was blacklisted we made *Rawhide* together and before that *Fourteen Hours*, a murder mystery written by the talented John Paxton. On the first day of filming *Fourteen Hours*, Henry kindly pulled me aside and in a whisper said, "Don't mind my yelling, kid. I respect your talent, otherwise I wouldn't have you on my set." I was honored and relieved and remembered this as we went into the tumultuous days of filming *True Grit*.

In *True Grit* I have a rather long, comical death scene in which Kim Darby, who played Mattie Ross, walks down a slope to a river to fill her canteen. She spies me across the river and aims her father's pre–Civil War dragoon revolver at me. She doesn't know how to use the gun, so in my role of the lamebrain Tom Chaney, I decide to help her out. "Cock your piece," I shout over the roaring river. She struggles with the gun and pulls it back one notch. "All the way back until it locks," I shout again,

163

barely being able to be heard over the racing water. At that point, to the surprise of both characters, she actually manages to shoot me in my ribs. Chaney, full of pity for himself, clutches his wound and mewls, "Everything happens to me," and whines about being "shot by a child!" The next day, Henry told me that an enthusiastic Hal Wallis had called him to say that he had watched the dailies and loved the scene. I told Henry, with a brazen smile, that the scene had gone so well because he was across the noisy river and I couldn't hear his line readings. He graciously laughed and then went on to interfere with the line readings of every other actor on the set.

I had worked with John Wayne in 1947 in *The Wake of the Red Witch* and had thoroughly enjoyed the experience. Though we obviously were at opposite ends of the political spectrum, I had a great deal of respect for his talent. On the first day of shooting of *True Grit*, the Duke put his arm around me and said, "Jeff, it's been too fucking long." We never mentioned the blacklist, but even through his conservative gaze, I knew he was glad to have me on the picture.

Robert Duvall, who played the nefarious villain Ned Pepper, had been warned about Henry's tempestuous disposition, and I think he was in an overweening state of alert when he did his first shot of the day with Kim. It was a difficult shot that took place on a steep hillside laden with aspens in full autumnal foliage. There was very little foothold for the crew, the equipment, or the two actors. Bobby was to grab Kim and wheel her around. In the first rehearsal, he grabbed her with his right hand and brought her down perfectly. Then Henry insisted he grab Kim with his left hand and bring her down to his right side because that action coincided with Henry's vision for the shot. When right-handed Bobby rather clumsily grabbed Kim with his left hand, Henry snapped at him and said, "No, no, really grab her and swing her to your right."

I never in my life witnessed anything like the scene that ensued. Bobby, at the top of his lungs roared, "I'm no fucking Martha Graham!" Something had been triggered, and Bobby went into a fit as the wooded mountainside echoed again and again with the irrelevant, irreverent reference to poor Martha Graham. Henry tried to pacify him, but Bobby held him at bay with his Martha Graham war cry.

The Duke approached Bobby in a fatherly way and started to say, "Now, look here, friend . . ." Bobby cut him off and again the aspens reverberated with the name of the first lady of modern dance. All of us—cast and crew—stood there frozen, waiting for another big bang. Henry very quietly said to Bobby, "Let's get this shot." Bobby settled down and did exactly what Henry had asked for in the first place. When the shot was finished, the assistant director got a nod from Henry and almost whispered, "That's a wrap, boys." We were all grateful to call it a day.

Bobby and I got into the station wagon that would take us back to our motel in Montrose. As we were about to leave, Henry appeared in front of the car and said, "Robert, I'd like to talk to you." Bobby slowly got out of the car, and the two of them stood in front of the station wagon. I couldn't hear a word they were saying, but Henry's manner seemed temperate and reasonable. When Henry finished, Bobby returned to the car. He grinned at me and said wryly, "I guess I overdid it, didn't I?" From that moment on, he and Henry got along beautifully, and his performance was an asset to the film. It was Bobby who threw that challenging line to the Duke, "I call that bold talk for a one-eyed fat man!" That line cued the Duke's greatest moment in film as he yelled, "Fill your hand, you son of a bitch!" and put the reins of his horse in his mouth and, holding his rifle in one hand and his revolver in the other, galloped toward his enemy.

I was concerned that Bobby's eruption would be the death knell of his career. Luckily for audiences everywhere, it didn't turn out that way. I don't mention this impasse between Henry and Bobby as idle gossip. Bobby was clearly out of line, for whatever reason, and he knew it. Fortunately for the entire crew, they were able to work it out. I mention it because how an actor behaves, whether on camera or onstage, is as vitally important to his role as the character itself. Professionalism dictates a certain amount of maturity and mental health, and regardless of how stressed or anxious an actor is feeling—or even insecure, for that matter—it is bad form to inflict that stress on the people around him. Come to the set or stage prepared. Know your lines and understand your character. If, for whatever reasons, the people around you—the director, the producer, whoever—have not yet achieved the air of respect the project deserves, don't dive into the fray. Be the sane one on the sidelines who keeps the creative process flowing. Don't be part of the problem.

Henry was marvelous and difficult to work with. Navigating his moods often brought to mind Edgar Lee Masters's line from "John Hancock Otis," in *Spoon River Anthology*, "Beware of the man who rises to power from one suspender." You never knew what was going to happen, and out of nowhere he would get impatient with someone on the crew who stopped to rest for a moment or to light a cigarette or to do anything Henry had decided was not to be done at that moment. Henry came up through the ranks as a poor kid from San Francisco and worked his way from a child actor in silent films to property man, assistant director, and then to the top echelon of directors. His favorite nudge was "Get that broom handle out of your ass!" Most of the crew had worked with him before and understood his straw-boss persona. They laughed at his testiness, but to the uniniti-ated, it didn't sit well. That said, however, Henry wasn't unfeeling. I often noticed that if he bruised a crew member's feelings, he would find a way to make amends.

During the filming of *True Grit,* we ran into an unexpected blizzard. Day after day it snowed, but Henry's entrenched work ethic would not allow him to "call it a wrap" until the scheduled quitting time. We took cover in our mobile dressing rooms and in a sheltering cave where we were trying to do some filming. The crew kept several cozy fires going, and at lunchtime, the catered hot food was served under protective tarps. We read; played chess, card games, and Scrabble; and waited for the weather to change. Wardrobe provided us with foul-weather gear, and there was always lots of steaming hot coffee and good conversation. At lunch, Henry would regale us with tales about the silent film days and the early talkies. He directed films like *The Lives of a Bengal Lancer* and *The House on 92nd Street.* One day, in the shelter of the cave and with the heat of a crackling fire keeping us warm, he told me that not since he did *Trail of the Lonesome Pine,* with Henry Fonda, Sylvia Sidney, and Fred MacMurray, in 1936 had he felt as good about a film as he did now about *True Grit.*

On the fourth day of the persistent blizzard, I felt like joking with him. I said, "Henry, I have a problem with Tom Chaney."

"What is it, boy?" he said brusquely.

"Well, the girl shoots me in the ribs, right?"

"Right," he responded.

"Then she scalds me with a huge tub of boiling water."

"Yes," he retorted, "I'm following you."

"Then Duke Wayne shoots me. And after the impact of the rifle shot, I fall into a snake pit."

"Come on, kid, what are you getting at?"

"Well, Henry, the next thing that happens is that the rattlesnakes in the bottom of the pit bite me. What I want to know is, would it be all right if I had a coronary seizure as well?"

Henry looked at me very seriously for a moment, considering his options. He shook his head and said, "No. That would be too much."

That was Henry's way. You ask a question, you get an answer. Even though Henry was often frightening, he got wonderful performances out of his actors with his stern manner and insistence on line readings. Personally, I do not approve of a director giving an actor line readings. I think it eliminates the space for art to happen. It unfortunately seems to be inevitable, however, so an actor must find the best way to deal with it without losing sight of his own creative instincts. If faced with a director who likes to deliver line readings, my suggestion is to find a way to make these directions inspiring rather than the imposition they really are. Find the hook for the line reading and then make it your own.

From there your performance can easily grow.

29

Styles, Isms, and Other Limitations

In 1955 I was invited to speak about acting styles at a weekend conference of the California Educational Theatre Association high up in the mountains of Idyllwild, California. The association gave me a ridiculous topic—style in the theater. I had been teaching for only a few years, but every instinct I had concluded there was no such thing as a theater style, and I stood up and said as much in front of hundreds of very distinguished acting teachers.

As a young actor in New York, I worked with a range of teachers and directors who defined themselves as avant-garde. At the Theatre Collective we did exercises in biomechanics and incorporated Dalcroze Eurhythmics in our performances. In the Theatre Collective's production of Philip Stevenson and Maurice Clark's *You Can't Change Human Nature,* Lazar Galpern, the gifted Russian choreographer, directed us in the style of theater of the grotesque. During our long rehearsal for the Federal Theatre's *Life and Death of an American,* each one of us, individually and then collectively, explored the nature of the play and discovered the most expressive way to shape our performances. Erwin Piscator, who had fled Germany and established himself as head of the Theatre Division of the New School for Social Research, worked in pre-Nazi Germany with Max Reinhardt on expressionist theater and with Bertolt Brecht on didactic theater. Piscator saw our production of *Life and Death of an American* and described it as the most significant American play he had seen in his years in America and categorically declared it was true "epic theatre." We were pleased with the compliment, but no one in the production consciously attempted to define our performance as epic theater. It grew organically out of our rehearsals and the work to discover the most creative and honest ways to play our parts.

The labels of style—avant-garde, naturalism, theater of the grotesque, and so on—continue to be bandied about and used to define plays and performances. What if, instead, there was no such thing as style at all and that the very conceit of a style served only to confine our creative impulses? What if it is as simple as form follows content? What if every performance—regardless of its place, era, or cultural ramifications—is only about a conscious, ongoing effort to do the play well?

In Bertolt Brecht's essay "Alienation Effects in Chinese Acting," published in 1936, he purported an anti-emotional stance he called the alienation effect—a process of making the action onstage removed or "alien" from the actors and the audience. The alienation effect attempts to fight against any kind of emotional manipulation onstage. After my trip to East Germany, where I witnessed profoundly emotional performances by actors in Brecht's Berliner Ensemble, I was perplexed.

I went to see my friend the former UCLA professor William Melnitz to help clarify my confusion. William had fled Germany in 1939 and had helped Max Reinhardt form a repertory theater group in Los Angeles. He arrived in America with a Ph.D. from a German university and had directed more than 150 professional productions in Germany, Austria, and Switzerland. He had worked with Brecht on many occasions. A diligent scholar, he completed a second Ph.D. at UCLA and then took over the role of dean of the newly formed College of Fine Arts. It was a delight to study with him there.

I described to William how, contrary to my expectations, the players in East Germany had displayed a profound and startling emotionality. I was confused by what appeared to be a contradiction in terms. William, in his grand and very kind voice, said, "Jeff, Reinhardt, Brecht, and Stanislavsky were superb directors." He looked at me carefully and continued, "I would not hesitate to say that they were geniuses. Their work transcended theory." After a moment he said, "Bertolt had a contrary nature. He liked to postulate outrageous notions and then disprove their substance over and over again. He loved contradictions."

I told him, as an actor, my guiding principle had been Brecht's interesting observation that a decision to do something must be involved with not doing something else. "Good!" William said. "Make use of that, but you must know that only if you can put an artist's theory into manifest practice does it amount to anything. Artistic axioms help only the artist who can embrace them." He paused for a moment and then said, "You must be free to choose what you, yourself, can make of it. If Brecht makes proclamations against emotional acting, it does not mean the very best performances by his Brechtian actors are devoid of emotion." I left William's home, reassured and content to live with Brecht's inconsistencies because it seemed to me the contradictions themselves opened the pathway to a myriad of views that were accessible in any performance.

It is easy to conclude that if a gifted artist carries a torch for a particular "ism" or "style," success is not guaranteed for another artist who adopts that same torch. While it may be thrilling—and even intellectually necessary—to study and explore the varieties of artistic styles, there are really no eternal verities. Instead, there are only good hunches fortified by experience on the part of imaginative directors, producers, writers, and performers. The range of human emotions that styles and isms attempt to capture is as regular as breathing. Even a person who claims, "I don't feel anything," is really experiencing levels of ennui, desolation, and resignation. No single approach will ever capture the bounty of that experience.

In film, the word *genre* often takes the place of *style* or *ism* as a way to identify a work. While the genre of a film may indeed have some importance, it is not its artistic defining light. Actors, writers, and producers should strive to make great films—films that speak to the creative struggle and human condition—not films that support a particular genre.

In the mid-1950s I interviewed Leonard Nimoy as a potential student. After our meeting I invited him to join one of my morning classes. At the end of the first class, Leonard approached me and asked, "Do you teach acting styles?" I think I was a little abrupt with him and said something like "Form follows function!" It's also likely that I elaborated briefly on that premise. At our next session, I apologized and said I was glad he came back because I truly thought I had been excessively curt with him. I explained to him that the endless search for style and labels often irritates me. As tools they are marvelous for the actor, but as standard-bearers for a performance, these labels invariably compromise the work. Every performance is unique. No style or ism can possibly define it or enhance communication.

Leonard did very good work in class and established close relationships with his classmates, Vic Morrow; Vic's wife, Barbara Turner; Peter Baldwin; and Mike Forest, and together they put together an exciting production of Jean Genet's *Deathwatch*. Appropriately enough, their production achieved a notable "style"—without laborious attempts to designate it by name. Over time, Leonard's work grew and continued to be inspiring. This was why, as the blacklist lifted and before he was too busy with *Star Trek*, I asked him to teach my classes whenever I had to take a break to work on a film. I knew my students would be in good hands with a teacher who had an open mind and a clear aim for good work.

I have had the good fortune to appear in a number of wonderful and interesting television shows and films. It was not a lack of perspicacity on my part, but I genuinely never approached a part in a so-called sci-fi project any differently from the way I would have approached a romance, mystery, or drama. The only questions that interest me when preparing for a role are: What is this screenplay about in terms of theme or meaning? In what way is my character's role a variant in the thematic scheme of the story? What, in the art director's extravagant cybernetic environment, is familiar to me? Have I not, all my life, dreamed similar dreams?

When I played Tom Sharp, the head of the Farmers' Grange in *The Devil and Daniel Webster*, in 1941, I never dreamed that many years later the film would qualify as science fiction. Everyone in the cast, including myself, just showed up and did the best work possible. This approach was true for *Seconds, Beneath the Planet of the Apes, Superman and the Mole Men*, and even, dare I say, *Oh, God!*—which has its own sweet foray into the supernatural. It also held true for *Conan, the Destroyer, The Next Voice You Hear, The Sword and the Sorcerer*, and *Something Evil*, a made-for-television movie Steven Spielberg directed ten years before *E.T.* I have received wonderful letters from *Star Trek* fans about my appearance in *The Cloud Minders*, and I apparently have been responsible for a number of sleepless nights owing to my appearance as Mr. Byron Lomax in the *Outer Limits* episode "O.B.I.T." I apologize to anyone I may have frightened.

I directed fifteen episodes of Rod Serling's *Night Gallery* at Universal and appeared as an actor in one episode with my friend Carl Betz. Even as a director, I don't think I ever thought to direct these phantasmagorical episodes in a sci-fi pattern. Each individual script prompted certain unique choices in terms of the environment and the nature of the characters in the story. It was important to me to have detailed discussions with the cinematographer and the art director, and to speak to the set dressers, the prop master, and the makeup artists to hear their takes on the story. These marvelous and talented people were all doing their jobs. I don't think one of them came to work thinking, "Today, I'm going to do sci-fi." I think all of us, including the actors, showed up and did the very best job we could. The fact that it resulted in a sci-fi piece is almost irrelevant.

While it can be delicious to delve into various creative styles and explore their nuanced, relative meanings, in the long run it serves little purpose to have them speak for an entire play or film. Styles and isms of any kind are nothing more than markers that can help an actor understand a certain temperament of a script or a character. They are not our whole understanding of a role. Used judiciously, these markers help orient actors and directors toward the themes and underlying meanings of a play, but they should never be used to focus the action or define a production.

To do so limits the creative instincts of the people involved in the production and will lead to a stagnant performance that does a disservice to the actor, the script, and his audience.

30

Be Yourself

In all my years as a teacher, I have stressed the importance of an actor bringing as much of himself to a role as possible—even if he has never experienced what his character is going through. In Patrick McGilligan's insightful book, *Jack's Life,* Jack Nicholson eloquently describes what he learned in my class in the following manner: "You have at least seventy-five percent in common with any character you'll ever play, if it's Hitler or Peter Pan. What you have to find is that twenty-five to five percent difference, and that's what you have to act. The other part you just forget it, 'cause it's there. You couldn't lose it if you wanted to."[1]

We all encounter roles that, at the outset, seem out of our habitual range, but the versatile actor learns to deal with the most variegated roles. Recognizing and describing the difficulty is the first step to finding answers, and no matter the panoply of roles offered, the personal style of the integrated artist will always be cogent in the performance.

A good actor should be able to imagine any human predicament and conclude, "I can envisage that circumstance. By engaging my fancy, I can comprehend the behavior of my character even though I never personally encountered it." There should always be something about the actor that allows the audience to imagine themselves in the same circumstances.

Michael Chekhov was really the source of my thinking about this. Mischa used to say when you play a part you must use 95 percent of yourself and then play the remaining 5 percent. This is not a new idea. The early Christian theologian Saint Augustine wrote, "The artist is the Man." If you see a Michelangelo fresco, you see the man Michelangelo in it. You can feel it, and it is transcendent. On the other hand, when you see a run-of-the-mill painting—devoid of passion and presence—the artist doesn't jump out at you from the canvas. The painting just sits there. The same is true of acting.

Developing an understanding of character is a matter of insight and balance, and to do that an actor must know himself. He must assume that he is an accumulation of collected stereotypes: a manner of walking, talking, thinking, and behaving. Starting from this richness, an actor then begins to retool his character. Not remake; retool. This is not *Pygmalion*. The object is for an actor to use his own self in the transmutation of a character developed by another self, the playwright or screenwriter. He must embody the role though the extension, intensification, modification, and negation of certain dominant personal mannerisms and characteristics. This idea echoes the Irish poet Yeats's query in "Among School Children," "How can we know the dancer from the dance?" A further inquiry into this can be found in the sage words Martha Graham spoke to her fellow dancer Agnes de Mille: "There is a vitality, a life force, an energy, a quickening that is translated through you into action, and because there is only one of you in all time, this expression is unique. And if you block it, it will never exist through any other medium and it will be lost. The world will not have it. It is not your business to determine how good it is nor how valuable nor how it compares with other expressions. It is your business to keep it yours clearly and directly, to keep the channel open."[2]

When *The Devil and Daniel Webster* was being filmed, Walter Huston and I were pitching horseshoes on the RKO ranch. I told him there was an actor who had been connected with the Group Theatre who was now a fledgling director at Columbia. No matter what I did, this man was critical of my work, and when I knew he was in the audience, I would freeze up. Walter laughed out loud and said, "Don't you know, kid, if there are fifty people in the house or five hundred, there's going to be someone who just isn't going to like what you're doing." He paused for a moment and then asked, "What the hell difference does it make? You just go out there, get excited about what you know about the part, and play the damned thing. Don't worry about some guy's opinion." Walter looked at me and grinned. "It's just not in the books that everyone is supposed to like your stuff." Coming from Walter, one of the great stars of American film, it was a liberating remark, and I diligently took it to heart.

The actor's vehicle, the instrument brought into a performance, is the total quality of the individual: the wit, the fancy, the mind, and the passion of that interesting human doing the acting. If an actor's personal resources are available, then it is possible, in permutation, to employ them in diverse roles.

The label *personality* is often used negatively, but, paradoxically, the actor's personality, in the best sense of the word, is critical to good acting. The performances we most enjoy are marked by a dual appreciation of the insightful human being who is doing the acting as well as the performance of the character itself. All the great acting we see on stage, film, and television in a lifetime is characterized by that double perception of the performer's self contributing to the performance. While I encourage young actors to listen attentively to what a director has to say, I also tell them to remain true to themselves. Actors, like the mythical Phoenix, can rise from the ashes only on the strength of their own fire.

Stark Young, the editor of *Theatre Arts Magazine,* in his book *The Flower in Drama* wrote:

> Actors remain artists, therefore, in proportion to the extent to which they remain themselves and translate into terms of themselves the thing to be created. They are firmly fixed at the centre. They remain themselves, even though it may not be their immediate selves. And so it follows that their art depends wholly on what these selves of theirs profoundly are. The greatness of a man's acting will depend on the extent to which the elements of life may be gathered up in him for the spring toward luminous revelation, toward more abundant life. Art is a perpetual growth of life in other terms than itself. And the individual quality of the actor must always determine the quality of the terms in which his particular art expresses life. That the sensibility and intelligence of an actor, his gift, his soul, his music, his miracle of talent, are the measures of his achievement, is indisputable. . . . If you amount to nothing, your art in the end amounts to nothing; that is a fact almost biological in its brutal certainty.[3]

As a teacher, my role is often as simple as helping direct an actor to move to new levels of trust, confidence, and self-awareness. I found a note I wrote to myself years ago in which I tried to set down what I had principally been working on in my teaching, acting, and directing. It read, "This is what I work for more than anything else: to help actors sanction their capacities." To do that, I have to help my students see who they are and help them believe in their potential for growth.

I looked through some random observations I wrote for a class back in the early 1950s. As had become my habit, I had typed out my notes on how to help individual students connect to their innate wisdom. In reviewing this single piece of paper, I was amazed at the diversity and talents of the students who filled my classes back then.

For a young, as yet unknown Jack Nicholson, I wrote, "Have to select more carefully what it is you are playing. There is a kind of undisciplined wandering. Too vague, not fixed enough. Make yourself a surer target. You move and filibuster as though to keep from committing yourself. Try more concretely to do 'a' thing. Don't rely on chance success. Think back on all the things you've done and it's hard to get a clear image of anything. Just a vague impression of charm and humor."

Jack more than took this to heart. There is never anything unfixed or uncommitted about his superb performances, and he has taken that vague impression of charm and humor and turned them into a career's worth of captivating and appealing roles.

For the talented Gene Reynolds, who went on to produce the television series *M*A*S*H*, in the same class notes I observed, "Exemplary effort. Loves his craft. *Have to avoid too much of the exceptional. Have to make comment on the ordinary.* No intending to discourage the poetic. . . . Make more characterization comment. We've discussed the tendency to overgeneralize and romanticize. More silences. Act as clearly nonverbally as verbally. Vocal dimensions are extraordinarily expressive."

Of the marvelous screenwriter Robert Towne, who at the time of the class had not yet tapped into his enormous writing resources, I observed, "Still controlled . . . almost shows it bodily—thinks as though caring too much what might show. . . . High-grade self-consciousness. Has much to give—personality rich—highly intelligent—feeling about imagery and metaphor has germ of contributing force. Has important talent—should experiment with writing in class. . . . Get more interested in other things—intellectual snobbish to a mild degree."

And of the beautiful yet self-effacing actor Sally Kellerman I wrote, "Enigma. Fights self. Must motivate on highly personal level. Too careful. Cares too much about doing it right. Wonderful when at ease. Ought to say what shatters her concentration. Not phlegmatic—safe—conservative—self-watching."

These notes are interesting observations about the extraordinary students who filled my classes in those early days, but they also give me insight into how I developed as a teacher. People are always central to the work, not the play or the screenplay, and certainly not the ism or approach. The intricacies of the magnificent self—whole and broken all at the same time—and our willingness to explore and expose those vagaries truly hold the key to remarkable performances.

31

Thematic Unity and How to Prepare

Good acting often comes from an actor's struggle to come up with a single compelling context for his role. It rarely comes in an instant. It comes with exploration and from the effort to search for thematic unity. We are the totality of our experiences and observations, large and small. For each of us there are literally thousands of occurrences, seen for no more than a flash, which seem to be inconsequential at the moment yet live in our minds and are part of the joy and sorrow of our lives. It is imperative for an actor to incorporate this abundance of detail and image in his performances; otherwise, he will play a one-dimensional character who speaks the lines accurately but has nothing underneath to support him. While there is no single approach to a role, it is wise for an actor to look for a single theme that underscores the meaning of a given play or film. Stanislavsky's phrase for thematic unity was "the super problem." At the Group Theatre they referred to it as the "spine" of the play.

It is not necessarily comfortable to search for thematic unity, and many talented writers, directors, and actors have experienced the pure panic of not knowing what to do or how to find it. Yet it is the very process of exploration that points us in the direction of our understanding. We have to be willing to stand in the unknown in order to get there. Excessive attention to breaking the parts down to beats or units can impede engagement with the subtext, which is infinitely more valuable to the actor. A shift in story does not mean a shift in purpose or objective, and it is more useful to regard the shift in plot and dialogue as another variation of the ruling theme.

I have a photo from the May 1, 1964, edition of *Life* magazine prominently displayed in my studio. It is of Laurence Olivier rehearsing *Othello*.

In the photo, the director, John Dexter; Frank Finlay, who plays Iago; and Olivier "rack their brains for a fresh idea," as the caption so aptly describes. Olivier is clutching his brow with both hands and is looking toward Finlay and Dexter for answers. Finlay is looking toward Dexter, his back turned to Olivier. And Dexter, his back to both actors, is staring straight down at the floor. All three of them are clearly asking, "What the hell do we do now?"

Olivier understood what Stanislavsky meant in *Stanislavsky Produces Othello* when he wrote:

A complicated psychological line with all its subtleties and nuances will only muddle you. I have the simplest line of physical and elementary-psychological actions and tasks ready for you. So as not to scare away sentiment, let us call this line *a scheme of physical tasks and actions* and use it as such during the performance, but let us decide beforehand once and for all that the essence it contains does not, of course, lie with the subtlest of psychologies, nine-tenths of which is composed of subconscious sensations. One cannot creep into the subconscious bag of human sentiments and rummage about in it as if it were your purse; subconsciousness wants a different treatment, the way a hunter treats his prey, luring it from the dark woods into the open. You will not find the bird if you look for it, but you will need a hunter's decoy to attract it. It is just these baits in the shape of physical and elementary-physical actions and tasks that I want to supply you with.[1]

While difficult to endure, that stymied moment is often where great performances come from. In the struggle to understand and develop a context, the actor can stretch his imagination to uncover untold riches in a script. Stanislavsky has been erroneously linked with actors feeling the role or finding the right emotion. What he meant was the process of unblocking the stymied moment.

In *The Story of a Novel*, Thomas Wolfe, the great American novelist, writes, "The quality of my memory is characterized, I believe, in a more than ordinary degree by the intensity of its sense impression, its power to evoke and bring back the odors, sounds, colors, shapes and feel of things with concrete vividness."[2] Wolfe's details are the undercurrent or jet stream that moves within our lives and leads us down unexpected paths. The flash of detail enabled Wolfe to see what was familiar in an entirely new light. The French writer Marcel Proust, in *Remembrance of Things Past,* dips his petite madeleine into a cup of tea, and the sweetness in his mouth brings back his entire childhood with such force that it takes seven volumes to tell the tale.

In his essay "The Family in Modern Drama," Arthur Miller conjectured, "All plays we call great, let alone those we call serious, are ultimately involved with some aspects of a single problem. It is this: How may a man make of the outside world a home? How and in what ways must he struggle, what must he strive to change and overcome within himself and outside himself if he is to find the safety, the surroundings of love, the ease of soul, the sense of identity and honor which, evidently, all men have connected in their memories with the idea of the family?"[3]

In *Art as Experience,* John Dewey, the eminent American philosopher, stresses that the structure of every work of art requires unity and diversity, but every variant must have a feeling of closure. Thematic unity not only must begin, it must end. It requires punctuation. It is not a cessation but a consummation. Thematic unity is the undercurrent that moves the story along and keeps an actor from stagnating onstage or onscreen.

Not all my investigations into thematic unity go over swimmingly in class. I once had an El Al stewardess named Ruth as a student. Ruth was a tough-minded sabra and a no-nonsense person. She had done her time in the Israeli army and nobody could push her around. Ruth and I often came to immovable impasses that to me showed her lack of trust in what I imagined was a very lively imagination.

On one occasion she did a scene and I wanted to rework it. As is my wont, I began to speak to her metaphorically. "Imagine doing the scene from the point of view that if your partner won't agree with you, you will end the relationship." I referred to the character of Nora in *A Doll's House* as a further example of what I was trying to communicate.

Ruth became very impatient. "Tell me what to do and I'll do it," she snapped. She insisted that all my allusions had failed to show her anything. She just wanted to know how to make it better. I stood my ground against her formidable resistance.

I concurred that I was trying to invest the scene with some pervasive assumptions that might provide more meaning than the script as written did. I further suggested, "This is what rehearsals are for."

"But the scene says such and such," Ruth shot back at me. "And such and such means what it says."

"No," I was forced to respond. "The words don't mean just one thing. The script can mean a thousand things."

Ruth, with the entire class at this point holding its breath, insisted I wasn't listening to her. "You have interrupted me fourteen times," she concluded in a huff.

I don't know what kind of tabulator Ruth had, but I gently suggested that it might have been fourteen interjections, not interruptions. I advised her that if she wanted to win this argument, it would probably be a pyrrhic victory—a victory won at too great an expense to her performance. I suggested she try listening to me instead.

With a great deal of patience and struggle, I finally succeeded in getting Ruth to rework the scene with her partner using a new set of assumptions. Once she softened to the idea and allowed her imagination to direct her actions, rather than insisting stridently on being shown what to do, she came up with an interesting performance. I thanked her for her cooperation and privately hoped Ruth would embrace the growth creativity had offered.

As a teacher, my job is to struggle with actors until they get the hands-on experience of knowing how important it is to rehearse and explore. Good acting never comes from anyone showing you what to do. I thought it relevant, in Ruth's case, to offer an Old Testament tale. I reminded her of how the angel wrestled with an obdurate Jacob all night and how Jacob prevailed, even though his hip was made lame. I explained to her that sometimes I won't let go as long as I feel that it's within a particular actor's range to improve a scene through clarifying the meaning and allowing the subtext or poetry of the scene to transcend the words. My goal was to make it clear to Ruth and the entire class that the art of rehearsal is essentially the art of acting.

That said, it is important to keep a balance. It is easy to overrehearse, and sometimes the most well-intended preparations for a play or film end in a performance that is so overplanned that it feels static and inert. This stuck feeling can occur in business and social encounters as well. Eden Hartford Marx, Groucho's wife, was a student of mine. She told me of a get-together between Groucho and the poet T. S. Eliot. The two great men had corresponded with each other over a period of many years. Eliot was charmed by Groucho's wit and ribaldry and made it clear he thought Groucho's droll humor had set the stage for the emergence of works by the playwrights Eugène Ionesco, Jean Genet, and Samuel Beckett. Groucho, in

turn, was a great admirer of Eliot's poetry, in particular his observations on
human vacuity.

After years of corresponding, the two men finally planned a rendez-
vous. Groucho and Eden flew to London to have dinner with Eliot and his
wife. Eden told me the evening was a fiasco. Groucho had prepared questions about poetry and spent the evening guiding the conversation in that
direction. Eliot only wanted to hear about Groucho's antics and his relationship with his brothers, Harpo, Chico, Gummo, and Zeppo. Eden said
Groucho could talk for hours about the Marx Brothers at the Lamb's Club
or with his old vaudeville and Tin Pan Alley cronies, but not in the exalted
presence of T. S. Eliot. Eliot, in turn, was reluctant to impose his views on
poetry on the mercurial Groucho Marx. Both men apparently left the dinner disappointed and unsatisfied.

Having a set idea of what a performance or encounter is going to be
just because it's what you've rehearsed is walking on thin ice. An actor
must rehearse and then be prepared for anything that happens. Props are
missing, cameras break, and audiences sometimes don't even show up. It's
not simply that the show must go on. It's more that, regardless of how well
you've rehearsed, the unexpected must be embraced and integrated into
the moment at hand.

32

Emotional Strangulation

When I taught at the Stage Society, actors auditioning for their classes were asked to prepare one or two pieces. At the end of the audition, the actor would be told, "Thank you, we'll let you know." This brutal phrase has become uncomfortably familiar in Hollywood. Even then, it was my feeling that we owed auditioning actors considerably more attention and respect than a cursory "Thank you" and dismissal.

I made the suggestion that if my colleagues and I could spend a bit more time with the auditioning process, we could rework an actor's audition material, which would allow us to ascertain more clearly the applicant's range and flexibility. My colleagues agreed and adopted that procedure. When actors audition for my classes, I always provide enough time to see what they can do, then reflect on what I saw in their work, and propose they do the scene again with a new set of assumptions.

The principal fault I encounter in auditioning actors is their almost endemic tendency to *feel* their disenchantment and to *show* me how shattered they can be. At its best, this search for feeling onstage perpetuates the myth that what the actor feels onstage is akin to the intensity we undergo in our personal lives. It is simply not true. One can take heed of the American philosopher Susanne Langer's postulate, "I think every work of art expresses more or less purely, more or less subtly, not feelings and emotions which the artist *has,* but feelings and emotions which the artist *knows,* his *insight* into the nature of sentience, his picture of vital experience, physical and emotive and fantastic."[1]

I have found through the years that many actors incapacitate themselves with an unreasonable search for emotional truth. Offhand, it seems commendable, but when it is unrelenting, it can lead to performances riddled by paralysis and despair. Some actors have an overly sensitized tilt mechanism, like a pinball machine, and no sooner do they start to play than the pinball is activated, and the emotional game is over before it begins. Such actors abort their rehearsals or performances by excessively declaring, "I'm not feeling it," or "My concentration is shot." Their hyper-obsession with truth suggests Diogenes carrying a lantern in broad daylight looking for one honest man. Stanislavsky's coproducer Yevgeny Vakhtangov described actors who take emotion too seriously as actors who "dig into the depths until they get corns."

To illustrate a character on a single level of emotionality is to nullify the real purpose of action. Stanislavsky put it succinctly when he wrote, "The undisputed bugaboo in the teaching of acting is the near feverish concern with the authenticity of feeling." We must also remember that the meaning of the Greek word for drama is "a thing *done.*" A performance needs to be active, and the circumstances of the given piece dealt with. Tensions must be alleviated and obstacles overcome. The goal is to let the audience feel in response to what the actor is doing, not tell the audience how to feel. Sometimes the most remarkable delineation of passion in dramatic literature is marked by an inability to feel at all. King Lear rails impotently against Regan and Goneril when he says, "I will do such things—what they are, yet I know not, but they shall be the terrors of the earth."

It can serve an entire production well if, from the top down, the men and women involved are willing to trust their instincts and emotions on the broadest level possible. Before being cast as Doc in *Home of the Brave,* I met with Stanley Kramer. Years later he wrote about our meeting in his autobiography, *A Mad, Mad, Mad, Mad World: A Life in Hollywood:*

Jeff Corey, who played the army psychiatrist, had been around Hollywood, taking supporting roles for long enough to become well known in the industry, but he had never played a role as substantial and important as this one. I had seen his work and admired him, yet I can't take credit for imagining him in this role. My uncle Earl, whose agency represented Corey as well, recommended him to me. When I interviewed him, it took little time for me to realize that he had a profound understanding of the psychiatrist's role and a deep feeling for the mood and meaning of our story. I soon decided the part was his. I could come to such quick decisions because my method of casting was so different from most Hollywood producers. I seldom relied on screen tests. Rather, my method was simply to find someone who made me feel that he or she was right for the role. . . . I felt that way about Corey, and he didn't disappoint me.[2]

It is also prudent to remember that the emotional life of a character is lived on many levels. The process of comprehending who and what a character is puts the actor into a direct and often difficult paradox. On the one hand, he must identify with his character on an emotional level. On the other hand, he must guard against letting his sympathy with the circumstances of the play engulf him. An actor must never forget that the emotional problems that beset a character are there for the purpose of discovery and resolution, not simply for the expression of pain, anxiety, anger, and so on. The playing of the part is active, forward moving, and complex. To understand a character on a single level of emotionality is to forget the very real purpose of the action being played.

To understand real emotion, one must understand and accept that while emotionality possesses us in times of personal crisis, there are rests between cyclonic dramas and that rarely, if ever, are we consumed with one single emotion. Gallows humor emboldens the doomed man or woman. A good joke follows volcanic eruptions. The French describe *le petit mort*, "the little death," following in the wake of passionate lovemaking. The most remarkable delineation of passion in dramatic literature is often marked by an inability to feel at all.

Young actors are often pressured into producing an emotion without earning it. Emotions and feelings are conditions the actor must explore, but too many actors work too hard to reach an emotional state as if it were something precise, circumspect, and different from the experience of life itself. The nursery rhyme "Little Bo-Peep" epitomizes the quietude that precedes discovery and intuition and, in its simple way, offers the very key to great acting:

Little Bo-Peep has lost her sheep,
And doesn't know where to find them;
Leave them alone, and they'll come home,
Wagging their tails behind them.

It is reasonable for an actor, upon the first perusal of a script, to identify on an emotional level. But, paradoxically, it is also wise to guard against letting sympathy and empathy obscure the drama itself. As much as it is vital to explore themes, hooks, assumptions, and thematic unity, in the end, the ability to *leave the performance alone* is where great performances live.

Ultimately, an actor works most impressively when emotion is organically engaged. Our understanding of *organic,* however, has to be somewhat altered. An organic connection to anger does not mean playing the anger with feeling. It means identifying the anger and then doing what people do every day—progress with the emotion. In reality, emotion is like a series of concentric circles. While anger may be at the center, from there comes an intricate array of feelings: fear, injury, rage, a sense of injustice, a desire to be alone, anxiety about being left alone, as well as the desire to transcend the anger.

At the risk of sounding dogmatic, I have told countless actors that a character should never be sad. What you must do instead is to try to extricate yourself from the circumstance that makes you sad—by combating it, adjusting to it, or pursuing actions that will ameliorate it. In *Stanislavsky Produces Othello,* Stanislavsky invokes this formula: "Forte is *not* pianissimo and pianissimo is *not* forte." Translated from Italian this simply says, "Loud is *not* quiet and quiet is *not* loud."

It serves the actor well to make use of these powerful distinctions.

33

Inner Monologue, Stream of Consciousness, and Free Association

There is a story I tell whenever I start a new class. A station wagon stops in the midst of very heavy traffic at the corner of Hollywood and Vine. A solicitous policeman, observing that the driver and his family seem lost, approaches the car and asks, "Can I help you?" The harassed driver says, "Yes, please. How do I get to Pasadena?" The policeman waits a beat and then says, categorically, "Well, you can't get there from here."

People in all walks of life often believe there is a better hypothetical launching place than where they are at any given moment for any given action or decision. This thinking has marred the progress of countless performances. When an actor comes to work with me, I am always quick to suggest he must not wait for some mystical insight that will be more amenable to creativity than the mood he is in right now.

There are three descriptive phrases I use interchangeably in my classes that are designed to tap into our random thoughts and put them to use in the development of a role: inner monologue, stream of consciousness, and free association. The terms are synonymous and describe the process of identifying passing images, colors, and associations that are not normally verbalized in daily life. This stream can bring great focus to things we sense yet never articulate. It helps us identify where we really are now and how to get where we're going.

The father of psychoanalysis, Sigmund Freud, originally devised the process of free association to ensure a patient was speaking for himself rather than just parroting the words of the analyst. Its purpose was to provide an environment for revelation. This same process of revelation is extremely useful to the actor's exploratory work on a role and offers a chance to glimpse the inner life of a character. It is important to remember, however, that when inner monologue, stream of consciousness, or free association is applied to the actor's development of a role, it is related to a fictitious premise involving imaginary characters in a dramatized or contrived situation. Its relevance or irrelevance is never judged, and, therefore, the actor is free to use his imagination to ignite the interior world of his character.

I make this distinction so as not to inhibit the actor who might otherwise be reluctant to air personal thoughts or feelings in a nonclinical environment. The images in free association are the images that form the myriad words and feelings that pile in, pell-mell, as emotions. Sometimes the uttering of a hitherto unspoken attitude or piece of information has an intensely clarifying effect. Out of nowhere, you realize that a person made you angry and you had not known it, or that some perplexing problem has an obvious solution that has been there all along.

The beauty of the creative imagination is that it overrides logical and linear order. Thoughts and images come in a jumble. If we welcome this cascade of images and associations rather than running from them or closing our minds to their cacophony, we can synthesize them into stunning congruity. No matter how much closer or more alluring another intersection might be, the driver mentioned above *is* at the corner of Hollywood and Vine. From right there, a logical procession of directions will get the family to Pasadena regardless of the objections of the kind policeman.

One evening, before the blacklist, Michael Wilson, Dalton Trumbo, Ben Barzman, and Jean Rouverol Butler—all remarkable, great screenwriters—asked me to go into one of my inner monologue "trances." Together they made up a premise for a fictitious screenplay, and I, in my trance, verbalized an incident in the story and its effects on the characters. The images I painted for my friends allowed them to discover new layers within the story that were not immediately apparent in the story line. This opening up of the amalgam of disparate and unlikely references often gives remarkable context to a scene, and the use of inner monologue can catapult an actor's or writer's creative output to unexpected and unknown heights.

Freud believed the actions of the brain fall into a very specific construct: consciousness, preconsciousness, and unconsciousness. Consciousness is the brain's awareness of immediate facts and elements, remembered experiences, faces, names, events, and so on. Consciousness is what enables us to know where we are at any given moment, as well as what happened last week or last year. The unconscious is the repository for everything we have forgotten or choose not to remember. We once knew the names of everyone in our grammar school class, but these specifics have no practical use to us now and have been relegated to the realm of the forgotten. On a more emotional plane, we often disremember events that were painful or difficult or block the details surrounding those events.

The most interesting area of the mind for the actor is the preconscious. Freud defined the preconscious as the area that lies between conscious awareness and the unconscious. Ideas are not immediately present, but they're not buried and, with focus, can be recalled. In the course of a given day, a thousand associations barrage the preconscious. Faces, names, and events all flash through our minds, yet we dismiss them, as we have no time for them. We cannot afford the luxury of dwelling on this passing parade of half-formed images and intonations. We have real things to do. At night, as we sleep, strange creatures inhabit our dreams. They talk to us, we talk to them without questioning their presence. Time ceases to exist. You cross a bridge in California and arrive in Maine and do not question the geography. Whether in sleep or in a daydream, the preconscious is the never-never land of the artist. It is the masquerade that slips past the sentinels of the unconscious. The disguise is total, and only with great thought and care are we able to remember the mask of these most mercurial, elusive visitors.

Richard Brooks, who directed *Cat on a Hot Tin Roof*, starring Elizabeth Taylor and Paul Newman, and *Elmer Gantry*, starring Burt Lancaster, cast me for the role of Walter Hickock in Truman Capote's *In Cold Blood*. Richard had written the screenplay and was going to direct the film. Walter Hickock was the terminally ill father of Dick Hickock, the man who teamed up with Perry Smith in the merciless slaughter of the Clutter family in Holcomb, Kansas. One evening before I left for the location in Kansas, I read the book at our very quiet country house in Ojai, outside Los Angeles. It was a dark, moonless night, and reading Capote's descriptions of these heinous crimes gave me a case of the jitters. As I sat by myself, I decided it would be a good time to employ an inner monologue on Walter Hickock.

The image that came upon me was not of the aging Hickock but of Walter as a young boy, living on the family farm. In my visualization, I saw Walter turning his head away in embarrassment and refusing to look whenever a bull mounted a heifer or a stallion mounted a mare in heat. From that invented image, I decided that Walter, as he grew up on this remote farm, learned to distance himself from things he thought were bad deeds or thoughts. Before the Clutter murders, Dick had already been in trouble and had been paroled into his father's care. While everyone in the community knew his son had a criminal record, Dick and Walter apparently never spoke about it, and the two men spent their time together watching football, baseball, and basketball on TV, which made it even easier for Walter to "turn away" from the reality of his son's behavior.

We filmed the scenes on location in Olathe in the house that Dick had actually grown up in. In fact, much of the film was shot at locations where the events of the story had taken place, including the house where the Clutter family had been murdered. It was chilling to be there. I still have the eight-by-ten photograph of Scott Wilson, who played Dick Hickock, and myself as Walter sitting in the farmhouse where the two men actually lived. I'm watching television, and Scott is almost hidden in the next room. The wall between us is significant and created an illusion of separation. My choice of the heifer-bull image was random. When I read the book that night in Ojai, I had no knowledge of Walter's personal life and certainly did not know there was a literal wall between father and son in the house they shared together. I discovered that only upon my arrival at the location. My observation was a useful hunch that came to me after reading Capote's words and trusting the images that came to me during my inner monologue.

It is our universal connections that allow us to communicate as artists. A good actor has a boundless capacity to invest the most ordinary lines with a poetically derived subtext. When that happens, the audience can sense that a good deal more is happening onstage or onscreen than what the skeletal words describe. Audience members can say to themselves: "Yes! I know these things. This comforts me, and I feel less alone because the things I sense on that stage or screen are actually about me."

Though images in inner monologue, stream of consciousness, and free association seem to come unbidden, the actor's imagination is his very own resource and is a reflection of his unique individuality. If he says too soon, "No, that's not what I want," there is nothing left for him but conventional choices. Take the risk. Trust your instincts. You will probably discover, just as I did in my inner monologue for *In Cold Blood,* that you uncover exactly what is needed to make a role compelling, connected, and available to your audience.

Learning to think for yourself and then trusting the outcome is difficult, but it is an essential tool for the actor. Through the implementation of inner monologue, the actor can be apprised of the boundlessness of his imagination as well as find ways to perceive the breadth of human fancy. It is also a way to reinstate the simple trust and belief of the uncluttered, free, leaping mind of a child. In *The Merchant of Venice,* Bassanio sings:

Tell me where is fancy bred,
Or in the heart or in the head?
How begot, how nourishèd? . . .
[*All:*] Reply, reply.
[*Bassanio:*] It is engender'd in the eyes,
With gazing fed; and fancy dies
In the cradle, where it lies.
Let us all ring fancy's knell;
I'll begin it—Ding, dong, bell.

James Dean used to audit my class. He was one of the very few people I allowed to do that. He was already a big star, but he was curious and very generous with my students. I remember one day there was a young kid in class who just couldn't get the hang of an improvisation exercise we were working on. Jimmy took him aside and worked with him and was able to help him relax and enjoy his part.

One day Jimmy wanted to talk to me after class. We stood under the camphor tree near the curb in front of my house, and he told me he was uncomfortable with his physical movements. He hated his walk. I stared at this handsome heartthrob of a man and wondered how such a presence could be so internally disassociated with what I perceived to be his physical reality. I had just seen *East of Eden.* I told Jimmy that I thought he was marvelous in the role and that he had possibly the third best outdoorsman walk, after Gary Cooper and Henry Fonda. I gently suggested he find ways to come to terms with his first-rate loping gait rather than reject it out of hand. As for his wish to find additional comfort in the physical life of his characters, I volunteered to demonstrate a strategy I had devised over the years.

To prime the pump for my illustration, I told him I would chin five times on the lowest branch of the camphor tree we were standing under and then ask him to suggest four other tasks. I don't remember them all, but one of the tasks he gave me was to wave my arms toward the house across the street and clap my hands four times. I rehearsed the sequence he offered up, explaining to Jimmy that I was concentrating primarily on the physical tasks—even bothering to take note of the distance across the street to the house, feeling the texture of the low branch, and being aware of the muscular tension involved in chinning on the tree. Then I asked him to suggest some dialogue. "Do a poem," he said.

With closed eyes, I ran through a Wordsworth sonnet I had put to memory in high school. As I recited the poem, I focused on the five sequential physical tasks we agreed on, making sure to define each task and then segueing into reciting the poet's words. Even though the tasks weren't necessarily consistent with what I was saying, there emerged a marvelous juxtaposition of word to action. I was able to choreograph my physical actions rather than just being mechanical as I recited the poem. The physical tasks, in fact, allowed me to bring a revelation to the words. Jimmy immediately understood the balance and distraction of connecting words with arbitrary physical tasks. The last thing he said to me as he got into his Porsche 550 Spyder he had driven to class that day was "I'm going to work on that." He died a week later in a terrible car crash. He was too young and so talented.

The Grammy Award–winning singer Harry Belafonte wanted to take a test run at acting. He was hired to star in *The World, the Flesh and the Devil*, a science fiction film written and directed by Ranald MacDougall that costarred Inger Stevens and Mel Ferrer. The story was set in a post-apocalyptic world after a nuclear explosion. In the first half of the film, Harry's character staggers alone through the rubble of lower Manhattan. There is no sign of life anywhere, human or otherwise.

Harry had wonderful ideas about how a man would relate to those unbearable circumstances. One day as we rehearsed in my backyard studio, we worked on an inner monologue about the part. Harry closed his eyes and found himself in front of the old Trinity Church in lower Manhattan. In the monologue, he entered the church and saw the bleeding figure of Jesus on the cross. Suddenly, Harry began to sing an old black spiritual called "Take My Mother Home." Halfway through the song, he began to cry. Through his tears he told me that the song is about Christ not being able to bear Mary's anguish as she watched her son crucified. He pleaded with his followers, "Take my mother home."

Harry told me he associated the song with his childhood. His mother had brought him to Harlem from the West Indies and supported the family by working as a domestic. One day, as she was descending the cast-iron elevated train stairs, she caught sight of young Harry being loaded into a paddy wagon. Before they closed the metal doors and hauled him off, Harry had one quick glimpse of his mother's horrified face. Her stricken look tormented his soul and changed his life. He decided right then and there to be a "good kid" whom his mother could be proud of. That spiritual was indissolubly connected with his mother, and he was able to connect it beautifully to his part.

The Swedish playwright August Strindberg had what he called intervals of unconscious writing. He'd fall asleep at his desk and find a sheaf of written dialogue sitting before him in the morning—yet he had no memory of writing it. In his preface to his drama *A Dream Play* he wrote:

> The author has attempted in this dream play to imitate the discordant but apparently logical form of a dream. Anything is possible and probable. Space and time do not exist. Based on a slight foundation of reality, imagination wanders far afield and weaves new patterns comprised of mixtures and recollections, experiences, unconstrained fantasies, absurdities and improvisations. Characters split, double and multiply; they evaporate, crystallize, dissolve and re-converge. But one single consciousness governs them all—that of the dreamer. For him there are no secrets, no scruples, and no laws. He neither condemns, nor does he acquit—he merely reports.[1]

In his book *Neurotic Distortion of the Creative Process,* the psychiatrist Dr. Lawrence S. Kubie suggests that a poet's mind is perfectly equipped for his work because he is constantly amalgamating disparate experiences. On the other hand, when the nonpoet experiences disparate events, he tends to fragment. The poet is able to take those fragments and form them into new wholes that serve him.

It is imperative for an actor to give his character an abundance of these delightful and arbitrary new wholes. Otherwise, he will play a one-dimensional, empty character. To be on the stage or in front of a camera without having come to a decision about the purpose of the scene and the function of the character inevitably results in self-conscious behavior and uninspired choices. An actor emboldened by evocative decisions often cannot wait for the opportunity to reveal what the performer knows about the character in the circumstances of the play.

Over my years of acting, I discovered a useful way of preparing for a role. Rather than making my work on the script at home an isolated process of running my lines, I say my lines OUT LOUD. This allows me to listen to the words and lets my mind wander to images and ideas sparked by the sound of my voice. In this preparation time, it is imperative to accept that these images are relevant to the situation of the story, even if they appear to be very remote from the plot. Invariably, when I take the time to explore these random and unexpected ideas, I discover that these seemingly unrelated images often lend great insight and relevance to my performance.

In 1979 the comedian Don Rickles was having trouble memorizing his lines for *CPO Sharkey*. He asked his writer-producer, Aaron Rubin, and the director, Peter Baldwin, who was an ex-student of mine, to see if I could work with him during his lunch breaks. As I came through the doorway of his spacious dressing room for the first time, Rickles, beaming his charming smile, said, "I feel better already." He really seemed to take a shine to me, particularly when he found out we had both attended New Utrecht High School in Brooklyn.

I had Don sit with script in hand. I told him, "Don't work on the lines. They will come to you in a context. Say the words out loud." Over the next month, Don and I worked like this, dissecting each new script and exploring all the lines and all the roles. I often stayed on after our sessions to watch him rehearse with the cast. His transformation was miraculous. Not only did he no longer have trouble memorizing his lines, but his performances grew each week by leaps and bounds as he settled more and more into his role and began to embrace his character rather than worrying whether he could say the lines correctly.

The great comedian and director Carl Reiner called me one day to tell me about a film he was to direct, written by Larry Gelbart, called *Oh, God!* The master of American comedy, George Burns, was to play God. The film had a brief scene where an interdenominational committee of religious leaders comes together to ascertain if the main character, Jerry Landers, played by John Denver, truly was, as he claimed, in direct communication with God.

Carl's open and generous nature probably rates him as the most popular and well-liked comedian-director-producer in Hollywood. He hand-picked a group of actors for the short sequence: Barry Sullivan played the Catholic archbishop, Paul Sorvino played the fundamentalist evangelist, Titos Vandis portrayed the Eastern Orthodox Church priest, and I represented the rabbinate. At our table read, we all joked we should switch roles around so that none of us played our expected part. If I remember correctly, it was suggested I play Paul's fundamentalist preacher and he take over my rabbinical duties, and Titos and Barry would switch as well. When we finally arrived on the set, we all played the roles we were originally assigned, but it was a great deal of fun to play around with the quirky idea.

Carl also asked if I would work with John Denver before the start of filming. By now, Hope and I had left our cozy home in Hollywood and had moved to the foothills of Studio City, in a lovely home on Brookdale Road, so named for the brook that ran along our street. After a few weeks of indoor work on the script, I suggested to Johnny that we take a walk along the brook to a waterfall that was about a quarter of a mile from our house. As we walked, I asked him to address his dialogue to the rocks and trees that we passed along the way and to include the wild watercress and tenacious rye grass that grew between the boulders. The purpose of this was for him to equate his character's perception of the glory of all growing things with God's love of people who embrace nature and never cease to see, as Shakespeare so beautifully says in *As You Like It*, "books in the running brooks, sermons in stones, and good in everything."

Johnny, who had been an environmentalist all his life, even before it was popular, loved those walks and used our work together as a ballast in his colloquies with George Burns. At the wrap party at the end of filming, George Burns came up to me and said, "Jeff, I can't thank you enough for working so well with Johnny."

It indeed felt like a salutation direct from the Lord.

34

Assumptions

In the brilliant children's book *Winnie-the-Pooh*, written by A. A. Milne, Pooh asks, "Hallo, Rabbit, is that you?" After a moment's pause, Rabbit replies, "Let's pretend it isn't and see what happens." Assumptions change everything, and the color of the lens we view the world through completely alters our perceptions of reality. What happens if it's not Rabbit who has entered the room? How does the scenario change between the two characters? Assumptions in a play or film have enormous power, and it is precisely when characters behave according to the prompting of their assumptions rather than objective circumstances that dramatic action begins.

Motivation in drama *always* leans toward the irrational. The tragic flaw, according to Aristotle, is derived from Hamartia (the error in judgment of an erstwhile heroic character) and from Hubris (arrogant self-assuredness). In the plays of Aeschylus, Sophocles, and Euripides the function of the chorus is to underscore that there is no second chance and no redemption. The ego, to sustain itself, embraces a system of beliefs compatible with itself and validates that system through all manner of experience. We literally see what we have come to believe. In real life that can cause trouble. In theater it begets drama.

For an artist, musing is a good vocation. The words inside our heads are not the facts outside. They are assumptions. Sometimes they are accurate, often they are inaccurate, and at times they can verge on paranoia. Characters in a play frequently perceive their circumstances through the tunnel vision of adopted viewpoints. These psychological misreadings create, on an internal level, as much chaos as cataclysmic events do in the external world. Shortsightedness prevails, small acts become catastrophic, and overwhelming events are reduced to pettiness. We assume things that are not necessarily so and live out our lives without relinquishing these assumptions.

Assumptions based on subjectivity have a direct effect on our personal biases as well as on world history. Supreme Court Justice William O. Douglas, a distinguished civil libertarian appointed by President Franklin Roosevelt, often quoted the advice Chief Justice Charles Hughes gave him the day he took office: "Ninety percent of any decision is emotional. The rational part of us supplies the reasons for supporting our predilections."[1] If all characters in a play were reasonable and farsighted, there would be no conflict. In real life, people circumvent conflict by withdrawing, swallowing their pride, and enduring their travail. Not so in drama. Drama deals with foolhardy impulses carried out by characters who should have known better. Excessive pride and stubbornness are the handiworks of assumptions.

Eugene O'Neill reflects this compelling need to take action in the very title of *Mourning Becomes Electra*. Lavinia *embraces* her grief and manipulates it as a weapon. Assumptions work the same way, even for less expressive characters. A character can be unreasonably reticent and fortify timidity with assumptions that, in their own way, have the vigor of the most volatile characters. The character of George Tesman, Hedda Gabler's self-effacing husband, displays a pinched tenacity that keeps him grooved in his world of pedantry and locked into a structured life. He is rooted to his regimen by the assumptions he makes about his world, and all attempts to force him out of his patterns of rectitude are fruitless.

It is exciting to read Sir Francis Bacon's seventeenth-century tome *Novum Organum* and consider his thoughts on the prevalence of assumptions over reality. In it he says:

For man's sense is falsely asserted to be the standard of things. On the contrary, all the perceptions, both of the senses and the mind, bear reference to man, and not to the universe, and the human mind resembles those uneven mirrors, which impart their own properties to different objects, from which rays are emitted, and distort and disfigure them. . . . The human understanding when it has once adopted an opinion . . . draws all things else to support and agree with it. And though there may be a greater number and weight of instances to be found on the other side, yet these it either neglects or despises, or else by some distinction sets aside and rejects, in order that by this predetermination the authority of its former conclusions may remain inviolate.[2]

The ego, to sustain itself, embraces a system of compatible beliefs and energetically validates that system through all manner of experience. Our assumptions are tested and retested in social and domestic contacts as they become more ingrained and give identity and contour to individual personalities. It is precisely when characters in plays behave according to the promptings of their assumptions, rather than to objective circumstances, that dramatic acting begins to take flight. In Clifford Odets's *Waiting for Lefty*, the real-life social conflicts and political stresses brought about by the Depression run parallel to the subjective and idiosyncratic viewpoints of the characters in the play. Characters become heroic or cowardly through an amalgam of external social pressures and internal psychological forces. The actor must see his role through the unyielding perception of his character's assumptions.

Social scientists have observed that perception is functionally selective. In its most simple terms, we see what we want to see and interpret objective facts to suit our assumptions. When *Home of the Brave* opened in 1949, the African American actor James Edwards played the protagonist. It was the first Hollywood film to break the stereotype of the African American as a caricature. Everyone involved in the production, myself included, was proud of the work we were doing.

In the film, Jimmy's character, Private Peter Moss, witnesses his buddy die in battle and becomes paralyzed by conversion hysteria. I played the role of Doc, the white psychiatrist who cures him through kindness and reveals how a background of racial hatred contributed to his breakdown. In the end, Moss is able to walk again. All across the country, and in the South in particular, audiences with enlightened views of racial relations applauded the film for affirming African Americans as decent, real human beings. Bigots, on the other hand, praised the film as proof of the African American tendency to crack under stress. Viewers' interpretation of the intent of the film was based purely on their personal point of view and their powerful ability to overlay these assumptions onto the screen.

The phrase "the power of suggestion" is another way of illustrating that strange, cerebral shift that occurs with strong assumptions. I tried an experiment in a class I had been teaching for some time. The class knew me quite well and knew a good deal about my family and my personal history. Nonetheless, at the beginning of class, I contrived an outlandish story. I told them there was part of my life that I rarely discussed but felt it was relevant to an exercise I wanted them to do that day. I told them that although my personal inclination and social viewpoint was intensely democratic, my father was connected to the royal Habsburg family and the Emperor Franz Joseph of the Austrian-Hungarian Empire.

I told them that as far back as I could remember I was at war with the ideologies of my family, many of whom were fervent royalists and spent much of their time trying to enlist me in their lifelong struggle to bring back the empire. The extraordinary acceptance by my class of this clearly preposterous idea alarmed me. Some twenty-odd students, armed with this fallacious information, began to adapt their understanding of me to fit this story. As the class discussed my disclosure, mannerisms I had were suddenly explained as regal. My rather direct and down-to-earth behavior was interpreted as a credible wish to overcome the trappings of my royal background. Their gullibility, aside from creating in me a character that did not exist, also invested me with tremendous power.

We believe things are as we see them. For the actor, this is a powerful and invaluable tool. Assumptions based on our emotions have a direct effect not only on our personal lives but on our world history as well. The great American philosopher John Dewey summed up the whole of life as the need to have the "stability of meaning prevail over the instability of events." This phrase suggests we can make use of the ideas and approaches we adhere to through reinforced experiences. We can never know all the answers, but we can make surprising progress with what we do know.

In 1993 I participated in a reading of *Twelve Angry Men,* by Reginald Rose. It was produced and directed by Matthew Modine, who hoped to establish the New Mercury Theatre. The cast was marvelous and included Matthew, Wallace Shawn, F. Murray Abraham, Leo Penn, Seymour Cassel, and Dirk Blocker. With the help of the William Morris Agency, Matthew was able to use a very posh building on Rodeo Drive in Beverly Hills that was still under construction as our performance space. It was a cavernous building that still smelled of unpainted plaster, and only the plumbing, floors, and electricity had been installed. The large room we performed in was shaped like the Pantheon in Rome. We decided on a horseshoe-shaped seating plan and hung a huge black tarp over the playing area to improve the acoustics. It was an invitation-only event and attracted studio heads, producers, directors, and a multitude of movie stars.

I played Juror Number Nine, described as "a mild, gentle old man, merely waiting to die." I accepted that information but felt obliged to have considerably more at stake than just resignation. My fictional assumption about Juror Number Nine was that he had been a Hebrew teacher. All his life he had functioned as a conscientious scholar trying to make clear to his students the importance of Holy Scripture and the commentaries. When the jurors meet in the jury room to discuss whether the young Puerto Rican boy is guilty or not guilty of homicide, Juror Number Nine is stunned by the abrasive behavior of the other panel members and their complete disregard for fair and rational decisions.

To the extent that combativeness prevailed in the room, my assumption allowed my character to sit quietly as others discussed the case. It allowed him to feel an increased obligation to make use of his lifelong experience with the Talmudic art of disputation and zealously sift through the accusations and distortions. In this context, he considers it wise to remain silent until he has carefully concluded there is something relevant to say. At the end of the play, Juror Number Nine makes clear that certain aspects of the testimony are simply untenable and that there is no way this boy could be guilty. His argument is so compelling that the jury unanimously renders a not guilty verdict. My assumptions about this character provided me with an active and immediate reason to listen, wait, and ponder while the interpersonal wrangling and caterwauling was rampant in the room. There certainly was no evidence to prompt anyone in the audience to guess that I had made the choice to make Juror Number Nine a Hebrew teacher. That was an actor's secret and it worked beautifully.

I played Edward Roundhouse in Romulus Linney's *The Love Suicide at Schofield Barracks* at the Odyssey Theater. Harris Yulin was the director. The play involves the double suicide of the commanding general of Schofield Barracks and his wife and the inquiry into their deaths. They leave a suicide note asking that in the event of a hearing, their friend Edward Roundhouse be called to tell their story. Roundhouse's backstory includes his being fired from a well-respected university post after being caught up in a New York City vice squad homosexual sting. Upon his release from prison, Roundhouse moves to Hawaii, and the general and his wife help him open a restaurant that caters to a gay clientele.

I decided that Roundhouse had had it with the United States. This was my own assumption as an actor and not at all indicated by the playwright. I further assumed that just before the hearing, Roundhouse sold his successful gay bar and had already crated and shipped his belongings to a new home in Aguascalientes, Mexico. I further assumed that before he entered the hearing, Roundhouse had put his suitcases in the trunk of his car and that directly after the hearing, he would drive to the airport for the flight to Mexico. None of this was indicated in the script. The hearing is irksome to him. He appears only because his friends requested it. Roundhouse's testimony, except for a few terse questions from the investigating officer, is an uninterrupted, seventeen-minute monologue. I tried to fathom Edward Roundhouse's state of mind. The details of his Aguascalientes escape helped frame my exploration.

In psychopathology, a nihilist delusion is described as "a fixed belief that nothing really exists." In my own experience—and this has been fortified in discussion with many people—most of us at times undergo that feeling. In performing Roundhouse's speech, I incorporated that nihilistic detachment. Spiritually, Roundhouse was not in the building. He had already left for Mexico. As an actor, I felt unshackled and never considered the consequence of what was said. Roundhouse was above the law, above decorum. In the course of the long expository passages, I kept observing mute but animated faces and noted whatever nonverbal rejoinders I perceived as I spoke. To the degree that I maintained this circularity with attendant faces, I believe the long speech seemed much shorter. The gracious reviewer in the *Los Angeles Times* said, "Sometimes a brilliant actor can salvage an otherwise pedestrian production. During a redundant military courtroom drama, 'Love Suicide at Schofield Barracks,' a distracted elderly gentleman takes the stand. He mutters, hesitates, considers each response, rarely gestures—yet we're hypnotized. How does Jeff Corey seize our breathless attention? His technique is subtle, imperceptible, mysterious, unforgettable."[3]

In truth, it had to do with my assumptions.

In each of us the psyche provides the battleground on which the war of perception is waged. We live our lives in the context of a universal myopia. We assume things that are not necessarily so and live our lives based on these assumptions.

So should the actor.

35

Words, Words, Words

For an actor, the text of a play is both enemy and friend. What the words say holds richness and meaning. On the other hand, the words open the trapdoor to the dullest, most one-dimensional performances imaginable. An actor must quickly learn to distinguish between the manifest content of speech—the words themselves—and the latent content of speech—what is actually meant by the words that are spoken. Actors often fall prey to the illusion that words are the support and ballast of a performance. They are often disarmed when I tell them it is safe to assume the words of a play, by themselves, say very little.

While the words may be remarkable and function as a window into the heart and soul of the play, to take them too literally is to assume the character consciously knows what he means to say or even, more preposterously, understands why he says the things he says. Taking the words too seriously is also believing that the ear has no function—either for the person speaking or for the listener. Thinking clearly and forming astute observations are difficult processes, and characters in a play rarely display that kind of clean objectivity.

To understand a character, an actor must grasp the multiple ways speech and thought develop. Actors must regard a play, as Susanne Langer put it, as "an embodiment of meaning." The performance takes on quality only to the extent that it transcends the literal structure of the text and the plot. In characterization, that process entails a profound comprehension of the psychological makeup of the role portrayed. An actor must simultaneously know more about the character's psychological modus operandi than the character does, and, armed with that information, make determinations about how responsive or reactive his character would be to the given circumstances and relationships within the play—without actually having that knowledge.

The British playwright Noël Coward, the master of acerbic speech, said, "Don't minimize the value of words. They are our only currency." The image is apt. We negotiate with words, barter our souls, relinquish our identities, and yield up our bodies through words. It's the irresistible medium of exchange. Sometimes our speech is literal, and we say what we mean. The shadowy organ in it all is the ear. The ear is a capricious instrument and often listens to what it wants to hear, making independent interpretations, filtering out the unpleasant, and receiving, almost too willingly, only what it favors.

In *The Hollow Men,* the poet T. S. Eliot writes:

Our dried voices when
We whisper together
Are quiet and meaningless
As wind in dry grass.

The dramatist Gordon Craig observed, "Speech is a lie. . . . We use words to disguise our thoughts." The inevitable irony implicit in human speech is that there is a gap between what we think we mean and what is actually perceived or understood. The opening phrase of the book of Genesis, "In the beginning," has baffled theologians and scholars for millennia. Even man's understanding of God is as varied as the number of believers.

Whenever I am aware of an actor "talking" his dialogue, I have to conclude it's because he is not giving me anything to watch. Paradoxically, to the extent that I can be watchful of what is occurring, the dialogue adds relevancy. In 1924, when the drama critic and editor George Jean Nathan saw the Moscow Art Players, he concluded, "The great drama of the world is not spoken by the characters so much as it is looked and, above all, felt by them." Words are actions. Words are deeds. They can inspire or demoralize. "Words can kill," as the saying goes.

It is useful to understand that the purpose of communication, even on the most minuscule level, is to effect change. When you communicate, you are trying to arouse an attitude in another person. Fortify your premise in every way you can and then evangelize. Be careful of disembodied reflection, exposition, or reverie. Get rid of the extraneous impulses and make the speech about one thing. Even if you are talking to yourself in a monologue, you must project yourself out in front and get a reaction back.

Words can have a range of meaning and adapt fluidly to any given context. An actor can use these disparate meanings to advance the action. Some words are more challenging than others, and exposition is an unavoidable element in a play. Its function is to acquaint the audience with events that transpired before the current situation and to render information concerning offstage characters involved with those events. Comments on facts, personages, and events not central to the immediate circumstances present a unique problem for the actor. He must use these references to render them pertinent to the solution of the play. In truth, however, they are merely background. For them to work onstage, the actor must channel the expository passages into the immediate physical and psychological environment.

Words register better in the dictionary than when spoken out loud. The spoken word is often convoluted by strange intonations, syntax, and self-mesmerization. Over the years, I've tried to illustrate that when you know whom you are talking to and understand what effect the words you choose have on the respondent, then monologue can suddenly become dialogue and a soliloquy converts to colloquy. Audiences do not remember the exact dialogue of a scene, but the meaning of the dialogue can remain fixed in their memory.

There's an epigram in regard to text. The process is not about familiarizing yourself with the text, but about making the text familiar. To this thought Jean Cocteau, the great French writer and playwright, contributes his succinct comment, "The point is not to put life onto the stage but to make the stage live."[1]

Exposition should never be merely reflection or reminiscence, and an actor must not hide the words from the audience by excessive self-absorption. At the Feagin School we were told by one instructor that when you recall a past experience, you should look for the bronze rail of the second balcony and be transported by the memory of the event. I now look on that as arcane. Such an exercise is inactive and will come off as self-indulgent unless you connect the recollection to an immediate problem to be solved. In his book *The Empty Space*, the director Peter Brook notes that many of his contemporaries complain, "Why don't you let the plays speak for themselves?" His epigrammatic retort was, "If you just let a play speak, it may not make a sound. If what you want is for the play to be heard, then you must conjure its sound from it."[2]

There has been much confusion in the training of actors over the importance of listening to another actor. I never tell an actor that he has to listen to the other actors. A more exciting interchange occurs when you don't listen to what the other person is saying but focus on all the things you are listening to inside yourself while the other actor is talking. Part of the challenge is the interpretation of what listening is. Most often listening, in this theatrical sense, is described as a literal hearing of what another actor is saying. We know from our own experience, however, that what people say is of much less importance than what we perceive they are saying or how they are saying it.

Listening that we care about is associative. If we are trapped in a conversation that bores us, we tend to hear only the words because there is nothing else going on that interests us. To maintain our interest we not only need to be engaged in what a person is saying, we need nonverbal cues—the intonations, the gestures, a clearing of a throat, a shifting in a chair, a tapping of a finger, and so on—in order to hear well. These nonverbal messages often communicate better than the literal words. I am not advocating for the artificial overlay of gimmicks and gestures onstage, but it is important that an actor understand the widest definition of listening.

There is a marvelous, almost ironic dimension that is distinct in certain actors' performances—an ability to seize on hidden and unexpected connotations in a word or gesture. They see the joke in tragedy and the pathos in the most outrageously comical interludes. These actors have the facility to listen beyond the fringes of lunacy and sobriety and "listen in" to the text beyond the words of the play—and it makes for the most interesting and intelligent performances.

If an actor allows the images in his mind's eye to precede the words and then finds the words to say the images, the relevance to the original story or given situation is unfailing. It reinforces the necessary faith an actor must have that the words, thoughts, and feelings that come to him do so because they are of his invention. They are produced for him. He doesn't have to make them up or contrive them. Dr. Wendell Johnson, the psychologist and semanticist, in his insightful book *Your Most Enchanted Listener* offers this observation: "The thoughts that we forbid ourselves to whisper and the feelings that we will not say we know are the measure of our self-abandonment. By stopping up our own ears against the sound of our own voices we achieve not the peace of inner stillness, but the unnerving disquietude of haunted consciousness."[3]

In Paul J. Moses's book, *The Voice of Neurosis,* he writes, "Volume in itself does not yield us the specific nature of the urge or emotion which gave it birth. It is merely a clue to the impact of this urge and the strength of the willed control that it encounters."[4]

When my students perform a scene in class, they often speak in a semi-whisper. I believe this is because the choices they have made do not excite them, and their hushed voice is an attempt to get away with a non-descript performance in which nothing of substance is happening. Why invest a lot of energy in something you know isn't working? On the other hand, I've seen these same actors, who, by probing intuitively into their characters, energize a desire to be seen and a passion to be heard that astounds. By finding the key to their roles, they find the range of their voice.

There are countless actors who live rather quiet lives and are not attention-getters but, when they perform, bring a compelling spectrum of energy and pertinence to their parts. Their onstage demeanor suggests a presence that asserts, "I love what I'm doing with this role." There's a reflection of that kind of chutzpah in Stanley Kauffmann's review of *Little Big Man* in the *New Republic* when he wrote that as he watched the film he had the feeling that at any moment Dustin Hoffman was about to face the audience and ask, "What do you mean I can't play an Indian?"[5]

The philosopher Susanne Langer observed that a play is "a complex of impending acts."[6] I take that to suggest that at the very beginning of a play a character is peripherally or marginally involved with anticipated events. Yet even as we search for context and layers, it is an actor's responsibility to incorporate the dialogue of the play as written and not to indulge in tailor-made renovations that accommodate the actor's shortcomings. In fact, actors *must* learn the lines exactly as they are written. The oft-heard protest "I don't talk like that" or "I can't say it that way" is irrelevant. It is not the actor's job to rewrite the text. It is the actor's task to find a meaningful context in which the words, in whatever syntax they've been formed, come easily and meaningfully.

The dialogue in *True Grit* had an unusual syntax, and there were no contractions. Instead of saying, "I didn't," all the characters said, "I did not." It was an arbitrary imposition by the writer, but it created an air of openness and ingenuousness. It wasn't my job to change the lines; however, it was my obligation to make Tom Chaney's words comfortable by finding a context wherein he would speak them as written. Another example is iambic pentameter. No one speaks in iambic pentameter. But there are ways, if the lines are invested with appropriate meaning, for the language to flow easily, maintaining its meter along with a resonating colloquialism. Thomas Jefferson's remarkable line, "We hold these truths to be self-evident," is a perfect example of iambic pentameter.

The aim is to invest the language of the play with such specific meanings in a particularized context that the actor will *possess* the words rather than have the literal meaning control him. The actor's function is to bring a revelation to the words that transcends the literal lines of dialogue.

Though it is the words that will ultimately delight the audience, it is the magnificent flow of ideas beneath the words that allows a performance to stand up and be heard.

36

Pathos-Logic

A good actor in the course of a career is bound to portray all sorts of pathological personalities. It is profitable for the actor to research the bizarre spectrum of misfits, perverts, emotionally impaired souls, recluses, and frantic folks who, fearing their ability to be spontaneous, indulge in what Freud called "a flight into reality."

The actor, however, is at a disadvantage. He knows the outcome of the play and is painfully aware of the consequences of his character's actions. Regardless, during the course of his performance he has to be in a mode of constant discovery. He has to take on the blindness, prejudice, proclivities, and desires of his character while maintaining intellectual control over the process. He may indeed weep, rage, or murder, but as Hamlet comments about the actors in the play within a play, "They do but jest, poison in jest."

It is a matter of insight and balance. It is wise for an actor to explore the underlying psychological dynamics of his character, and it is important for him to make adaptations that are logical and consistent with his character's world and viewpoint. He must also possess a wealth of imaginative devices so he can incorporate and enact the particular individual behavior of the character in the performance. For example, knowledge of abnormal or pathological behavior is critical in playing a so-called normal character. An integrated persona that can understand and resist irrational conduct will not be tempted to play the fool or indulge in tantrums. But he will understand the complexity that "normal" carries with it. He will also understand how the confusion and anger that simmer beneath the surface of a seemingly normal character provide conflict and tension.

Once an actor is in touch with the inner psychological workings of a character, it is important to incorporate these understandings on a level that is attainable by the audience—not as shtick or gimmick, but as an ongoing discovery of who the character is. Too often, actors try to achieve this through verbal or physical mannerisms. A grimace that worked one night or a gesture that received a laugh suddenly gets thrust into an entire run. Like Pavlov's dog salivating at the sound of the bell, an actor succumbs to old devices to get out of new problems rather than uniquely engaging the challenge of the current situation and finding appropriate solutions. It is called playing it safe, and it is the worst thing an actor can do to himself or his audience.

Even worse is when he borrows from other actors, thinking if this is the way Laurence Olivier or Marlon Brando or Katharine Hepburn did it, it must be right. In the meantime, devices, which may have had some valid function at their initial inception, suffer from overexposure and arbitrary use. They become an actor's recognizable clichés and idiosyncrasies that call too much attention to the actor and not enough illumination to the character. Nothing is worse than seeing an actor playing the same part over and over again regardless of the story line.

An actor's research cannot match the range of insights accrued by professionals through thousands of clinical hours, but psychology is not the exclusive province of the licensed therapist. Abnormal behavior has been dramatized as far back as the great Egyptian "passion" plays and certainly held center stage in the Golden Age of Greek drama. The behavior of any character has its basis in a number of conditions and situations. Contemporary and historical drama is notable for its range of intricate characters beset by abnormalities and difficult psychological conditions. This, on both overt and subtle levels, has a powerful influence on a character. Not all characters are mad, but it behooves an actor to ferret out the deeper complexities, motivations, and causes that beget his behavior. An intimate understanding of how the intricacies of the mind impose their will on a character's actions will bring depth and richness to a performance that might otherwise go unnoticed.

Inspired bouts of lunacy can sit well with almost anyone on certain occasions. Shakespeare certainly understood divine lunacy. Preceding the nuptials of Theseus and Hippolyta in *A Midsummer Night's Dream*—a seemingly inappropriate time for the groom to comment to his bride-to-be on the nature of artistic strivings—he says:

Lovers and madmen have such seething brains,
Such shaping fantasies, that apprehend
More than cool reason ever comprehends.

The lunatic, the lover and the poet
Are of imagination all compact.
One sees more devils than vast hell can hold:
That is the madman. The lover, all as frantic,
Sees Helen's beauty in a brow of Egypt.
The poet's eye, in fine frenzy rolling,
Doth glance from heaven to earth, from earth to heaven.
And as imagination bodies forth
The forms of things unknown, the poet's pen
Turns them to shapes and gives to airy nothing
A local habitation and a name.

Max Reinhardt, the German régisseur-director, once said that the actor "is at once sculptor and sculpture; he is a man at the farthest borderline between reality and dream, and he stands with both feet in both realms."[1] It requires enormous energy for an actor to play dissociative neuroses. The actor must establish a depth of passion and then, just as energetically, repress it, layering over it a controlled mode of behavior that does not recognize the hidden volcanic seething that lies beneath the surface and affects so much of his behavior. To be clear, the actor does not play the understanding of multiple personalities. He knows that his character is three or four people but that each individual persona does not display this wisdom as part of his performance.

To dynamically play amnesia or a fugue (a rare psychiatric disorder characterized by reversible amnesia), there must simultaneously be a need to know the source of fear: an ability to recognize the options and face the fear or run from it, and the reconciliation of those opposing impulses by conveniently forgetting that they exist. The psyche needs to disremember a life it chooses to relinquish. In *Home of the Brave*, the character Moss has no recollection of the events in combat that led to his amnesia and subsequent paralysis. To play the role, James Edwards had to make a vigorous attempt to recall the events and then make an equivalent attempt *not* to recall the events, something he pulled off brilliantly.

When an irrational fear becomes so preoccupying that one is distracted from the real stress of the situation, it becomes a phobia. The implementation of a common phobia can be used by an actor in myriad ways in the shaping of a character. For example, a prisoner suffers from acute claustrophobia, but in the course of the film he makes extraordinary adjustments so that the claustrophobia gives him an additional element to play against.

The obsessive-compulsive, so as not to wander into forbidden behavior or fantasies, must keep busy no matter how irrational it is to do so. A workaholic who cannot allow himself to take time out for any other aspect of his life is a prime example of how obsessive-compulsive behavior can control an entire existence. This need to control the environment is beautifully illustrated by Ibsen's characters Solness in *The Master Builder,* Gregers in *The Wild Duck,* and Rosmer in *Rosmersholm.* The power of the obsessive-compulsive provides an intensely dramatic condition that propels a character into action. In Leonard Melfi's *Birdbath,* Velma is so obsessed with the impulse to pierce her mother's chest with a knife that she is finally driven to commit the act.

In many instances the power of obsession acts nonheroically on a character as intensely as hubris acts on a character in a Greek tragedy. Jack Nicholson perfectly illustrated the layers of an obsessive-compulsive pattern in his stellar performance in *As Good as It Gets.* A less insightful actor might have played only the single dimension of obsessive and none of the richness that probably resides in all people who live with this condition. His wide range offered us something to chew on and allowed us to experience the mixed emotions that are in fact present in almost everything we do.

There's such adventure in entering into Ingmar Bergman's dream of mythological scenes and heraldry in *The Seventh Seal.* One can imagine Bergman must have learned his lessons from Strindberg, who wrote, "The characters split, double, multiply, evaporate, condense, dissolve and merge. But one consciousness rules them all: the dreamer's; for him there are no secrets, no inconsistencies, no scruples and no laws."[2]

37

Mythology and Postcards

When I teach, I make frequent references to mythology, not as some high-toned parlor game but as a practical device to help the actor's search for a more impelling thematic core. For example, it might be useful for an actor who is playing Dr. Stockmann in Ibsen's *An Enemy of the People* to equate the travail of Stockmann with the struggles of the Greek deity Prometheus. Prometheus brought fire as illumination to the people of the Earth and was cruelly punished by his vengeful father, Zeus. Regardless of Zeus's wrath, Prometheus would not yield.

The Promethean myth is reflected in a whole gamut of plays, including Arthur Miller's *The Crucible* (in the character of John Proctor), Shaw's *Saint Joan,* and Lillian Hellman's *Watch on the Rhine* (in the character of Kurt Muller). The refusal to yield to adversity is clearly expressed in Hamlet's plaint: "The time is out of joint—O cursèd spite, That ever I was born to set it right!"

The classicists Robert Graves and Edith Hamilton and the social anthropologist Sir James Frazier have all provided us with a compendium of ancient myths that, without fail, are possible to link to the main body of plays in the contemporary and classical repertory. The modern expression "What a way to die" epitomizes the reckless and heedless submission to the Sirens' call as described in Homer's *Odyssey* and the irresistible call of the Lorelei in German mythology. The medical student Philip in Somerset Maugham's *Of Human Bondage* knows no rational way to resist Mildred's near-fatal enticements. Quentin in Arthur Miller's *After the Fall* willingly puts his life in chaos at Maggie's behest. There are elements of the Sirens' call in Lady Macbeth's exhortation to Macbeth to murder King Duncan.

The myth of Minerva, the goddess of poetry, wrought from the brow of her father, Jove, suggests countless characters spawned by the intellectuality of formidable fathers and then forever confined to their father's orbit.

The myth of Cronus, who swallowed his own children, is suggested in countless plays and films. In *Oedipus Rex* Sophocles describes how the Theban King Laius removes his son Oedipus from the physical environs of Thebes because the seer forewarns him that his son will slay him. The thrust of the Cronus metaphor can apply to the brutal fistfight of Montgomery Clift and his adoptive father, played by John Wayne, in Howard Hawks's *Red River*, as well as the father-son confrontations in Arthur Miller's *Death of a Salesman* and *All My Sons*. During the German occupation of France, Jean Anouilh's adaptation of *Antigone* was viewed by the German military as a respectable treatment of a classical play. The French, however, viewed it as a paean to resistance fighters. The same is true of Jean-Paul Sartre's *The Flies*. It played all over France during the war and was received by the Germans as a brilliant telling of the Electra story. It was understood by patriotic French as an analogy to the heinous collaboration of the Vichy government under Nazi occupation.

When George Roy Hill cast me in the role of Sheriff Bledsoe in *Butch Cassidy and the Sundance Kid*, it occurred to me that Bledsoe was the Greek chorus of the film. As such, his character's function was to acquaint the audience with the tragic consequences of the protagonist's willfulness. Two and a half millennia after Aristotle and Sophocles devised this dramatic interplay, the screenwriter William Goldman's dialogue foretold the predestined demise of Butch and Sundance. In the film, the two outlaws visit Bledsoe to ask for help:

Bledsoe: You should have got yourselves killed a long time ago when you had the chance.
Sundance: We're asking for your help, Ray!
Bledsoe: Something's got you panicked, and it's too late. You may be the biggest thing ever to hit this area, but in the long run, you're just two-bit outlaws. I never met a soul more affable than you, Butch, or faster than the Kid, but you're still nothing but a couple of two-bit outlaws on the dodge. . . . It's over. Don't you get that? It's over and you're both going to die bloody, and all you can do is choose where.

Images of art on postcards work similarly to mythological figures, and over the years I have collected thousands of postcards of paintings, sculptures, and drawings from museums around the world. Whenever I want to understand a particular character, I reach for a stack of miscellaneous postcards, select a handful at random, and lay them out in front of me. As I view the postcards, I begin to look for indications of my character in the nature of a given work of art. The image need not correspond literally to the character in question, nor does there need to be congruity in terms of time and period. The list of possibilities is endless. From Edgar Degas to Max Beckmann, Henri Toulouse-Lautrec to Jean Ingres, William Hogarth to Thomas Hart Benton, Henri Matisse to Chaim Soutine, the visual arts provide an unlimited resource of archetypes for the exploration of a character. Fortunately, most of the great paintings, frescoes, sculptures, and bas-reliefs of the world have been excellently reproduced in postcards and are readily available in museum bookstores at a small cost. An actor should eagerly and actively collect hundreds of these cards and make use of them in exploring and creating a role.

Working with postcards allows an actor to free up his thinking and invites his creative instincts to make associations that might not otherwise be possible.

38

Metaphors, Opposites, and Details

Whatever evolutionary process brought speech to humans brought in its wake a need to go beyond words as reflections of literal things and facts. Aristotle in his *Poetics* affirmed that "the greatest thing by far is to be master of metaphor. It is the one thing *that cannot be learned from others;* and it is also a sign of genius, since a good metaphor implies the intuitive perception of the similarity in dissimilars."

This need to intricately state that one thing is similar to another is universal and prevails in all languages and all cultures. It is insufficient to declare that a woman is beautiful. The pioneer of the Romantic movement, Robert Burns, wrote instead, "My love is like a red, red rose." Shakespeare's Juliet in *Romeo and Juliet* declares, "My bounty is as boundless as the sea, my love as great." Conversely, the poet T. S. Eliot describes J. Alfred Prufrock's deadly existence as being "like a patient etherized upon a table."

It is appropriate, if not inevitable, for a good actor to think metaphorically. As you read a script for the first time, ask yourself, "What are these words about? What's behind them? What is it in this scene that is familiar to me? How frequently do I say what I mean but keep unexpressed associations that flow unuttered in my mind?" The connection to metaphor comes about intuitively. It is not the product of laborious imposition of ponderous symbols. It is part of the cognition process.

When an actor asks me, "What is my subtext?" I can only say that the question is as irrelevant as asking, "What will I dream tonight?" What we call subtext comes unbidden and involves the search for metaphor, which is exciting and inventive. It is always available to an actor who has defined a play in thematic terms and understands what problems beset his character and what the character proposes to do about them. When a connection is made, an actor can stumble onto unexpected areas that might not have been explored. It is also important to remember that though the exploration of metaphor is important, it must never be taken too literally. As the actor works on a role and discovers one metaphor after another, a logic-of-metaphors begins to be revealed. He will discard those images that are not useful and maintain those that add depth and quality to his performance.

The imagination has the capacity to link what is immediate and remote. The smallest idea, the finest trace of color in the mind's eye, can affect the nature and circumstance of a character. Just as assumptions and images are derived from stream of consciousness, metaphors are not meant to blare out at the audience like a transistor radio or unfurl like a pageant flag. They are to be subtly worked into the character until they become an integral part of his nature. The images they evoke are intended to add dimension and depth. They are the colorful inner dialogues that make the role an actor plays real and infinitely more interesting.

The miracle of ordinary things is an act of piety. In general, absorption with a word, a glance, a small gesture can create a sense of wonder and curiosity for the character. The way a room smells, the quality of light through a window, flower petals on a tablecloth—all allow for a rich and multidimensional character configuration. Details are the undercurrent, the jet stream that moves within our lives and leads us down all kinds of unexpected paths. Our lives are not simply a series of large, clear ideas. We are the total of all experience and observation, massive and diminutive, and for each of us there are literally thousands of details we have seen for no more than a flash that seem to be of no consequence whatsoever at the moment. Yet these images live in our minds forever and are somehow part of all the joy and sorrow of our human destiny. In preparing for a role, an actor must access the depths and heights of these details and use them to round out his character and his performance.

Many spectacular writers, from E. M. Forster to Lewis Carroll to Raymond Carver, have explored the profound question "How can I know what I think till I *see* what I say?" The remarkable British actor Sir Ralph Richardson in his own fashion expressed a similar awareness of the connection of imagery and speech when, in an interview with the *New York Times,* he said:

Acting means dreaming at fixed moments in fixed places. . . . The difficulty in acting is that the dreaming must take place on a deadline—8:40, six nights a week—and this requires discipline. The fact that there's specific dialogue and action makes no difference. The actor must dream his own dreams underneath the playwright's dialogue. The dream is the main part of the iceberg under the speeches. What you see and hear on the stage is not all that the playwright has written. Beneath his words lie the dreams of the actor. Even if you say a simple line, like "Hello, my darling" without a dream behind it, without a personal fantasy of some sort, you are not acting.[1]

In Max Frisch's *Sketchbook 1946–1949,* he writes about the effect of reading on the reader, and I think it applies to the effect of a good acting performance on an audience as well. He observes:

Perhaps it is one of the main joys of reading that the reader should above all discover the wealth of his own thoughts. At least he should be permitted to feel that he could have said it all himself. All he lacks is the time—or, as a more modest person might put it: all we lack are the words. And even that is a slight delusion. These hundred things that the author did not think of—why do they occur to me only when I am reading him? . . . We blossom from our own branches, but on the soil of another.[2]

The nineteenth-century American philosopher Ralph Waldo Emerson had his say on this construct as well when he wrote, "The poet has a new thought: he has a whole new experience to unfold; he will tell us how it was with him, and all men will be richer in his fortune."[3]

J. Middleton Murry, the prominent English critic and publisher of the literary review *Rhythm,* wrote an essay on Shakespeare's imagery and properly asserted, "Metaphor appears *as the instinctive and necessary act of the mind* exploring reality and ordering experience. It is the means by which the less familiar is assimilated to the more familiar, the unknown to the known."[4]

There are so many ways to view the so-called given circumstance of a play, and any word in the language can be made to fit in any given context. The word *cow* refers to a bovine creature, but it is also a synonym for intimidation and a vulgar description of an overweight woman. The word *table* describes a flat surface braced by any number of legs but can also pertain to a chairperson deferring part of an agenda to another time. It serves an actor or director well to seize on the myriad allusions of words in the dialogue and weigh their metaphoric connections.

To do so will unravel the mystery of the words and keep them alive and well as the script unfolds.

39

The Mystique of Acting for Stage and Film

In terms of acting itself, what is required of a film actor is essentially no different from what is required of a stage actor. The accommodations are truly minimal, and I've always shied away from the idea of classes in film acting because it betrays ignorance. It just means you don't understand acting. Obviously, there are practical adaptations that one must be aware of when working on a film set versus a theater stage, but those adaptations never pertain to the acting itself.

Acting requires deep reverence. I tell my students, "Wipe your feet before you enter a theater." This is true for a soundstage as well. The stage in any form is sacred space. An actor working in a play gives essentially the same performance in a five-hundred-seat house as in an Equity-waver ninety-nine-seat house. An actor working on a soundstage with the chaos of the production staff teeming all around gives essentially the same performance he would if he were standing on that stage alone. Of course, there are modifications that need to be made, but those modifications should never throw the ship off course.

When I toured with Leslie Howard in *Hamlet* in the 1930s, we played in a boxing arena in Wichita, Kansas, accompanied by chirping swallows nesting in the eaves. Adaptations were made and we got on with the performance. Two nights later, we played in a midsize vaudeville house in Ogden, Utah, with all the elegant trappings of beautifully built theater. It was easier but not that much different.

Throughout history actors have always made accommodations. Imagine the Grecian actor wearing the larger-than-life mask with a megaphone attachment. Imagine being an actor wearing cothurnus, the thick-soled boots worn in Greek tragedies. The ancient theater of Epidaurus, built in the fourth century BC, was admired for its exceptional acoustics and boasted a stage that was sixty feet wide and sixty feet deep. Actors performed for upward of 14,000 spectators at a time.

Medieval guild players traveled from village square to village square to perform. Elizabethan players acted in inn yards before untutored groundlings. How cozy it must have been for the Restoration players to appear in the comfortable enclosure of four walls and a ceiling and have their performances illuminated by candles. Much later, gaslight and finally electric footlights came into being. Ultimately, overhead spotlights replaced footlights, and in most cases modern lighting obviated the need for makeup at all. And throughout time, actors rose to make these accommodations regardless of the circumstances.

Acting is a serious matter, but the actor ought to approach his craft with a great deal of prankishness, capriciousness, and fooling around. Most of all, he should love it! It doesn't matter if it's a comedy or a tragedy; joy should define the experience. I've been on the set with temperamental, difficult stars, and one can only assume that their fear of failure or distrust of their creativity was running the show. What would happen instead if they were drenched in the pleasure of the opportunity to work and explore? No matter what the topic, when you're doing a play or a film, the process of the work should be full of delight. That doesn't make it frivolous or unimportant, but it ought to be fun. Too many actors take the process too seriously; not only do they miss out on all the joy, but they often make it miserable for everyone around them.

The various accommodations an actor has to make should in no way compromise this joy. The directors of the silent movies, wearing their leather puttees and wide-brimmed Stetson hats, had megaphones handy to talk their actors through a scene. According to a 1920 volume of *Screen Acting*, written by the silent screen idol Mae Marsh, actors conscientiously memorized their dialogue to match the printed titles on the screen. They learned to accept being talked through a shot, and as an actor spoke his dialogue, the director might yell, "Get down on your knees very slowly, now raise your arms as though in prayer, waft the letter in your right hand, and slowly turn to make sure that Jack is looking at you, smile at him as you talk—broader—good; now tear the letter into shreds. Fine! Print that!"

It was my good fortune to work with some of the great silent directors who had successfully segued into talkies. Whenever I arrived on the set, Allan Dwan, Robert Z. Leonard, William Wellman, or W. S. Van Dyke would invariably ask me if I knew my "titles." It was delicious to be connected to that great era and a delight to work for all of them. Their perspective was unique, and as they had defined much of what film is even today, it was thrilling to be on the set with them.

Movies are a collaborative expression, and the set of any film is populated by brilliant cinematographers who exhort actors not to cast shadows on their partners' faces and to "feel out" their key lights in the course of playing a scene. Skilled and talented camera operators urge actors to hold a particular prop for a zoom insert and to position the prop in such a way that it is framed properly and catches optimum light. Hardworking hairdressers and makeup artists make last-second adjustments to the actor's appearance with the rapidity and energy of pit-stop personnel at the Indianapolis Speedway. Accomplished sound technicians attach and conceal short-wave transmitters to an actor's garments so that no bulges show. There is, indeed, a lot going on during filming, but it serves no purpose for the actor to complain about these inevitable intrusions. Instead, an actor should learn to live graciously with these constraints. In fact, it would serve everyone on the set well if, instead of complaining, an actor understood, with deep respect, the time and energy each film artisan—from director to best boy—contributes to the whole. Once the film is finished, an actor must understand that the wise editor will not necessarily use his best performance but will select the takes that best match in the cutting room. Film, if nothing else, is the delightful and remarkable result of collaboration.

Even before an actor arrives on the set, an attitude of cooperation is well advised. When a script is delivered to his home, he may have only a day to work on it. In some rare instances, an actor might have weeks to prepare a role. Either way, this first work is most likely done isolated from the cast, director, and screenwriter. The contemporary film actor, generally denied the luxury of long rehearsals, must be his own teacher, director, and collaborator. The isolated actor must learn to rehearse with illusory figures that look and talk to him directly and specifically. The actor must not merely go over his lines. The dialogue should be spoken out loud, to characters that appear in his mind's eye. As I suggested to Don Rickles, performers must create their own ensemble. This is not a burden. It is the gift of the creative art.

When the day of shooting arrives, it is time to rehearse with colleagues. Let us presume that they, too, have done their individual preparatory work; only on the set, amid the chaos of shifting props, makeup, hair, camera rehearsals, lighting, and sound checks, do they have their first run-through. All involved, including the technicians, are attempting to merge their individual and diverse efforts into a coherent, creative form. Lines may be modified, deleted, or added. The nature of the set or the angle of the shot may require a totally new physical activity. The intervention of new props might require additional adaptation. A cumbersome costume might contribute to the confusion. Through this process, in collaboration with the director, well-prepared actors, more often than not, succeed in fusing their separately prepared efforts into an ensemble relationship.

The demands of a single setup in a film put a unique stress on performers. The relatively short fragment of a shot requires its own color and dynamics. Unlike working on stage, where the actor sustains a performance for two or three hours, working in film requires the actor to do it again and again, perhaps as many as twenty times. The redirection of energy for the inevitable retake requires conscious alterations in the actor's approach. There is compression, a meting out of energy in small or perhaps extravagant doses. But the approach the individual actor subscribes to, if applied practically and intelligently, serves equally in the three-minute vignette on film and the three-hour performance on stage.

Many of us have had the experience of a first reading of a play that turned out to be magical. As a consequence, there is the burden of trying to seize the flame again. But it eludes you. You will have to forget the ephemeral lost chord and explore new avenues. That moment is gone. The joy of film is that sometimes those rare rehearsals are captured and you have it forever. You don't have to rediscover the alchemy.

Sometimes an actor is lucky and a film director treats the film process as if it were a play. When we filmed *Home of the Brave,* our director, Mark Robson, rehearsed with us for two weeks and then we shot the entire film in three weeks. The director John Frankenheimer sat with our cast for a full week before shooting *Seconds.* Arthur Penn arranged for the entire cast of *Mickey One* to fly to Chicago for a week's rehearsal. Then he sent us all home to wait for our respective work calls back to Chicago.

In playing for film, it is wise for an actor to learn the capacities of the camera lens and the range and mobility of the dolly, the crane, and the incredible shortwave lavaliere microphone that enables an actor to perform easily and colloquially in the most distant long shots. Just as an actor accommodates his stage performance to the size of the playing area, it behooves the actor to be keenly aware of the frame encompassed by the lens that is being used and where he is cut in the frame. Knowing that, he can intelligently modify his performance to the size of the frame. If it's a three-inch lens, he imagines that close-up frame. If it's a master shot, he automatically feels less confined and might logically amplify—ever so sub-tly—what he's been doing in earlier cuts of the same scene. An actor work-ing in television or a film ought to follow the editing process as well in order to learn how to anticipate the next shot. Will they go back to a mas-ter, go for a zoom or dolly shot, or go to a series of over-the-shoulder shots—and so on.

Whether working onstage or in a film, don't take the physical set for granted. Observe the furniture and the props. The sofa isn't just a piece of furniture. It has a history. It belonged to an aunt whom you disliked but learned to live with. You never imagined you'd ever bring one of her belongings into your home, but here it is—central to the milieu you live in. Notice the curtains—do they need changing, are they filled with dust? Is the bric-a-brac on the shelves the sort of items your character would choose? Would the lack of good books be a comment on your character's lifestyle? Does it mortify you to live in this run-down part of town? Do you park on the street and worry about delinquents breaking into your car?

Movies are easy because you get the trophy with the job. You don't have to wait for opening night and good reviews, and you get paid, no mat-ter what. It's easy on the set, and you have the chance to do it over and over again, if needed. A play presents another matter. When we enter the first day of rehearsal for a play, we feel avalanched. The magnitude of the drama or the comedy can be intimidating. And the mass of words! It may take an eternity to get the first ten pages to make comfortable sense, not to men-tion the remaining hundred pages. As rehearsals progress, and if you work well, you begin to get a sense of cohesion. Your character gets centered. Both the size of your role and the play itself go through a process of com-pression. Likewise, you reduce the sheer mass of the play into three or four relevant ideas. Sometimes you discover one unifying theme, and, sud-denly, it all becomes reachable and playable.

I've always been impatient with actors who feel their creativity and spontaneity are being stifled by the obligation to hit their marks or hold still for a rack shot. Any physical imposition can be justified and can often reveal a hitherto concealed dimension. It is unreasonable for actors to complain about the imposition of movement to accommodate the camera or to gripe about the script supervisor's need for them to match the use of props. Rather than complaining, actors can invest some purpose in duplicating the handling of the prop as it was in the opening shot.

In *Seconds,* I ate twenty-eight grilled chicken wings as we went from master shot to two-shot and a sequence of reverses and close-ups. Even when I was off-camera, I felt an obligation to eat my chicken wings exactly as I had done in the master shot. It did not impinge on my spontaneity at all. If anything, it enhanced it. In a 1978 film called *Jennifer,* I played a religious pet store owner who spends most of his time listening to Christian radio as he works with his prop—a live, wriggling seven-foot king snake draped around his neck and shoulders. Even with an unpredictable prop, an actor must commit to matching shots and investing purpose in the action.

In Henry Hathaway's *Shoot Out,* starring Gregory Peck, I played a saloon and brothel keeper who is confined to a wheelchair. In one sequence I demonstrate to one of my sporting ladies how to relieve her blackened eye by applying Mexican leeches. The prop master provided me with two Mason jars full of live leeches and showed me how to place them on my cheek. Fortunately, I'm fond of props and, to my surprise, was not as appalled by the leeches as I thought I would be.

The set of *Beneath the Planet of the Apes* was the subterranean Saint Patrick's Cathedral, buried deep under the dross of the atomic bombing of the planet Earth. The outer surface was inhabited and ruled by the apes, personified by Maurice Evans, Roddy McDowall, and Kim Hunter. I played Caspay, one of the four human spiritual leaders, who, in a moment of religious fervor, peels off his face and reveals the network of nerves, blood vessels, and capillaries called the ganglia that is all that is left of his human skin after radiation had its way with him.

A week before shooting all four actors playing the spiritual leaders went to the makeup department, and the brilliant, Academy Award–winning artist John Chambers made a cast of our faces. It was no fun having our living and breathing faces heavily coated with plaster of Paris. We could breathe only through a single straw thrust into our compressed lips. We were encased for over an hour. The plaster molds were shaped into a latex replication of our faces and then deftly colored to look like porous skin. The mold was used again to make the latex mask of the subcutaneous ganglia.

For over a week we had makeup calls that took four and a half hours. It was distracting to see a latex reproduction of one's face and a ganglia mask on two wig stands. We were shooting in August and we were sweating under the masks. Lunch was impossible because while the masks allowed for speaking, we couldn't eat with them on. At my suggestion, we were fed eggnog several times a day. When he starting working on *Star Trek,* Leonard Nimoy told me how he hated the many hours spent in the makeup room to ready Spock's face. I don't know how he did it all those years. Regardless of the makeup or props or any other mimetic devices imposed on an actor, he must learn to cope with them cheerfully and with curiosity, which I did, and I know Leonard did as well.

I want to add one last piece of wisdom that is universally true and essential for any actor or public speaker to believe: there is no such thing as stage fright. Stage fright is merely our premature reaction to an expected adverse response from the audience that has not yet occurred. It's what we *think* the audience will think of us and has nothing to do with the reality of how they perceive us. In the midst of stage fright, we are literally scaring ourselves about a future we imagine. Before a performance, an experienced actor has devices that can protect him against stage fright. He can generate such excitement about what it is he wishes to illustrate with his role that he simply can't wait to reveal it. He doesn't have time to be afraid of mythical responses from his audience.

The variety of skills that it takes to put a film together is remarkable, and I have nothing but respect for the talents of all involved; everyone approaches his work from a unique perspective. When I was on location in Eugene, Oregon, filming *Getting Straight,* I'd sometimes see a movie at one of the local cinema houses. One day on the set, I told the cinematographer, the great Lázlo Kóvács, and his camera crew that when I see a particularly bad movie, I distract myself by looking at the set dressing, listening to sound effects and music, and noting the film editing and selection of shots. The young man who was Lázlo's film loader said to me, "I know just what you mean, Jeff. When a picture is really lousy, I watch the actors."

It is a gift for any actor to be performing in a film or in a play. Art is never easy, but the complexities involved with our performances create such an exciting journey. Anyone lucky enough to wander down this path should be grateful for the opportunity to witness the marvelous, brilliant, and enchanting landscape along the way.

Part III

Études—
The Acting Exercises

Every blade of grass has its angel that bends over it
and whispers, "Grow, grow."
—*The Talmud*

The Exercises

So much of what the actor does has to do with life itself. We all playact throughout the day and take on various roles within our private and public personas. The following études, or exercises, while designed for the actor, can also be used by the layperson to explore the events, relationships, and actions that fill his days. As we peel away the levels of our personal creative onion, we can learn much about ourselves and discover unexpected actions and solutions we might not have realized existed.

The études work best when supported by a total lack of censorship, a desire to embrace your most random thoughts, and a willingness to believe that your inner voice has a wisdom and intelligence beyond the limits of the often self-effacing self. A process of exploration, the études offer a creative respite to the weary and the possibility of being artistically ignited once again.

I encourage everyone to explore the études freely and with an open mind. Use them to unearth the hidden meanings in a character. Use them to discover solutions to challenges in your personal or business life. Regardless of your occupation, the études can help you uncover the rich fabric of your inner self that has been waiting for you all along.

Sigmund Freud offered a construct called psychic determinism, which suggests there is no such thing as a random thought. Instead, whatever you are concerned with in your mind at any given moment is, in fact, deeply connected to some important aspect of your life and can offer great insight into solving a problem and letting you know what you actually feel about a person or event. While useful in everyday life, these random thoughts are gold for the actor. They are a powerful means of traveling inside to the imagination and allowing it freedom of expression.

The purpose of the études is to reveal the choices and multiplicity of meanings available to the actor who wishes to go beyond the literal words of a script and to illustrate that it's not so much what the actor says as what the actor means.

Many of the études are based on my belief that we generally don't know anything until we articulate it. The object is to discover the unspoken images and ideas that can help frame a character and build creativity. Études can help an actor learn how to improvise and, in the process, make no direct reference to the given story itself but make allusions to the thematic connotations of the story.

A few suggestions before you begin. No editing. There is no such thing as a wrong image. If you see "nothing" describe the nothing. Embrace it. Some of the most compelling scenes in dramatic literature occur when characters go blank, when the effect of circumstance is so great that all they can feel is no feeling at all.

The études are designed for a class situation with a teacher offering support and guidance; however, they can be easily adapted to be used independently. I prefer to use the traditional blackboard and chalk when they are called for in an étude, but a whiteboard or Post-it Wall Pad can also be used.

Étude No. 1: Blackboard and Chalk

An actor is asked to select a character he has played or would like to play. He is given a piece of chalk and asked to stand in front of an empty blackboard. The first direction is to go absolutely blank, to put all thoughts of the character he has chosen out of his mind and prepare nothing.

After a few seconds, he is directed to write any fragment, detail, or word association that comes to mind about the character he has selected. The object is to actively avoid censorship or editing and to put the ideas down as they form in his mind, using the blackboard freely and writing the words helter-skelter, not set down in orderly columns.

If the words prompt an illustration, the actor is asked to draw the image or pattern. If he momentarily hits a block, then he must write the word *block* or *blank* or *nothing* and continue on with the exercise. The trick is not to stop.

When the blackboard has been completely filled, the actor turns away for a moment and then, with eyes closed, is asked to turn back again to the blackboard and point blindly at a chance word. He is asked to speak the word out loud and then share with the class the associations that come to mind about his character on the basis of this word alone.

He then turns away again with eyes closed. He turns back to the board once again and points to another random word. From here he begins enlarging its implications within the whole of the play and his character.

Next he builds a phrase from three random words on the board and begins to synthesize their disparate meanings as they pertain to his character. As these words and arbitrary phrases are explored, the actor begins to deliberately fragment and isolate the parts of his character and the play and then vigorously considers their relationship to the entire piece.

This exercise is designed to be antilinear in thinking. The intention is to spurt in random directions and allow the actor's thoughts to take him by surprise at remarkable and unexpected twists and turns.

Its very obliqueness is calculated to take the actor far away from the tendency to approach a role in literal interpretations and literal causes and effects. This étude works also by opening a dictionary over and over again and randomly selecting a word on a page and discovering how the selected words reflect the qualities of any given character.

Étude No. 2: Random Thoughts and Images

The actor is told a made-up story and is asked to portray a particular character within the framework of a conflict implicit in the story. The focus of the exercise is to encourage the actor to give voice to any and all images that are prompted by the fictional circumstances.

These are not necessarily tidy thoughts that come in a coherent order. The object is to say and identify everything that cascades through the actor's brain before he discards or edits it. For example, take the fictional situation of taking a drive to the country with your wife and kids. Let your mind go. Perhaps what you see is "Dirt, bluebird, a river, a baby, a farmhouse, etc."

The actor's job is to call up his own images and name as many of them in the order of their appearance as he can. Regardless of the part he is playing, these images will invariably reveal the life and soul of the play. Again, if a blank or nothing emerges, he should describe the nothing: outline its color, its intensity, even its dimension. As he describes it, out of that nothing other images will randomly appear. The mind never rests, and the actor must embrace the fact that even the blank has intensity and purpose.

At the conclusion of the exercise, the actor is asked what images came to him that he chose not to say. Time and time again, I find that even after the process of omission has been pointed out, students still edit their thoughts and reject perfectly useful images.

It is essential to remember how perversely we screen out certain images that arrive too unexpectedly, seeming to be inconsistent with the logical flow. Almost without effort, we pick and choose the overtly sensible and congruent images while eliminating what we conveniently call way-out, crazy, or wild.

It is important for the actor to bear in mind that it is precisely these way-out associations that impart the poetic quality of dreaming and day-dreaming, or in the case of a role, insight into the character he is playing. It is also important to remember there is no image that should be rejected during the exploration process.

Another step in the étude is to play out the same free-associative improvisation, but midway through ask the actor to stop and direct him to go blank. It immediately becomes apparent that he cannot will himself to do this. The consciousness will not allow a void. After another fifteen seconds, ask him to have a silent daydream and let his mind wander freely, without constraint. Then ask him to share his daydream with the class. These daydreams seem to course widely across the spectrum of the imagination, but no matter how disparate the isolated images, we can invariably find a connection to the original story or role.

In another variation of the same exercise, at the conclusion of the daydream, the actor is given ten seconds to think of three irrelevant words and speak them out loud. At first, they are seemingly disconnected; however, I have found that upon exploration, even these three seemingly unrelated words can be tied to the original idea of the story in magnificent ways.

Étude No. 3: Two Mirrors

Two actors sit in front of two mirrors as they act out an improvised scene. The task is to look at themselves throughout the scene and never remove their eyes from their own image in the mirror. It's disconcerting at the outset, but once the actors overcome the discomfort of staring at themselves, they begin to accept the reflected presence in the mirror and the quality of acting becomes more focused. Additionally, the simple act of looking at oneself in a mirror often increases the ability to hear what the other actor is saying.

Étude No. 4: Emotional Thermostat

A useful tool for the actor is to learn how to set up an emotional thermostat for himself and his character to identify the range and quality of possible emotions. The following étude may appear intrusive on the surface but is intended only to help this process along.

Actors are asked to improvise a situation that has a conflict. Before beginning, they are asked to clarify for themselves what positive actions should be played to achieve their respective objectives in a scene. The rest of the class is instructed that once the scene begins, they are to break into the scene any time they observe one of the actors playing an emotion without actively doing something to relieve that emotion.

The response of the class might be "Oh, come on. You're whining." Or "If you're sad, why don't you do something about it instead of complaining?" The task for the class is not to pull a power play over the actor's work or intrude arbitrarily. It is to listen very carefully and interrupt any glimmer of self-pity or static emotion. While this can be unnerving for an actor working the improvisation, the exercise is designed to bring out a "tilt" mechanism that lets an actor know when he is slogging in self-pity or undue emotion. This étude also illustrates how easy it is to fall into the static condition of emotion versus the active condition of reaching a solution.

Étude No. 5: Assumptions

One way to explore assumptions is to invent a situation and then create an assumption of opposites. To do this, we ask two actors to improvise a scene. First, we create assumptions that are a total distortion of circumstance and explain these assumptions, privately, to each actor. For example, one actor (female) is told she has been forced into a car by a stranger and has been driven to a remote cottage. Though the man who abducted her is relatively kind to her, whenever she mentions words relating to family—mother, sister, brother, father, and so on—he strikes her.

The other actor (male) is told the woman is his wife. He has to convince her to spend Thanksgiving weekend with his family; however, throughout their marriage, any time he mentions his family, she gets her back up and refuses to talk about it.

As the improvisation begins, the female actor is careful to omit any

233

words pertaining to family from her speech. The male actor brings up the issue of spending the weekend with his parents. She responds with extreme caution, afraid she will inflame him. When he tries to touch her, she is careful not to agitate him by any overt resistance. The improvisation continues, based on two completely different and opposite distortions. As the improvisation moves through these diverse states of mind, the assumptions direct and mold the nature of the action.

Another way of exploring assumptions is to improvise a simple scene. For example, character A requests that character B repay an old loan, and character B doesn't have the money to pay it right now. The actors improvise this scene a number of times, each time privately choosing a new assumption about the other character. For example, assume the other character is:

1. Hard of hearing
2. Recovering from a terrible illness
3. Sexually aggressive
4. Very timid or combative
5. A bigot
6. A thief
7. Mentally slow and needs everything to be reiterated

In this étude, the situation remains constant, but as the actors commit to their assumptions, the approach and dialogue begin to shift. As an actor prepares for a role, his assumptions about his character and the other characters in the play allow him to believe in his performance. Once you believe in your performance, your audience will happily follow.

Étude No. 6: Listening and Feedback

For an étude in listening and feedback, have up to ten actors sit in a semicircle. Give them a premise to work with. For the purpose of illustration, let's say they are asked to enact the following story, although any random story will do. At a staff meeting your boss pressures you and your coworkers into donating one hundred dollars to a political candidate you don't support or be fired. As he expects, everyone writes out a check. The first actor in the semicircle begins the exercise by making a statement about how he feels about this turn of events. For example, "Now I know what they mean when they say, 'If you eat a toad for breakfast every morning, in time you get to like it.'"

The discipline of the étude is, without editing, to have the next actor pick up the last few words uttered, in this case "like it," and repeat it rapidly, almost as gibberish, "Like it, like it, like it, like it," until an image appears. When an image comes to that actor, he describes it out loud. The object is to let the image flow easily and without censorship. For instance, in the case of the reiterated phrase "Like it, like it, like it," one student responded with, "Like it, like it, like it, I am like Edgar in *King Lear*. I am standing in a green, slimy marsh. Out of nowhere, the slime rises up into my mouth. I want to spit it out of my guts." The next actor continues, "Out of my guts, out of my guts, out of my guts, I reach into my guts and I come up empty-handed. The cupboard was bare, Old Mother Hubbard sat on a cupboard eating her curds and whey—wrong poem—wrong ditty—all confused."

And the next actor, "All confused, all confused, all confused—blew a fuse, short circuit, circuit breaker, blow out black out dim dark fathomless deep, deep, deep drying pit falling through dark, dismal dark, nowhere." Next actor, "Nowhere, nowhere, nowhere, what's happened to 'where' where is when, there is nowhere anymore, fresh out of where, are you interested in when or why or what? I can give you lots of what." And so forth. As the actors learn to listen to the words coming out of their fellow students, they are also forced to trust their first instincts about the words they hear. This étude loosens up the imagination and supports the flow of stream of consciousness while increasing an actor's ability to really hear what his fellow actors are saying.

Étude No. 7: Endless Words

I composed a series of études to clarify the endless meanings for every word in the lexicon. At the outset, I describe an arbitrary conflict. For example, a man is making an obligatory visit to his parents for Sunday brunch. His wife doesn't want to go. First I provide two actors—male and female—with separate dictionaries and lay down the ground rules. Each actor will open the dictionary, randomly select a word on the page, and use the definition of that word as the dialogue to act out the scene.

1. The man opens his dictionary and, with eyes closed, points his finger to the word *singe*. He pursues his argument with the words "to burn superficially or slightly scorch."

2. The woman opens her dictionary, closes her eyes, and chances on the word *geranium*. She avails herself of its definition, "plants having regular white, pink, or purple flowers with elongated styles and glands that alternate with the petals," easily alluding to the random pattern of his family's dysfunction.

3. The man responds with *parasol*, another randomly selected word. "A woman's slight sun umbrella," implying the measures his wife takes to shield her delicate, self-protective choices from her imperious in-laws.

4. She responds with *fulsome,* listed as "offensive, disgusting, and base." She immediately integrates this into their quarrel.

The dialogue in this étude continues, the actors using only the randomly selected dictionary definitions until the scene is finished. Invariably, the astonishing result is the discovery of how disparate words can be fused metaphorically together to evoke abstract thoughts that, in turn, induce further abstractions and ultimately begin to make sense. An exercise in words can elevate an actor's confidence in his choices and make it very clear that the words themselves are not necessarily where the meaning of the character or play lies.

Étude No. 8: Recalled Words

I ask four actors to take the stage and address their fellow students with the following task: recall an event that really occurred during the first six years of your lives. (I advise them not to make it too personal.)

The first actor remembers being panicked by circus clowns. Actor two remembers the praise he received for dancing around the living room like Gene Kelly in *Singin' in the Rain.* The third describes camping with his family in the midst of a hailstorm. The fourth remembers getting a bad case of the chicken pox.

The four actors are then given the following fictitious scenario: each actor has borrowed a huge sum of money from the three other actors, telling them he was going to open a chain of discount shoe stores. Instead, he spent the money on a luxury cruise around the world.

Each actor's task is to excuse what he has done by using his childhood story as a rationale or parable in which a spiritual force brings forgiveness.

As the actors individually begin to make their excuses to each other, it is remarkable how easily these four random and disconnected childhood memories can be used to explore an equally randomly invented improvisational scenario. "You have to understand, I went to the circus expecting it to be fun, and instead I had nightmares. That's how everything I do turns out." Another actor might say, "I danced around the living room and everyone loved me, but no matter what I do as an adult, I can't get anyone to pay attention to me or believe in anything I do." Another actor might say, "We went camping. The sun was shining and then everything went dark. The hail was so strong it dented our car and tore holes in our tent. I don't believe anything I plan will ever work out the way it is supposed to." Another actor might say, "I got chicken pox the day my class was supposed to leave for a weeklong field trip to Washington, D.C. I stayed home in bed while my classmates visited Congress and the White House and stayed in a hotel. There was no way I was going to miss out on this cruise, no matter what it cost me." The words used become relevant and everyone in the class is able to understand exactly what the four actors are trying to accomplish with their words.

Étude No. 9: Personality Inventory

While I was studying at UCLA, I prepared for my certification as a speech therapist from the American Speech and Hearing Association. One day I came across a copy of the University of Minnesota's *Multiphasic Personality Inventory*, a psychology test that assesses personality traits and psychopathologies. The original version included 567 simple statements, such as "Once in a while I think of things too bad to talk about" and "I never played with dolls."

I made use of the potency of these marginal idiosyncrasies to design an étude in which conflicting situations are improvised. I ask an actor to state his character's objectives and describe, in the most precise language, what action or infinitive phrase most clearly represents what he plans to achieve with his goal. Once he determines his objective, I ask the actor to pick a random number from 1 to 567. I assign him whatever "trait" in the *Multiphasic Personality Inventory* corresponds to the number he picked. For the sake of discussion, let us assume an actor picks number 316, which reads, "I think nearly everyone would tell a lie to keep out of trouble."

I then ask the actor to restate his original objective and start an improvisation while integrating the additional inventory characteristic into his work. The subtlest inference of a trait or tendency can invest surprising dimensions in a character.

On a more heroic level, the essence of Aristotle's idea of a tragic flaw is incorporated. In this exercise the considerations are less dramatic than a fall from pride, but the process is essentially the same—a basically stable character distorts and convolutes his actions and discovers his life is based on the most meager character flaw or idiosyncrasy, such as "I think nearly everyone would tell a lie to keep out of trouble."

If the *Multiphasic Personality Inventory* is not available for this étude, I recommend the instructor create a list of random personality quirks and traits to use instead.

Étude No. 10: Postcards

For another étude, I spread out up to one hundred art postcards at a time on a table. I ask an actor to choose a random postcard and, without showing it to anyone else in the class, begin an inner monologue while taking on some of the imagined traits of the character depicted in the artwork on the postcard, along with the environment in which the character lives. For example, I might arbitrarily pick up a postcard of *A Franciscan Monk* by the seventeenth-century Spanish painter Francisco de Zurbarán. My inner monologue to the class begins, "My faith sustains me. I want no intrusions from the querulous world's nagging questions. I have found solace in obeisance."

The class, not knowing I am working with the image of Zurbarán's monk, begins to ask me random questions. They may be light years away from my character, but my responses must always be relevant to the character as I perceive it in my postcard image.

Q: Do you like rock music?
A: Your question confuses me.
Q: Have you any children?
A: I live a monastic life.
Q: Have you ever been laid?
A: I have known the sin of adultery and have been absolved by a
    merciful Christ.
Q: Do you have any kids?
A: Kids? What do you mean?

Q: Children?
A: As numerous as the sands of the sea.

Though the question-and-answer is focused on the image in the postcard, it is easy for an actor to do the same exercise with any role he is playing.

In another example, I select a postcard that portrays the full-length figure of the *Prince of the Lilies* in the restored frescos in the palace of Knossos on the island of Crete. He is a long, lithe figure with a blue cloth wrapped around his waist. His chest and limbs are bare, and a feathered helmet adorns his head. The inner monologue begins:

"I am the source of all the vital forces in the earth and air and sea. I teem with my own youth. My head is light, my arms expand, and my limbs abound with power. My eyes! I cannot resist the look of my own eyes. They captivate, hypnotize, they glow. I am life. I am sex. I am me."

The class begins its questions:

Q: Have you ever been married?
A: My dear friend, the world is my spouse, the air is my bride.
Q: Do you have a wife?
A: I have slept with every woman I have ever desired.
Q: Are you good at sports?
A: Sublime.
Q: Do you play baseball?
A: I don't know what it is, but I'm certain I'd excel at it.
Q: Do you go to church?
A: What is church?
Q: A place to worship God.
A: Oh, yes. I am a priest of the Gods. I serve them and their spirits live in me.
Q: Do you like red meat?
A: I love the meat of the goat and the sheep.

We all live guided by constructs that enable us to penetrate the complexities encountered in a lifetime. Art offers enlightening images that support our character's complexity and open the pathway into a deeper understanding of these constructs. All actors should have a significant collection of art postcards from as many artists and styles of art as possible. Besides being beautiful to look at, they offer an endless supply of images that can spark the imagination and jump-start the creative investigation into a role.

Étude No. 11: Surrogate or Alter Ego

In this étude, the object is to clarify, underscore, and heighten the message of the scene by employing the aid of an imagined surrogate figure or alter ego to address your dialogue to. To start, there are four actors onstage, two characters and two surrogates or alter egos.

Perhaps it is an improvisation about a disagreement between a husband and wife. The two actors begin. The conflict in the scene is so untenable and hopelessly irreconcilable that the actor asks the imagined surrogate figure to intercede on his behalf and help communicate with his partner. In other words, rather than play the scene directly one-on-one, the actor enlists the help of a third and fourth party to play the scene.

For example, a woman describes the futility of reaching her husband to her alter ego and explains to her that her husband has become unreachable. "I want you to warn him that his excessive infantile demands revolt me."

The alter ego absorbs the import of what she has said and turns to the husband and explains that his wife has asked her to talk to him because in her mind her husband is unreachable. The alter ego then paraphrases what the wife thinks of her husband and alerts him that she's ready to give up.

The husband thanks the wife's alter ego and then talks to his own alter ego and says, "I'm really disturbed by all her prattle. Will you tell her that I'm not a vain man, but in my own mind I truly believe that I am a paragon, and I regret that she is so terminally myopic."

The husband's alter ego tries to make clear to the wife that her husband's attitude is "as he just delivered it to me." She then turns again to her alter ego, and the feuding continues in that oblique manner.

The surrogate étude creates a great deal of comic tension. Each character, by using an alter ego, takes on a position of power as well as martyrdom, as if to say, "I'm really trying to help the situation, and his ridiculous alter ego can't hear it." Often this exercise illustrates the human capacity to create a tempest in a teapot or, as Hamlet says, "To find quarrel in a straw when honor's the stake." This is the core ingredient of drama, tragedy, and comedy. The virtue of the exercise is the intense quality of listening on the part of the alter ego or surrogate and the maximum attention paid by the quarreling spouses. It's wonderful to watch actors trying so hard to figure out how to really understand what needs to be communicated.

Étude 12: Metaphor

For an étude in metaphor, each actor selects a character he has either played or is working on. A dictionary is opened at random, and a noun is arbitrarily selected. In the exercise, the actor must liken the character and the incidents in the play to the particular noun. The images are deliberately remote and will, in most cases, not connect easily with the character and circumstances. When a connection is made, however, the actor can stumble onto unexpected areas that might not have been explored.

For example, take the character of the manservant Jean in Strindberg's *Miss Julie*. The noun selected at random might be *pickax*. The actor begins to find in Jean the qualities of pickax. When the actor can let his imagination run wild, it turns out *pickax* exactly exemplifies Jean's ambitions, his manipulations of Julie, his need to undermine and "cut" Miss Julie and the societal forces that sustain Swedish aristocracy. He figuratively and literally "picks" away at and digs her grave. These metaphors suggest an additional dimension for the role and present an unexpected yet logical aspect of Jean's true nature.

An extension of this exercise is to again assign a character to an actor that he has played or is working on. Spread out a selection of photographs and illustrations of animals on a table and ask the actor to randomly select one. Rather than integrating a random noun from the dictionary, the actor is asked to incorporate the traits of the selected animal in his performance—for example, a caged tiger, an orangutan, or a Dalmatian. Like randomly selected words from the dictionary, these randomly selected creatures help an actor, as he explores their images, discover unexpected relevance to his character.

Étude No. 13: Daydreams

In this étude I ask two actors to improvise on a fictional scenario—perhaps the story of parents struggling with a fretful child. A minute or two into their improvisation, I ask them to go blank. After fifteen seconds or so, it becomes quite apparent they cannot will themselves to go blank—their consciousness will not allow a void. I then ask them to have a daydream, to let their minds wander freely, without constraint. After about thirty seconds of silent introspection, I ask them to reconstruct the daydream and share it with the class. Invariably, within the daydream there is an image or action that easily connects to the fictional scenario at hand.

A variation of the exercise: at the conclusion of an inner monologue, give an actor ten seconds to think of three random words and say them out loud and then connect them to the fictional scenario. At first the words may seem irrelevant; however, I have found that upon exploration these three seemingly unrelated words can be tied to the original idea of the story in magnificent ways. Inner monologue will unlock the mind and provide the actor with an astonishing insight into a role.

Étude No. 14: Semantic Stretching

Two actors are asked to improvise a situation. For example, Actor A has decided to return to the religious practices he was brought up with. Actor B is skeptical about this return and considers it an evasion of everyday problems. Each actor states his character's basic premise out loud, incorporating a strong goal-directed action.

As they begin their improvisation, they are assigned various topics, and their task is to incorporate the random topics in the conflict at hand. The topics, if properly integrated, serve as parables or analogies. Below is a list of possible topics that can be used to implement the exercise. Keeping the original premise in mind, the actors explain to the class what happened when:

1. Your best friend came over to spend the night and your parents fought
2. You were kissed for the first time
3. You tasted the best food you had ever eaten
4. You felt sicker than you had ever felt before
5. You ran away from a fight
6. You achieved a great athletic feat
7. You spent New Year's Eve alone
8. You met a relative you were supposed to like but could not tolerate
9. You did not leave a party even though you had nothing in common with anyone there
10. You saw the worst movie ever

11. You were unfairly kept after school
12. You stole merchandise from a store
13. You lied to your parents and blamed a sibling for something you had done

The overlay of random topics onto the improvisation forces an actor to move out of his comfort zone and away from the expected dialogue that might emerge from the original premise.

A final note about working with the études: play with them; adapt them; make them your own. Remember, when doing an improvisation, there must always be a problem to be solved. Play the *problem*. We want to see the struggle. What is the premise or theme of your character? The problem of the scene will arise from your premise coming into conflict with the premise of another actor.

When you are working on a role, it is important to remember that every scene must involve two things: something immediate and the ego. The ego involved in a scene is more important than the immediate plot. Use the études (as well as your work in rehearsal) to find out where the ego is involved. What is the threat? What is at stake? Ask yourself, "How is what I am doing involved with my own self-interest?" Most important, you must always be on the side of your character. Never make judgments against him.

In my life as an actor and as a teacher, I've had reasonably good success. I've learned to trust my hunches and hope that I've encouraged my students to do the same. In retrospect, my life itself has been a series of études, sometimes sought-after, sometimes thrust on me. And through it all, the search for creative expression has helped keep me on an even keel.

As actors, we all encounter roles that at the outset seem way out of our habitual range. Life, too, comes in unexpected jumbles. This is certainly true of the blacklist and my tenure as a teacher. To paraphrase a line attributed to Mark Twain, I've had a lot of trouble in my life, but very little of it ever happened. In fact, I've had quite a bit of trouble in my life, along with so much more that is wonderful. I hope that, like a versatile actor, I have dealt with these various roles in the most creative and imaginative ways possible. I encourage you to do the same.

Afterword

Jeff Corey was an American stage and screen actor, as well as a major act-ing teacher. His professional actors' workshop began in the 1950s after he was blacklisted. His classes, attended by Hollywood's most talented actors, directors, producers, and screenwriters, have been described by Wash-ington's *National Observer* as "a major influence in the motion picture industry."

Jeff cared deeply about film, actors, teaching, his students, his friends, and his family as well as every flower that bloomed on the Malibu coast, where he lived with his wife, Hope. His teaching was legendary. His mem-oir, which he wrote with his daughter Emily Corey, offers his personal per-spective on life, craft, and the art of integrity.

A gentle giant who walked the earth, Jeff had a moral core and intel-ligence unequalled in the theater and film business. More than anything he was a man whose ear was turned to the sound of the universe. He had, I believe, a direct line to the human heart. Jeff heard the music the Earth makes and had the grace of language and wisdom to lead us all out of the wilderness to some Promised Land, like a kind of Moses piercing what is our aloneness and making us all more human. The major action of Jeff's life was to capture the human heart: in conflict, in terror, in love, and in all its small triumphs.

Jeff lived most of the last century, the century of the automobile and motion pictures, the computer, the spaceship, the Great War, the War in the Pacific, the Cold War, the Vietnam War, the Depression, and the repression known as the blacklist. And through it all, the arts flourished because artists like Jeff refused to settle for any prescribed formula. I think of him as a Renaissance painting of the Madonna sheltering us all under his wings.

If anyone's life is a testimony to the transformative power of love, his was. Jeff says in this memoir that his hope was always to keep his ship on an even keel, steady as she goes. For those of us fortunate enough to have known him, he was our Captain.

Janet Neipris
Playwright and Educator
Professor of Dramatic Writing
Tisch School of the Arts

Acknowledgments

Thank you to:

Michelle Cohen for knowing where the gold was on our property. This would have never happened without you.

Patrick McGilligan for showing up at the eleventh hour and pointing the way to a new direction. Adam Nimoy and Susan Nimoy for your kindness and support. Janet Neipris for never losing faith. Deborah Robison Cohen and Nena Couch and Beth Kattleman of the Jerome Lawrence and Robert E. Lee Theatre Research Institute for giving my father's papers a safe home. Anne Dean Dotson, Patrick O'Dowd, and the University Press of Kentucky for your insight and support. Ann Twombly for your compassionate copyediting.

Mark Adachi for taking such good care of us all and for never doubting I could do this.

My sisters, Eve and Jane, who lived this remarkable journey with me. My husband, Randy, for believing in me. Nora, Maia, Ben, and Nat, and my amazing children, Ryland and Jed. You reflect the grace and wisdom of your grandparents every day.

And to my parents, Hope and Jeff Corey. The life you lived absolutely astounds me.

Notes

2. Hope

1. Hallie Flanagan, *Arena: The Story of the Federal Theatre* (1940; repr., New York: Limelight Editions, 1985), 9.
2. Statement of Hallie Flanagan before the House Un-American Activities Committee (HUAC), December 1938.
3. Flanagan, *Arena*, 342.

4. Hollywood at Its Finest

1. *Life*, July 9, 1945, 93–97.

8. The Possibilities Narrow

1. *Hearings before the Committee on Un-American Activities, House of Representatives*, 82nd Cong. (April 21, 1951).

10. It Arrives

1. *Communist Infiltration of Hollywood Motion-Picture Industry*, United States House of Representatives Sub-Committee of the Committee on Un-American Activities Committee, Los Angeles, September 21, 1951, transcript, 1736.
2. Richard Erdman, "The Stage Society: Footnote from Oblivion," *Los Angeles Times*, January 7, 1979, 42.

13. The Act of Teaching

1. John Joseph Brady, *The Craft of the Screenwriter: Interviews with Six Celebrated Screenwriters* (New York: Simon and Schuster, 1981), 400.

16. The Doors Open

1. "Jeff Corey Comeback," *Hollywood Reporter*, January 6, 1961, 1.

24. Exits and Entrances

1. William Henry, "Corey's Vibrant 'Lear' Evokes Ravages of Age," *Boston Globe*, May 4, 1973.

Notes

25. The Past as Prologue

1. Neal Gabler, "Life Outside the Lines," *Los Angeles Times*, October 3, 1999.

2. Patrick McGilligan and Paul Buhle, *Tender Comrades: A Backstory of the Hollywood Blacklist* (New York: St. Martin's Press, 1997), 299–300.

3. Timothy Dwight, "An Essay on the Stage" (London: Sharp, Jones, 1824), 165.

4. Leslie Hotson, *The Commonwealth and Restoration Stage* (Cambridge: Harvard University Press, 1928), 51.

5. Sterling Hayden, *Wanderer* (1963; repr., Dobbs Ferry, N.Y.: Sheridan House, 1998), 389.

26. Infernal Methodists

1. Nikolaï Gorchakov, *Stanislavsky Directs*, trans. Miriam Goldina (New York: Funk and Wagnalls, 1954), 119.

2. Søren Kierkegaard, *A Kierkegaard Anthology*, ed. Robert W. Bretall (Princeton: Princeton University Press, 1951), 145.

3. *Players Magazine* 26–27 (1949): 44.

4. Joseph Jefferson, *The Autobiography of Joseph Jefferson* (New York: Century, 1889), 448.

5. Aristotle, *On the Art of Poetry: An Amplified Version*, ed. Lane Cooper (New York: Harcourt, Brace, 1913), 24.

6. Sonia Moore, *The Stanislavski Method: The Professional Training of an Actor* (New York: Viking, 1960), xvi.

30. Be Yourself

1. Patrick McGilligan, *Jack's Life: A Biography of Jack Nicholson* (New York: W. W. Norton, 1994), 90–91.

2. Agnes de Mille, *The Life and Work of Martha Graham* (New York: Random House, 1991), 264.

3. Stark Young, *The Flower in Drama: A Book of Papers on the Theatre* (New York: Charles Scribner's Sons, 1923), 14.

31. Thematic Unity and How to Prepare

1. Constantine Stanislavsky, *Stanislavsky Produces Othello*, trans. Helen Nowak (London: Geoffrey Bles, 1948), 184.

2. Thomas Wolfe, *The Story of a Novel* (New York: C. Scribner's Sons, 1936), 6.

3. Arthur Miller, "The Family in Modern Drama," *Atlantic Monthly*, April 1956, 35–41.

32. Emotional Strangulation

1. Susanne Langer, *Problems of Art: Ten Philosophical Lectures* (London: Routledge & Kegan Paul, 1957), 91.

Notes

2. Stanley Kramer with Thomas H. Coffey, *A Mad, Mad, Mad, Mad World: A Life in Hollywood* (New York: Harcourt Brace, 1997), 39.

33. Inner Monologue, Stream of Consciousness, and Free Association

1. August Strindberg, "Author's Note to *A Dream Play*," in *A Dream Play* (N.p.: N.p., 1902).

34. Assumptions

1. William O. Douglas, *The Court Years, 1939–1975: The Autobiography of William O. Douglas* (New York: Random House 1980), 8.

2. Francis Bacon, *Novum Organum* (1620).

3. Richard Stayton, "Mesmerizing Actor, Prosaic Plays," *Los Angeles Times*, June 4, 1993, 23.

35. Words, Words, Words

1. Quoted in Eric Bentley, *The Life of the Drama* (New York: Applause Theatre Books, 1964), 169.

2. Peter Brook, *The Empty Space* (New York: Atheneum, 1968), 38.

3. Wendell Johnson, *Your Most Enchanted Listener* (New York: Harper, 1956), 21.

4. Paul J. Moses, *The Voice of Neurosis* (New York: Grune & Stratton, 1954), 65.

5. Stanley Kauffmann, review of *Little Big Man*, *New Republic*, December 26, 1970, 25.

6. Susanne Langer, *Feeling and Form: A Theory of Art* (New York: Charles Scribner's Sons, 1953), 312.

36. Pathos-Logic

1. Max Reinhardt, "The Actor," *Encyclopaedia Britannica* (1949 ed.).

2. Strindberg, "Author's Note to *A Dream Play*."

38. Metaphors, Opposites, and Details

1. Maurice Zolotow, "English Knight to Gallic General—Continental Dash," *New York Times*, February 10, 1957, 119.

2. Max Frisch, *Sketchbook 1946–1949*, trans. Geoffrey Skelton (New York: Harcourt Brace Jovanovich, 1977), 81–82.

3. Ralph Waldo Emerson, "The Poet," in *"Essays: First Series* (Boston: James Munroe and Co., 1844), 11.

4. J. Middleton Murry, "Metaphor," in Warren A. Shibles, *Essays on Metaphor* (Whitewater, Wisc.: Language Press, 1972), 28.

Jeff's Recommended Reading List for His Students

Of Particular Interest

Brecht, Bertolt. *Brecht on Theater: The Development of an Aesthetic.* Edited and translated by John Willett. New York: Hill and Wang, 1957.

Clurman, Harold. *On Directing.* New York: Macmillan, 1972.

Cole, Toby. *Acting: Handbook of the Stanislavsky Method.* New York: Crown, 1955.

Cole, Toby, and Helen Chinoy. *Actors on Acting: The Theories, Techniques, and Practices of the World's Great Actors of All Times as Told in Their Own Words.* New York: Crown, 1970.

Diderot, Denis. *The Paradox of Acting.* Translated by Walter Pollock. New York: Hill and Wang, 1957.

Gassner, John. *Producing the Play.* New York: Dryden Press, 1941.

Hagen, Uta, with Haskel Frankel. *Respect for Acting.* New York: Macmillan, 1973.

Jones, Robert Edward. *The Dramatic Imagination: Reflections and Speculations on the Art of the Theatre.* New York: Theatre Arts Books, 1941.

Marowitz, Charles. *Stanislavsky and the Method.* New York: Citadel Press, 1961.

Spolin, Viola. *Improvisation for the Theater.* Evanston, Ill.: Northwestern University Press, 1963.

Stanislavsky, Constantin. *Stanislavsky on the Art of the Stage.* New York: Hill and Wang, 1961.

Strasberg, Lee. *Strasberg at the Actors Studio: Tape-Recorded Sessions.* New York: Viking, 1965.

Additional Basic Books on Acting

Boleslavsky, Richard. *Acting: The First Six Lessons.* New York: Theatre Arts Books, 1949.

Carnovsky, Morris. *The Actor's Eye.* New York: Performing Arts Journal Publications, 1984.

Chekhov, Michael. *To the Actor: On the Technique of Acting.* New York: Harper & Brothers, 1953.

Funke, Lewis, and John E. Booth. *Actors Talk about Acting.* New York: Random House, 1961.

Lewis, Robert. *Method—or Madness?* New York: French, 1958.

Redgrave, Michael. *The Actor's Ways and Means.* London: Heinemann, 1953.

——. *Mask or Face: Reflections in an Actor's Mirror.* London: Heinemann, 1958.

Rosenstein, Sophie. *Modern Acting: A Manual.* New York: S. French, 1936.

Stanislavsky, Constantin. *An Actor Prepares.* Translated by Elizabeth Reynolds Hapgood. London: Geoffrey Bles, 1936.

——. *Building a Character.* Translated by Elizabeth Reynolds Hapgood. New York: Theatre Arts Books, 1949.

——. *Creating a Role.* Translated by Elizabeth Reynolds Hapgood. New York: Theatre Arts Books, 1961.

——. *Stanislavsky Produces Othello.* Translated by Helen Nowak. London: Geoffrey Bles, 1948.

——. *Stanislavsky's Legacy: A Collection of Comments on a Variety of Aspects of an Actor's Art and Life.* Edited and translated by Elizabeth Reynolds Hapgood. New York: Theatre Arts Books, 1958.

Young, Stark. *Glamour: Essays on the Art of the Theatre.* New York: Charles Scribner's Sons, 1925.

Essays on Acting, Directing, Dramaturgy

Brook, Peter. *The Empty Space.* New York: Atheneum, 1968.

Cole, Toby, and Helen Chinoy, eds. *Directing the Play: A Source Book of Stagecraft.* Indianapolis: Bobbs-Merrill, 1953.

Fergusson, Francis. *The Idea of a Theater: A Study of Ten Plays.* Princeton: Princeton University Press, 1949.

Gilder, Rosamond, et al. *Theatre Arts Anthology: A Record and a Prophecy.* New York: Theatre Arts Books, 1950.

Gorchakov, Nikolaï M. *Stanislavsky Directs.* Translated by Miriam Goldina. New York: Funk and Wagnalls, 1954.

Saint-Denis, Michel. *Training for the Theatre: Premises and Promises.* Edited by Suria Saint-Denis. New York: Theatre Arts Books, 1982.

Shaw, George Bernard. *Our Theatres in the Nineties.* Vols. 1, 2. London: Constable, 1932.

Theater History

Cheney, Sheldon. *The Theatre: Three Thousand Years of Drama, Acting and Stagecraft.* New York: Longmans, Green, 1929.

Clark, Barrett H. *European Theories of the Drama.* Cincinnati: Stewart and Kidd, 1918.

Jeff's Recommended Reading List

Clurman, Harold. *The Fervent Years: The Story of the Group Theatre and the Thirties.* New York: Knopf, 1945.

Gassner, John. *Masters of the Drama.* New York: Random House, 1940.

Gorchakov, Nikolaï. *The Theater in Soviet Russia.* Translated by Edgar Lehrman. New York: Columbia University Press, 1957.

Gorelik, Mordecai. *New Theaters for Old.* New York: S. French, 1940.

Hamilton, Edith. *Mythology.* Boston: Little, Brown, 1942.

Hartnoll, Phyllis. *The Oxford Companion to the Theater.* New York: Oxford University Press, 1951.

Macgowan, Kenneth, and William Melnitz. *The Living Stage: A History of the World Theater.* New York: Prentice-Hall, 1955.

Nagler, A. M. *A Source Book in Theatrical History.* 1952. Reprint, New York: Dover, 1959.

Playwriting

Brady, John Joseph. *The Craft of the Screenwriter: Interviews with Six Celebrated Screenwriters.* New York: Simon and Schuster, 1981.

Cole, Toby. *Playwrights on Playwriting: The Meaning and Making of Modern Drama from Ibsen to Ionesco.* New York: Hill and Wang, 1960.

Egri, Lajos. *The Art of Dramatic Writing.* London: Pitman, 1950.

Lawson, John Howard. *Theory and Technique of Playwriting.* New York: G. P. Putnam's, 1936.

Aesthetics and Communication

Dewey, John. *Art as Experience.* New York: Minton, Balch, 1934.

Freud, Sigmund. *Wit and Its Relation to the Unconscious.* New York: Moffat, Yard, 1916.

Ghiselin, Brewster, ed. *The Creative Process: Reflections on Invention in the Arts and Sciences.* Berkeley: University of California Press, 1952.

Johnson, Wendell. *People in Quandaries: The Semantics of Personal Adjustment.* New York: Harper & Brothers, 1946.

———. *Your Most Enchanted Listener.* New York: Harper, 1956.

Kubie, Lawrence. *Neurotic Distortion of the Creative Process.* Lawrence: University of Kansas Press, 1958.

Langer, Susanne. *Feeling and Form: A Theory of Art.* New York: Charles Scribner's Sons, 1953.

Meredith, George. *Comedy: An Essay on Comedy;* and Bergson, Henri. *Laughter.* Garden City, N.Y.: Doubleday, 1956.

Moses, Paul J. *The Voice of Neurosis.* New York: Grune & Stratton, 1954.

Steiner, George. *Death of Tragedy.* New York: Knopf, 1961.

Jeff's Recommended Reading List

Voice, Speech, Phonetics, and Dialects

Hahn, Elise, et al. *Basic Voice Training for Speech.* 2nd edition. New York: McGraw-Hill, 1952.

Kenyon, John S., and Thomas Knott. *A Pronouncing Dictionary of American English.* Springfield, Mass.: G. & C. Merriam Co., 1944.

Wise, Claude Merton. *Introduction to Phonetics.* Englewood Cliffs, N.J.: Prentice-Hall, 1957.

Shakespeare

Chute, Marchette Gaylord. *Shakespeare of London.* New York: Dutton, 1949.

Granville-Barker, Harley. *Prefaces to Shakespeare.* London: Sidgwick and Jackson, 1927–47.

Jones, Ernest. *Hamlet and Oedipus.* London: V. Gollancz, 1949.

Shakespeare, William. *The Complete Plays and Poems of William Shakespeare.* Boston: Houghton Mifflin, 1942.

Spurgeon, Caroline. *Shakespeare's Imagery and What It Tells Us.* New York: Macmillan, 1935.

Play Anthologies

Bentley, Eric. *The Modern Theatre: A Study of Dramatists and the Drama.* London: R. Hale, 1948.

Gassner, John. *Treasury of the Theater: From Henrik Ibsen to Eugene Ionesco.* 3rd edition. New York: Simon and Schuster, 1960.

———, ed. *Best American Plays* (series). New York: Crown, 1952–.

Ibsen, Henrik. *The Master Builder/The Wild Duck/Peer Gynt/Hedda Gabler/Pillars of Society/A Doll's House/The League of Youth/Ghosts/Rosmersholm/John Gabriel Borkman/An Enemy of the People.* New York: Modern Library, 1935.

O'Neill, Eugene. *Nine Plays.* New York: Modern Library, n.d.

Theatre Guild. *Theatre Guild Anthology.* New York: Random House, 1936.

Tucker, S. Marion. *Twenty-five Modern Plays.* New York: Harper & Brothers, 1931.

Cinema and Film Acting

Bergman, Ingmar. *Four Screenplays.* Translated by Lars Malmstrom and David Kushner. New York: Simon and Schuster, 1960.

Eisenstein, Sergei. *The Film Sense.* Translated by Jay Leyda. New York: Harcourt, Brace, 1942.

Froug, William. *The Screenwriter Looks at the Screenwriter.* New York: Macmillan, 1972.

Gassner, John, and Dudley Nichols, eds. *Best Film Plays, 1943–44.* 1945. Reprint, New York: Garland, 1977.

———. *Best Film Plays, 1945.* 1946. Reprint, New York: Garland, 1977.

———. *Great Film Plays.* New York: Crown, 1959–.

———. *Twenty Best Film Plays.* New York: Crown, 1943.

Jacobs, Lewis. *The Rise of the American Film: A Critical History.* New York: Harcourt, Brace, 1939.

Pudovkin, Vsevolod. *Film Technique and Film Acting.* New York: Lear, 1949.

Spottiswoode, Raymond. *Film and Its Techniques.* Berkeley: University of California Press, 1951.

Thomas, Sam. *Best American Screenplays.* New York: Crown, 1986–.

Index

Index

Index

265

SCREEN CLASSICS

Screen Classics is a series of critical biographies, film histories, and analytical studies focusing on neglected filmmakers and important screen artists and subjects, from the era of silent cinema to the golden age of Hollywood to the international generation of today. Books in the Screen Classics series are intended for scholars and general readers alike. The contributing authors are established figures in their respective fields. This series also serves the purpose of advancing scholarship on film personalities and themes with ties to Kentucky.

SERIES EDITOR
Patrick McGilligan

BOOKS IN THE SERIES

www.ingramcontent.com/pod-product-compliance
Lightning Source LLC
Chambersburg PA
CBHW020338100426
42812CB00029B/3178/J